GW01110639

Spirals

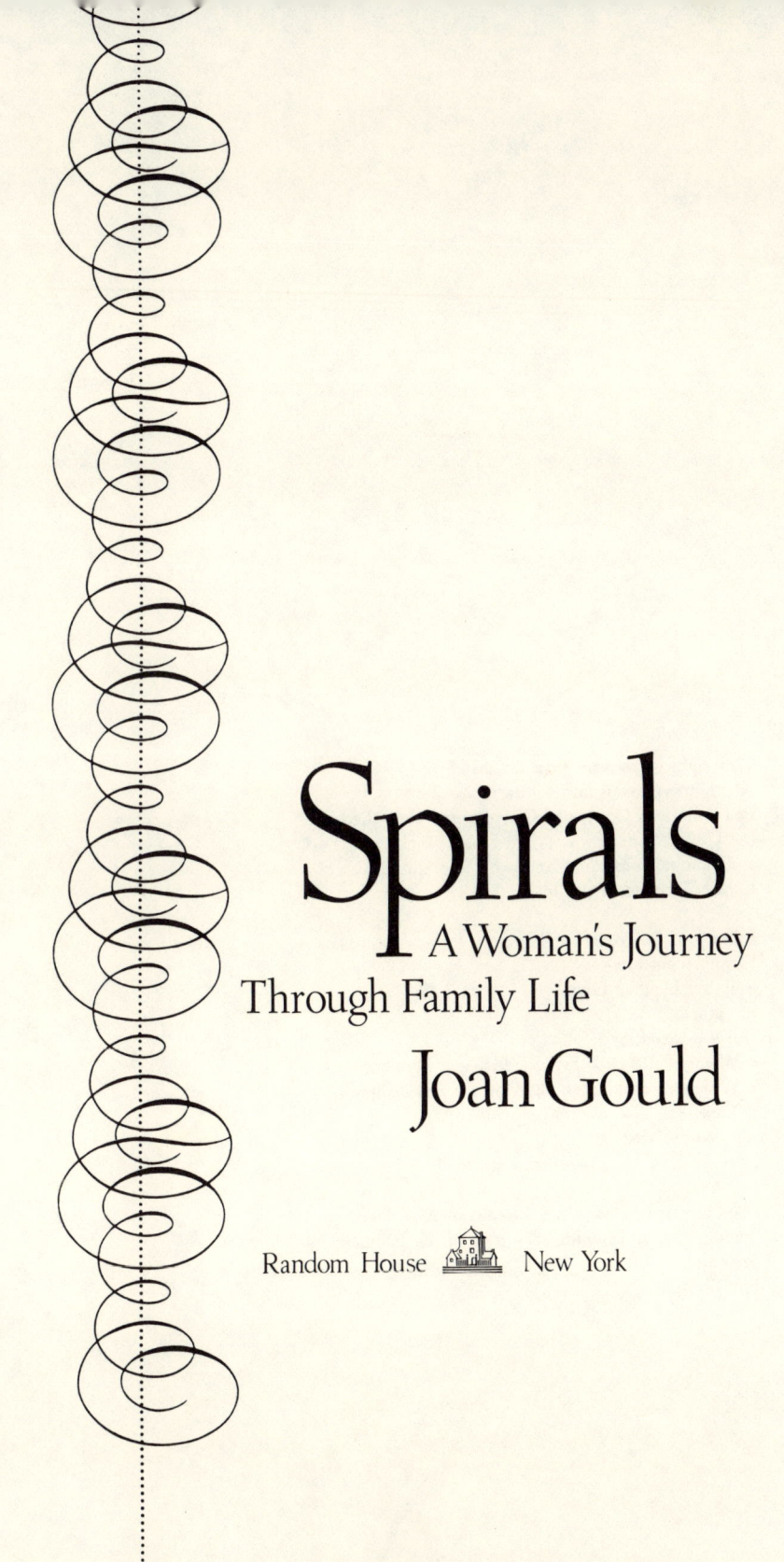

Spirals
A Woman's Journey Through Family Life
Joan Gould

Random House New York

Copyright © 1988 by Joan Gould
All rights reserved under International and
Pan-American Copyright Conventions. Published in
the United States by Random House, Inc., New York,
and simultaneously in Canada by Random House of
Canada Limited, Toronto.

Library of Congress Cataloging-in-Publcication Data
Gould, Joan, 1927–
Spirals / by Joan Gould.
p. cm.
ISBN 0-394-55497-3
1. Women—Psychology. 2. Life cycle, Human.
3. Widows—Psychology. 4. Mothers and daughters.
I. Title.
HQ1206.G72   1988
155.6'33—dc19   87-28352

Manufactured in the United States of America
Typography and binding design by J. K. Lambert
98765432
First Edition

TO MARTIN

With. Without. Within.

ACKNOWLEDGMENTS

The author gratefully acknowledges the hospitality of the Corporation of Yaddo and the assistance of the following scientists: Dr. Jay S. Rosenblatt, director of the Institute of Animal Behavior of Rutgers University, Newark, N.J.; Dr. Lawrence Nathanson, professor of medicine at the State University of New York at Stony Brook, L.I.; and Dr. J. H. Kennell, chief of child development at Rainbow Babies' and Children's Hospital, Cleveland, Ohio.

Spirals

Introduction

FAMILY. Familiar. Only my family isn't familiar at all. My friends are familiar, my friends are as dependable as telephone poles, but the members of my family change in size, looks, powers, burdens and expectations, when all I ask of them is that they remain the same.

Children grow, gather power while their parents lose it, leave home, travel in other orbits. Parents move, remarry or don't remarry, dwindle away, die. Spouses may stay around for a long while—mine did, for twenty-eight years—but sooner or later they leave.

And I keep changing too, even though I'm the one who stays home. I picture myself in the role of mother, particularly the mother of young children, because this is a self I like—distracted and short-tempered, I grant you, but well-meaning in spite of outbursts. Still,

I have to recognize that this is different from the self who was a daughter or wife—and these don't have much in common with the new, apprentice selves, who have to learn a whole set of limits, as mother of adults, mother-in-law, widow and grandmother. One thing these selves have in common, however: They're not the same as my self when I'm alone.

THIS BOOK, which is fact, not fiction, is based on a journal that I've kept for years. I haven't invented anything except a few background details about people who aren't members of the family, in order to protect their privacy, and false names for everyone involved except my husband, Martin, and our collie, Ralph. Those two don't admit displacement. I couldn't think of either of them under another name, and, as it happens, neither of them is in a position to object.

A few months after I began keeping the journal, Martin became fatally ill, which raised a series of questions: Should I tell him the truth about his condition—in other words, does truth have some virtue that imposes obligations of its own? If he knew the truth, would he stop working, and if so, what would such a decision say about the way he'd spent his life up to that point? Most important for me, how was I going to survive without him?

I meant that question in the literal sense. Until the day I was married, I saw myself as a daughter opposed to my mother. After that day, I saw myself united with Martin and then as the mother of three children, but now I was about to lose not only my husband but my job. Two of my children—Ted and Karen—were already grown-up; Ted was married, and Karen was as-good-as-married, which her father and I considered not-quite-as-good. Peter, our youngest, who was born sixteen years almost to the day after his older brother, was ten years old at this point, so that not even he would need me much longer. I was about to become either the whole of my own life or nothing at all.

Two years after Martin's death, when I started this book, I planned to write about my husband and children, and about myself as a wife and mother. But that's not the book that I've written. Instead, I've concentrated on the one subject that I didn't want to touch, which shows what exotic and dangerous territory we cross as soon as we venture into the subject of family. I'd forgotten that I was a daughter, after all, long before I was a wife, and what's more, I continued to be a daughter after Martin was gone. The only question was, what sort of daughter was I?

My mother had never liked me, I was sure of that, or at the very least, she'd never approved of me. We'd never spent a peaceful afternoon together. How was I to deal with someone I might love but didn't necessarily like—in particular, how was I going to deal with her impending death? I couldn't simply distance myself, as I'd done in the past. The bond between us was real. If she died while I was unable to mourn for her, I felt that I would wipe out her existence as a mother (she'd never been much of a mother, or anything else, for that matter, except too much of a daughter), while at the same time I would diminish my own life in a way I couldn't yet understand.

This problem bedeviled me so thoroughly that I wasn't able to finish the book until I'd resolved it. For all I know, it may have been the reason why I undertook to write the book in the first place. At last, to my astonishment, a time came when I simply stopped agonizing about our relationship and realized that on a more significant level, it didn't matter whether my mother and I liked or even loved each other or not; there was a deeper bond than liking or not-liking between us. A child needs parents to give him life and to nurture him—but a father or mother has an equally urgent need for a child to complete the parent's life and give him a proper death, through the consummate act of seeing him whole. When I was able to see my mother whole, I was able to finish this book.

Birth, when I looked straight at it, seemed as tangled with problems as death. Why should a mother love the particular lump of flesh that's handed to her in her hospital room? I asked myself. Later my question became even sharper: Can a grandmother honestly claim to love an infant seen behind glass in a hospital nursery if she doesn't know which infant she's supposed to love without reading the name on the index card? Would we need all those bibs with "Grandma Loves Me" embroidered on them, if our responses were so predictable?

WRITING a book about family means writing a book about time, I discovered, since time is the dimension that families live in, but friends and lovers lack. (If friends and lovers stick with us long enough for us to perceive changes in them and for them to perceive changes in us, why then, according to my definition, they are not just friends and lovers any more; they are transformed into family.) But what shape is time? An image floated into my head, and this image became not only the title but the shape of the book.

When I was young, I assumed that time had to be a straight line, like a railroad track that would carry me from the past into the future: from school to career, from marriage to parenthood, at which point it would become a double track, heading up as long as my husband and I were hardworking and lucky, running downhill or staying level for certain stretches, of course, but sloping up in general, up and up, until . . . Why, until the day came when the line didn't head up any more. Until the day came when it headed down much more abruptly than it had headed up. But that was a day that no one chose to talk about, wives least of all.

The only alternative I'd heard of was a circle, which was the usual picture of marriage for women in the 1950s: the family circle, safe as lamplight and sure as the seasons; the daily grind of the kitchen cleaned up tonight so that it can get dirty tomorrow; groceries carried into the house and garbage carried out in the saved paper bags; the wheel of time spinning and spinning but getting me nowhere.

I dreaded the circle, but had no need to worry. True enough, events in my life seem to twist on their tails and come back at me again, but they're never quite the same; they've changed in the interval, and so have I. (If they didn't change, if my life were really a circle, I might learn more from experience and do everything better the second or tenth time round.)

A year after I began my journal, there I was, husbandless again, sleeping alone again, thinner and tougher than I'd been as a wife . . . racing my small sailboat as I'd raced it for twenty years, always without Martin, but for all that, decidedly not a girl again. I lived in a house with a young son some sixteen years after I'd lived in the house with another young son, but this time I was also the mother of a woman who was of childbearing age herself. I was my mother's daughter, and yet, as she grew weaker, I was my mother's mother.

My life has a swing to it, but also an unending surprise—it's not a circle but a spiral that I feel. And why shouldn't I feel a spiral, which is the natural pattern of growth and motion on a spinning planet? Winds move in spirals, ocean currents travel in spirals, sunflower seeds grow in spirals, our galaxy itself is a spiral. Why should my life be any different?

I may not get ahead, but I get around, I swing in loops, always kept in my path by my relation to my family, which is the spiral's core. With each circuit, I find myself at a level higher than the last, while the levels of my husband, children, parents are also changing. Scenes disappear and reappear, sometimes so close beneath my feet that they knock the breath out of me—but I'm not in them any more, I'm up here, detached in an orbit of my own, with chillier air and a broader view.

While the loops of the spiral rise, they also grow wider, but they spin more slowly. I feel the loss of power. The central core doesn't exert as strong a pull on me as it did before. What do I count for, after all, now that my daughter is a wife and mother herself and a working woman besides, now that my son is a professional man and the equal of his father, who isn't a professional man any longer, while

I'm without employment? There must have been a moment when power was equally balanced between me and my children, just as there must have been a moment when it was equally divided between my mother and me—but I was looking somewhere else at that moment, or I may have blinked and missed it.

Now, when I look for my children, I find them, but they're at a distance, and their heads aren't turned in my direction. With each circuit I make, I swing wider and higher, losing strength but gaining vision, generating less energy than I used to, seeing less of my family, but seeing more of the stars.

Chapter 1

BEGIN then, as everything always began in my life, at the moment when Martin comes through a door.

Start in fog on an October evening in 1978, past the time when the lamppost at the end of the front walk ought to be lit, nothing to be heard except the foghorn lowing on Execution Rock—two seconds out of every fifteen, but the sound stretches itself out to slide under the fog—a chesty tone that flows through the bottom layer of air without inflection, as if Long Island Sound itself is breathing in and out. At this point in the year, my sailboat is out of the water. The racing season has ended.

Suddenly, tires come rushing down the street from the Post Road, a heavy whirring recognizable to me as soon as it is to Ralph, the collie: an old Thunderbird barely slowing for the turn into the driveway, then braking. A few seconds later, the garage doors are thrown open one at a time, the car roars again (a man's foot, too heavy on the accelerator, not a good driver, not a person who cares about engines). The dog barks frantically and jumps up from beside my chair as one car door thumps shut and then the other (a lot of packages tonight, too many for the front seat). Ralph hurls himself against the front door, which my husband, Martin, is about to fling open, his overcoat slung over his shoulders, his suit jacket unbuttoned and flapping, a briefcase under one arm, two cake boxes in one hand and a shopping bag in the other, and silence is shattered into a thousand fragments lying in small heaps around his feet, which he kicks aside as he and the collie mount the stairs.

Reaching the bedroom, he flips on the overhead light, flips on the air conditioner (never mind the fact that it's autumn already, he likes the hum), tosses his briefcase and packages on the bed, twitches his finger through the mail on his night table, pushing aside the few that interest him, before he takes time out to kiss me.

"I didn't remember the dry cleaners until too late," I say. "You'll have to manage without your plaid bathrobe this weekend." Martin takes a crumpled shirt out of his briefcase, along with a stack of papers that he arranges on the table to be read after dinner, then runs the water in the bathroom sink full blast, before the dog has even stopped barking.

"Pete," I call to our son as I leave the room, "did you take in the badminton set the way you promised?" He's in his room with the door closed.

"Is it any wonder I love you best?" Martin says to Ralph, as I go downstairs.

Twenty minutes later, at the dining-room table, Martin demands some oak leaves, ordinary dry oak leaves, which I go out and get from the backyard. He steps into the kitchen, returns with a plate covered with a dish towel, and makes up a chant on the spur of the moment:

> "Abracadabra, bric-a-brax,
> Bonwit Teller's, Bergdorf's, Saks,
> Hoop-la, hope-la, water and soap-la,
> Hey, I say, Presto!"

Snapping his fingers, he whisks the towel away—and what do we have? Not crackly old oak leaves any more but chocolate leaves, straight from the best New York bakery. Peter looks warily at the plate. He's ten years old, on the verge of eleven, during the season that I'm talking about, and chocolate leaves are his favorite, but he's old enough now to see through the trick—that's what his father mustn't be allowed to realize—and not yet old enough to pretend that he doesn't.

This is the child we had no right to have, born two days before the sixteenth birthday of our older son, Ted. "Never have your youngest until your oldest can drive you home from the hospital," I told our friends when our daughter, Karen, was fourteen and I was forty. Strangers meeting us, way back then, were sure this little one must be the product of a second marriage. Neighborhood women, carrying tennis rackets or attaché cases, were convinced that he must be an accident, and that I must be bizarre or slovenly or devoid of inner resources to be so out of keeping with the times. Delayed motherhood wasn't due to come into fashion for another decade.

"We didn't trust our children to do right by us," Martin used to say to new acquaintances, "so we decided to produce our own grandchild." The strangers would look from one of us to the other, while I waited for them to laugh entirely too vigorously, to show that they understood this to be a joke. Martin enjoyed flashing his family life in front of people in the same spirit in which he stuffed a colored silk handkerchief in his breast pocket, coordinated to match his tie, even though he knew this had gone out of fashion, and what was worse, out of taste, some time ago.

But how could I prove that I wasn't this child's grandmother? Easily, easily. Not because I'm young or pliant—God knows I'm neither, especially not on autumn evenings, and most especially not on this one—but because, when I'm with Peter, I'm irritable, impatient, vainglorious, prideful, furious, niggling, passionate and, above all, full of remorse that I should be filled with such ungraceful feelings. My vision is knocked silly by the force of my desire that he should go get a Kleenex and blow his nose, instead of sniffing up into his sinuses or dripping down on to his plate.

Now I begin to understand why there's something wary in his nature, a protective coating that shields him from the overboiling of my love. How else did I acquire a son who has already asked for a filing cabinet for his room, in which to keep papers of interest to him laid away in alphabetical order? How account for a boy who hates circuses, mistrusts foreign travel, likes butcher's-shop lamb chops and chocolate truffles, but curbs his desires and asks for nothing that transcends the supermarket? When he sleeps, he lies flat on his back with his head turned to one side, folded away for the night as neatly as one of the papers in his file.

He's small for his age, and a year younger than the rest of his class, and this affects not only the way he sees himself but also the way in which we treat him. Of course, he never suspects that I'm the one who has done this to him, I'm the one who has betrayed him by willing his body to remain small a while longer, because of the intensity of my need for a child in the house. How much taller would he be today if I'd been ten years younger when he was born?

I remember the day that Martin fell in love with this child. It was a Sunday at noon, a year after the baby's birth, an hour that existed in no one's schedule, like a hammock slung between two weeks for us to lounge in.

"Gross," said Karen, who was fifteen at the time and skinny, and hadn't come into her beauty yet, "absolutely gross," riffling her hair to show us her dandruff, which was unbelievable, unbearable, and bound to get much, much worse because no one was doing a single thing to cure it. We were sitting in the kitchen, the only spot in our 1920s Tudor house that catches the sunlight on a winter afternoon. Or rather, four of us were sitting at the table in our accustomed symmetry, Ted and Karen, Martin and I, a junior couple and a senior couple, while the baby stood in his playpen at our side, stretching his neck over the rail like a pony to take any tidbit that might come his way. I don't remember if Karen was cranky because she'd slept too long that morning, beyond her usual bounds, or because she still had to go to Sunday school that year and hadn't slept long enough.

Martin, on the other hand, sat in his bathrobe, greatly at his ease, his abundant straight brown hair not yet combed but falling over his forehead. It may have been that straight hair, so thick and flip and casual, so unusual for a Jew and yet in perfect harmony with the line of his nose, that made me fall in love with him in the first place. Apparently he was pleased by the number of hours of sleep that he'd banked in his account that night, helped by pills, I was sure, but what else were the pills there for, he'd have demanded. Martin feared insomnia the way other people fear starvation; in fact, in his mind there wasn't much of a gulf between them. If he didn't sleep well, he wouldn't be able to work well, and if he didn't work well, he wouldn't hold on to his rank in his law firm; he wouldn't be able to supply this family with the food, the table, the Tudor house within walking distance of Long Island Sound, the garden with winter sunlight glinting, and beyond the yew hedge, the shapes of college tuitions and weddings and calamities still to come.

When I saw him asleep on a Sunday morning with the shades pulled down to the sills and the air conditioner humming even in midwinter to drown out any stray household noise, I never felt that I recognized this man. During the night, his face, with no body to be seen beneath it, flattened out into a seamless mask, vast and still, twice as large as the face I knew and as empty of thought as the heads on Easter Island. No, not like the heads on Easter Island. Like his mother. That was his trouble, although we didn't know it yet. He looked like his mother. His mouth was half open, but no sound came out of it. His smell—the smell of this man who used Binaca mouthwash and French cologne in astonishing quantities—condensed wet and middle-aged in the folds of his pajamas.

But now, here in the kitchen, he was restored to us, he was back from that dense and primitive land in which he traveled alone; from his look of relaxation, the night's journey had been a good one. He handed a potato stick to the baby in his playpen, and Karen offered him a sip of grape juice from her glass, which the baby accepted with equal good will. While she was distracted, I slipped an extra slice of cold leftover steak on to her plate.

Ignoring the juice, Martin went to the cabinet and took out a giant bottle of Coke, which he opened. He must have shaken it first, because it frothed all over the table. Bits and pieces were always flowing or falling from this man. At that very moment, if I went up to the bedroom, I'd find Seconal or Dalmane or Miltown or Maalox, quite possibly all four of them, scattered on the night table or lying on the floor ("Don't you ever worry about the baby? Or at least the dog?"), bath towels tossed on the bed, dimes that had dropped through holes in his trouser pockets lying on the carpet, tissues, which later clogged up the washing machine with lint, stuffed in the breast pocket of his pajamas, and dollar bills that he kept on hand for a quick tip or taxi left in the pockets of suits on their way to the cleaners. There was too much of him to be contained. He emitted a steady stream of memos to his associates and secretary, writing at night with a battery-lighted pen. Even his beard needed shaving twice a day, on the nights that we were due to go out.

"I must've gotten this dandruff from you," Karen accused her father, as she wiped the purple mustache off the baby's mouth. It was true, father and daughter faced each other with the same head of hair, the same reddish undertone. I noticed that she'd already put the extra meat I'd tried to feed her back on the platter.

"You don't have dandruff," I said crossly, because Ted had gotten up to help himself to peanut butter, ignoring the cold cuts laid out on the table. Ted was always a dazzling child, with golden curls when he was little, darker curls as he grew older, which seemed less like curls than like electric coils, as if so much energy sparked inside him that it had to erupt through his scalp. It was hard to admire his good looks, however, since he was forever in motion. Karen, on the other hand, was as self-contained as an egg.

"The hen laid only two devilled eggs today?" Martin asked.

"Look!" Karen pointed dramatically at the white specks that littered her plate. It was no use, she couldn't get away with it. We'd seen her sprinkle the salt herself. She sputtered protests, while the baby chomped with relish on a piece of steak that Martin had given him.

"Stop him, he's going to choke!" Ted exploded, our firstborn child, the first grandchild on both sides of the family, first in his class at school every year, first in everything, and always the burdened one in the family. Martin laughed, but took the steak out of the baby's mouth in the interest of safety and consoled him with a sip of Coke instead.

"He won't like that," I pronounced. "Babies hate carbonated drinks." But already this little one, enchanted by bubbles, was guzzling out of his father's glass, and as we laughed at my error and his rapture, liberated by joy, Martin sprang up from his seat and began to sing.

"My mother gave me a nickel . . . To buy a pickle . . ." he sang, jigging up and down wildly in front of the playpen. Suddenly, holding on to the railing of his pen, the baby began to sing and jig too, facing his father, bending his knees and bobbing up and down, and as he did this, Martin's heart flew out to him—I could almost feel the air part—in a violent rush of love, but also of admiration for one so little and yet so gallant that he dared hold his own and demand his glory against the claims of four such tumultuous giants. Martin had seen his son for the past year, but this was the first time that he had truly seen him. After that, the baby came into his name. We spoke of him as Pete, or Peter.

On the evening that I'm talking about, however—which was the last evening that Martin turned oak leaves into chocolate—Peter was ten years old, and Ted was a lawyer already, like his father, and married to Felicia, and Karen was living with Kurt, who was another lawyer, Ted's roommate from law school, in fact, but she wouldn't marry him for reasons that Martin and I couldn't understand; they seemed to have something to do with her intelligence and independence. Both grown-up children had apartments in New York City. Only Peter was left at the dining-room table with us.

I remember that Martin brought home more than cookies that evening. He brought rum babas for me and a poundcake for himself, to keep in the freezer, his taste moving in those days toward butter cookies, poundcake, custard—everything eggy and simple that might have been used fifty years earlier to fatten a skinny child. He also brought a bottle of Borghese hand lotion that I'd mentioned but hadn't bought because it was expensive, then excused myself by saying I wouldn't be able to find it in the suburbs anyway.

Bringing home gifts was important to him—I wish I'd seen this at the time—partly for the pleasure of giving, but chiefly for the power of buying. All day long and often on weekday evenings and Saturdays, he worked in his New York office as a litigation lawyer, battling over cases that in the last analysis came down to money, but money made terrible by what men went through to get it and hold on to it, and yet money that remained intangible. Only for a few moments at the end of a day or on a weekend could a little of that money become visible, like fairy gold at dusk, taking on twilight shapes of new shirts or ties for which he had no room left in his drawers, packages of Nova Scotia salmon and cream cheese that we ate sitting in bed at midnight, long-stemmed lilacs for me, and for the children chocolate turkeys covered in colored foil, marshmallow eggs in cardboard egg cartons, candy valentines or Droste chocolate apples that we tapped open, each in season.

Entering a store, Martin breathed in the smell, the way that other men breathed in the smell of woods or surf before plunging. His eyes shone. His voice rose. He expanded his soul. He was as old now as his father had ever been, a diamond dealer who had adored his family with a doggish adoration but was too honest and irritable to be anything but a failure at business, a man who had quarreled with his customers and never been able to buy for his wife and child what his son was buying at that moment.

It was Martin who picked out my good dresses, as if I were a cripple, which in a sense I was. I was capable of buying only everyday pants and sweaters for myself, and not enough of those, never having learned as a child that it was all right to spend money, least of all on myself. That was a lesson my mother, Marion, could hardly have taught me.

I might have learned something about giving and getting if I'd taken lessons from the collie. On Saturday mornings, Martin would take Ted and Karen when they were small, or Pete in his turn, and drive into the village, with Ralph in the back seat, where he'd buy a toy for each child and a rawhide bone for the dog. Ralph never chewed his bone after the first day—I don't think he really liked them—but whenever company came, he'd rush to produce it and prance around the room carrying it in his mouth, to show what a well-loved creature he was.

This must have been the reason I picked Martin in the first place: because I had no idea what I could afford in life without him; indeed, without him, I could afford nothing at all. It was no surprise when he came through the door that Friday evening in October, carrying cookies for Peter, rum babas and hand lotion for me, poundcake for himself, even though he was going into Mount Sinai Hospital the next morning to spend his weekend in the cancer ward.

Did I say that he brought treats even though he was going into the hospital? I should have said he brought treats because of it. The luxuries of life weren't trivial for this man. He was too much of a child of the Depression for that. They were his assurance that where there was cake, there would always be bread; they were his margin of safety. Like a taxi on a rainy night, they sheltered him from evil, from the fatigue, wet feet, chills, wrinkled suits, stolen wallets, muggings, stabbings, smoke inhalations that wore down people who were forced to use the subways, and eventually destroyed them, as he, too, would be destroyed one day in some precinct where it would be impossible to hail a cab.

There are good men who are men of substance, who exist like rocks, perpetually in the shadow of truth, and then there are men like Martin, also good men, who are men of style, and who must live and die with their own sparkle, like water running fresh and flashing in the sun. I thought it the duty of love to know which was which. And so nothing was different at our dinner table that evening, except that Martin broke off part of a cookie he'd brought home and fed it to Ralph under the table, then leaned over and whispered baby talk into the dog's ear.

"It won't do you any good," I said. "No matter how hard you try, that dog'll never learn to talk."

"How do you know?" Martin answered. "He's very young yet."

WHEN Martin flung the garage doors open, I heard the hinges creak, a sound inconsistent with the thunk of the doors of the Thunderbird. Of all the houses on Shad Point, ours may be the only one that doesn't have an electric garage door; what's more, it's the only house in the neighborhood with a one-car garage with old-fashioned wooden double doors. The house stands on so little ground that the narrow garage, with its wrought-iron hinges, is obliged to face the street, instead of being tucked around to the side, where it belongs. What's visible of the other houses here on the Point—most of them Tudor, built in the twenties to share a common beach—are half-timbered façades and tapestry brick and casement windows set with an occasional rondel of stained glass, glimpsed behind rhododendron bushes that are twice as tall as the gardeners.

We were a young couple with two small children when we moved from the city and bought this house, but we never moved on to another that had more land, even when we could have afforded it. In part, this was because Martin had never outgrown the Depression—he always regarded his income, no matter how large, as a temporary state of grace—but in part it stemmed from a different kind of depression. Martin's was the gaiety, the extravagance, of a truly melancholy man. He was amazed by the present; he'd spend any amount of money on present pleasure, but he mistrusted the future, and not without reason. The squeak of those hinges, every time he came home, was a reminder to both of us that he never expected to make old bones.

The trouble, as I say, was that he looked like his mother. Sixteen years earlier, he'd developed a growth in his private vegetable patch, the colon, family territory of a sort, the kitchen garden right next to the back door. One spot, one crop.

"Like a mushroom," said the doctor who detected it. "A nice neat stem."

"This isn't the time for it," I answered. Martin's mother had died two months earlier. He was an only son, whose hair was reddish-brown, like hers, and dipped to a widow's peak on his forehead, just like hers.

"Fifty-fifty I'd say his chances were," the surgeon told me in the hall outside the hospital room the day after the growth had been removed. I hadn't asked him to quote the odds.

"In that case, we have to make sure he never finds out," I said.

"I feel my patients have a right to be informed." The surgeon was a man who made a point out of truth with which to prick a vulnerable spot.

"You've cut out the tumor," I argued. "If it was really a benign polyp, which is what I told him, there wouldn't be any difference in aftercare, would there? Then what more do you want from the man?"

"This isn't the way I usually handle these cases." The doctor's tone made it clear that never again would he lower himself like this.

There are luxuries in life that we confuse with virtues—cleanliness and ambition are two that come to mind—and chalk up to character, until they disappear under the pressure of circumstances. Truth is one of these. Truth is a luxury that comes out of a smug throat and serves the truth-teller well, whereas lies are wrung from the belly of anguish and don't have a sense of choice about them. I was perfectly willing to lie outrageously, if I could prolong Martin's life by twenty-four hours.

"We mustn't be discouraged," the surgeon added meticulously. "Each year that he lives improves the odds. If he pulls through for five years, you can consider that he's—"

"Cured?"

"That his chances are the same as yours or mine." I'd been warned that doctors, especially surgeons, especially eminent surgeons like this one, were apt to exaggerate the seriousness of a situation in order to make themselves bigger heroes if the patient lived. "There are certain things, though, that you'll have to make sure that your husband never does."

"Such as what?"

"Apply for life insurance. He'd have to submit his medical history. Including the record of this operation. And then he'd be turned down."

So I tore up solicitations from insurance companies, and considered myself lucky that Martin never brought home any on his own. At the end of five years, the surgeon who lopped off the mushroom was dead, and Martin was fine. Eleven additional years passed before he fell sick again.

I MUST have been the only person in the world praying for lymphoma. Lymphoma was terrible, of course, but lymphoma was treatable, or at least treatable compared to carcinoma. Lymphoma was "indolent," in the pretty phrase used by Martin's cousin by marriage, Stanley Berkman, who's a doctor himself, although not an oncologist. He meant that lymphoma takes its time while doing its job of killing somebody off.

It was April 1978, and Martin was on an operating table, and my daughter-in-law, Felicia, was with me. I'd asked the children not to come to the hospital that morning, for my sake, not theirs—they were too real to be bearable at that hour—but Felicia had surprised me and showed up anyway. Martin's hospital room had pale-blue walls and a desk with Queen Anne legs. The curtains were looped up in the middle and fastened with rubber bands, like ponytails—to keep them from gathering dust, I suppose.

Carcinoma, not lymphoma, was what Martin's doctors expected. I'd seen the mortality curve on a graph by that time, a sharp climb to a peak at the fifth or sixth month, then an even steeper descent until the foothills were reached at the end of a year. After that, nothing but rock.

"What are you reading?" I asked.

"*Ada,*" Felicia said, pronouncing the name "Ah-dah." "Whenever I want cheering, I go back and reread *Ada.*" Felicia is the tallest, most elegant woman I have ever seen, with the longest neck, around which she wears a silk scarf knotted at the side. My long-eyelashed giraffe, I call her, my willow tree, my Theodora of Ravenna, my Byzantine mosaic, her black eyes outlined in still darker black and her impossibly pointed toes, in their Italian shoes, suspended in the glittering air above our heads.

"I never read it. I've never read any of the books you've read. But you shouldn't have missed work today, silly." Felicia is the publications director of a major auction house.

"Nonsense. Plenty of people are dying to cover for me. Don't you think I'd rather sit here with you and read a book than work?" She snuffed her cigarette in the ashtray, as if to snuff out any objections. While most girls I know reach their full bloom at twenty-five or even twenty, some when they're thirty or forty and some when they're only twelve, and then spend the rest of their lives forgetting the glory they've left behind them, Felicia longs to be an old woman. In her case, she's right. She won't reach her full grandeur, her face won't live up to the full promise of her cheekbones, for another fifty years. Sometimes, when she gestures, I think she's in training for her future, for the time when she'll stand at the head of a grand staircase, dressed in chiffon and leaning on an ivory-headed cane.

"There's just a chance, Stan says, that this could be an atypical lymphoma," I said in gratitude. "It doesn't sound like a lymphoma. We have to face it. It would have to be a freakish one. Almost unheard-of." But only the freakish was unpredictable, and only the unpredictable had no place on the chart I'd been shown.

"Of course there's a chance," Felicia echoed.

"An outside chance." Years ago, at some family dinner or other, when discussing the prognosis for a mutual friend, Stan had quoted his old professor in medical school, who used to say that when you heard the sound of hoofbeats, you should prepare yourself to meet horses, not zebras.

"I brought *The Master and Margarita*," Felicia added. "I thought you could reread the best parts. Where Margarita smears her body with magic ointment and becomes twenty years old and a shining beauty? And then she flies out of her bedroom window mother-naked on a broomstick, and as she goes, she drops her slip on the head of the dirty-minded old man who sits and moons on a bench in front of her house?"

"I never read it in the first place. Don't you know that I've never read anything?"

"Really? What luck! You can lean back, and put your legs up on that footrest, and let me read to you. I always feel better when I lie down and let someone read to me." Neither of us touched the bed, whose top sheet was folded into accordion pleats at the foot.

Martin's doctor, Ephraim Bentwick, came into the room, unbearably pure in his hospital whites. "Lymphoma," he announced triumphantly.

There are people for whom any chance, however slight, is the same thing as victory, and a little stretch of time carries inside it a promise of immortality.

Martin was a fighter by training, not only a lawyer but a trial lawyer, and not only that but a lawyer's lawyer, getting his business from house counsel or other colleagues who were afraid that they'd lose not only the case but their client as well. He agonized over every comma in a brief, but once an argument was done he left the decision to the court. For thirty years, he'd made his living chiefly by beating the odds.

As for me, I'd never given failure any thought. My optimism may have been genetic, inherited from my father, but it was also part of the era in which Martin and I grew up. It's not accurate to say that we were children of the Depression; we were children of Depression parents, which is something quite different, and so we weren't depressed in the least by our future. When Martin was in high school, non-farm unemployment was thirty percent, but he never doubted that he'd find a job. Four years later, only one person every year was admitted from City College to the law school he wanted to attend, but he knew that he'd be the one to get in. Before he graduated from law school, the dean called him into his office. It was almost impossible that year for Jewish graduates to find work in law firms unless they had relatives in the profession—didn't Martin have at least an uncle in his file? No, he didn't. But Martin didn't even have to look for a job. World War II intervened. By the time it was over, the law business was booming along with all others. Our philosophy, or else our luck, must have been shaped by the movies of the period, in which the gallant little plane, riddled with bullets, staggers back to the airfield, where it lands safely against overwhelming odds, as everyone knows it must. We were all revved up to land safely against the odds.

It was the same in our personal lives. From what I saw in my mother and father's home, I had no reason to believe that love could exist within marriage, and yet I found and married Martin. With him, I bore children whenever I wanted them, the last when I was forty, not so much betting against birth defects as never stopping to give them the slightest thought. Sure enough, our children turned out kindhearted as well as healthy, intelligent and good looking as well as hardworking and vigorous, high in SATs and low in draft number. Apparently they inherited the family luck.

"Lymphoma!" Felicia cried. "You see?" We fell into each other's arms. I held her responsible for the miracle.

"We'll beat this thing yet," I said. "It was the azalea bush that scared me." She looked at me. "The white azalea that you and Ted and Karen gave us."

"For your twenty-fifth anniversary?"

"Next to the front door. Taller than I am. But you wouldn't know an azalea from an oak. I'll show you, next time you're at the house." We smiled at each other lovingly. "Every other azalea in the neighborhood is blooming, or at least budding, except that one." And its top branch is brown and crippled, I didn't choose to add. Each morning, when I go out to pick up the newspaper from the driveway, it mocks me, but tonight, when I go home, I'll mock it back, I'll spit in its branches. "Of course, it faces north. And we've had a rough winter." This was the level I had come to in little more than a week, superstitious as a peasant, a seeker after signs.

Two days later, I was eating breakfast in the kitchen when the telephone rang. A mistake had been made, said Doctor Bentwick. By the laboratory, that is. The answer was carcinoma. Widespread. A matter of months.

Chapter 2

DAYLIGHT saving time moved in on us while Martin was in the hospital. It came as something of a shock to me, all that light and wind rolling around in the sky, and the dogwood bursting into bloom, and the river glittering under the Triborough Bridge when I drove into New York, as if to remind me that the shad were running silver through the fish stores. For three weeks now, I'd seen the afternoons only through the barred window at the end of the hospital corridor, but this afternoon I was leaving Martin early to go visit my mother in her apartment.

The results of Martin's liver scan had come back a few hours ago—good, almost astonishingly good. Who could tell what was going on? How could this be a metastasized cancer if the liver was unaffected? And if one test result was abnormal, then nothing was proceeding according to schedule, nothing was predictable, nothing at all.

May sunlight struck the top of my head as I walked to the garage. A drugstore window showed stacks of suntan lotion and polarized goggles under a cardboard beach umbrella. Martin would be coming home soon, maybe in a week or less. I'd better have his car inspected and serviced before he needed it. It was time to take the storm windows off the screened porch and buy impatiens to plant near the terrace and wash the garden furniture. He'd spent enough time lying indoors.

Is it possible, I wondered, that each of us has his inner thermostat, his own emotional range of temperature—mine ten degrees higher in May and in sunshine than in November and the dark—and tends to revert to it, no matter what the circumstances? Is it possible that if all my feelings were laid out on a chart over a long period of time (not ignoring my depression the year before, when Martin was healthy but the book I'd been working on for three years had been rejected) I'd find that the average was nowhere near as erratic as I imagined?

Maybe this is how concentration-camp victims survived, I told myself, by hanging on to their habit of happiness, finding as much of it in a scrap of potato as they used to find in a banquet. Or maybe I had everything backward. Maybe survivors are people with low happiness temperatures by nature, who are better adapted to scraping through without it. Like my mother, Marion.

"I'd better have a quick supper with my mother," I'd said to Martin that morning. "She hasn't seen a soul in weeks, she says. Except Sylvia." Sylvia was her housekeeper, a highly groomed young black woman who was taking a computer course at Hunter in her free time.

"Ah, the dear Raven," Martin said, flourishing his arm to show that he gave his permission for my venture. "Enjoy yourself." He was working in bed, his attaché case open beside him and a yellow pad propped on his knees, flinging his hand across the page as he wrote, underlining his words or circling them and drawing long swooping arrows to show where he wanted them inserted. It was contrary to his nature to write more than a few lines on a page.

The Raven was Martin's private name for my mother—The Raven because her eyes were black, her expression was black and her essential message was "Nevermore." He wasn't apt to care for a woman who was incapable of walking into a store and spending a dollar on a present for any of her grandchildren, even though she was willing to hand out substantial checks. Checks didn't count; checks made out to the family weren't gifts but transfers of funds, like water moving from one reservoir into another—the supply wasn't reduced, so long as we weren't foolish enough to tell her we had cashed them.

"What do you want for Christmas?" she asked Ted one winter when he was little. Being Ted, he named something marvelous but expensive. "We'll have to see," she said, pretending to be shocked at the enormity of what he'd asked for. "I never thought about anything like that. But maybe . . . if your grandfather and I eat a little less for lunch every day . . ." She swelled up in front of us with the treasure she was withholding, a sly look in her eye that meant I was supposed to go ahead and make the purchase (I'd do it anyway, she knew) and she'd pay me back, but first we'd have to make this young one suffer and crawl, because he'd never learn the value of a dollar unless she taught him. Heaven knows he'd never learn it from his parents.

Marion doesn't believe in happiness, or rather, she doesn't know what happiness is like, any more than a tone-deaf person knows what music is like except in theory, which makes it sound absurd. She doesn't believe in romance, either; romance is nothing but puppy love, romance is falling in love with love, she told me when I was single. In any case, no boy would ever fall for a girl who liked books and got good marks, so I wasn't even worthy of her warning. When

I married Martin, she changed her tune. Romance lasts as long as the honeymoon, she assured me, which is about the same length of time that a married woman's figure lasts. My trousseau slips and nightgowns—pure silk, trimmed with lace—were ordered two sizes too big, because she was sure that I'd become as flabby and shapeless as my future, once I was married and my youth came to an end. So far as she knows, no woman of her acquaintance has ever had an affair.

She doesn't believe in the reality of money, either, although she'd violently deny this. Since she has never confronted money head on, she regards it as some sort of ogre that will either devour her or defend her beyond all reason, depending on her past behavior.

It was a cruel twist of fate that made her marry a moderately rich man rather than a poor boy while she was only a teenager herself, so that she never had an excuse to go out and earn a dollar, or at least to exercise the real talent for scrimping and begrudging—but ultimately making ends meet—that might have justified her existence.

It's even more unfair that if she has to have money, she can't at least use it to patronize her married daughter. One of the many things she finds unforgivable about me is the fact that Martin has always made what her generation called a "comfortable" living.

"Another new sweater! Tell me the truth just once," she demands every time I see her. "Exactly how many sweaters [pocketbooks, coats, skirts] do you own? Martin must have some income!" She puffs out her lips in disbelief when I tell her this sweater isn't new, it's years old, and what's more, I've never stopped to count how many I own. "Well, thank God!" she adds with a pious sigh, which means she never believed she'd be able to afford a daughter who could give such an answer.

No, Marion believes in only one thing: She believes in mothers and daughters. Marion's mother—my grandmother—married a brilliantly sarcastic man with the face of a hawk, in order to make a home for her own mother. Marion's father—my grandfather—was a German immigrant who went into business as an importer of toys and novelties, made money, saved money and went blind before he was fifty. His own fault, my father said; the man had such a temper he jumped up and down in his rages at business until one day his retinas were jarred loose and snapped up like window shades—and there he was, blind for the rest of his life, and all because of his temper. His own fault, my mother and grandmother said: My grandfather was so stingy with himself that he wouldn't spend the money to see an eye doctor, but bought his eyeglasses off the rack in the five-and-ten, a stronger pair every couple of months, and look what happened to him, will you? A few years later he went crazy and tried to kill himself by jumping out of his apartment window, but never let go of the sill. Instead, he lived on his savings for the rest of his life, as his widow lived on them for the rest of hers, as his only child, Marion, lives on them to this day.

Marion worshipped her mother. She sat at her mother's feet. She never lived more than three or four blocks away from her mother from the day she was married; she went to visit her mother every day and demanded that her husband have dinner with her mother at least once a week. Well, of course she did. What other way was there for a daughter—an only child—to behave, especially with a mother who was so sympathetic, never minding her own troubles living with a crazy blind man and trying to keep him in line? Marion could give you an earful about her mother's troubles, which were plenty, but plenty, and still that woman was always good for a giggle over a dirty joke or some gossip and a drink on a rainy afternoon— why, it was unbelievable to Marion how many friends that woman had. Wasn't it only natural for a daughter to feel this way about her mother? Wasn't her own daughter—wasn't I?—bound to feel the same way about Marion one day?

I, too, was an only child, but I was the unnatural daughter who never did anything right in her life. I never managed to please my mother, but I was too dense to figure out where my offense lay.

"I can't leave her sitting alone forever," I said, as if Martin was arguing the point. Marion broke her kneecap a year ago and walks with a cane, but finds less and less reason to go out. Her husband divorced her fifteen years ago. Her friends, who turned out in the final crunch to be his friends, abandoned her. Her daughter comes to visit her once a week for two hours, but has missed the past three weeks because her son-in-law is in the hospital.

"Of course, nothing keeps her from coming to the hospital to visit you," I said to Martin. "Except she wouldn't spend the money on a taxi. But at least she plays fair. After all, she didn't go to the hospital to see Karen either, when Karen had her appendix out last year. And Karen's her favorite."

"Count your blessings," Martin answered, picking up an opponent's brief.

LOOKING back from here, I can see that it must have been losing Martin that changed the way I felt about my mother. This wasn't because he didn't like her. It wasn't as simple as that.

After I graduated from college, I found a job in a public relations firm, but I still lived in my parents' apartment. I dated many boys at the same time, because seeing the same boy twice in a week was tantamount to announcing my engagement to him (they were known as "boys" in those days, no matter how old they were, until the day they were married). Night after night, bored by the whole routine, I dragged home trophies of matchbooks and swizzlesticks. A girl's popularity rating depended on how many times a week she went out, rather than whom she went out with.

Most of my dates were mine because none of the other girls wanted them. They were tiny accountants from Brooklyn, who wore jackets with padded shoulders and handled me with wet palms because I lived in Manhattan. "P.H.G.," they would tell their friends on the other side of the river the next day—"Papa hat Gelt"—but it was admiration for that fact, not avarice, that made their hands sweat. They were heavy-lipped, homely boys cursed with good-looking older brothers who were already doctors. They were nephews of my father's secretary, or they were homosexuals dating me to keep their parents quiet, but always they were the unloved, and while they were with me their eyes shone like those of wounded animals who knew when they were in the presence of someone who wouldn't hurt them. Whenever a man said that he was in love with me, I could see all too clearly the deficiency in his own life that I was supposed to plug to be fooled into believing him.

Over all of us girls, over all of us professional virgins, there hung a delicate lack of innocence. Twenty-five was the generally accepted cutoff age, by which time a girl had to be married or else run the risk of being forced out of the group, like a child at a birthday party playing Going to Jerusalem, who wasn't quick enough to grab a chair at the moment the Victrola stopped. Now that I look back, I suppose that I didn't believe in romance very much more than my mother did, or if I did, I believed in it only for other girls, those who were beautiful and sexy, or I believed in it in the way that I believed in God, with no more expectation of waking up and finding one kind of lover in my bedroom than the other. The best that I could hope for was to meet a kind and decent man, with whom I'd set up a kind and decent home, which was better than anything my parents ever had.

Then I met Martin, who was thirty at the time, and who'd been interviewing applicants, as he put it, ever since he got out of the army. We became engaged that first night.

He found what he was looking for in a wife, which was no more than he'd counted on while he dated so assiduously, but I found what I'd never believed existed. I didn't so much fall in love as hurl myself into it, swapping one universe that was lopsided, passionate and vulnerable for another equally lopsided, passionate and vulnerable, but one that offered me a chance for happiness.

"We'll never quarrel," I said fervently. "No matter what happens, I promise I won't go home to Mother." I had no way of knowing—

and, of course, he didn't tell me—that I'd said one of the cruelest things a woman can say to a man.

After that, for as long as Martin was with me, I paid very little attention to my mother or to anyone else other than Martin and my children. I worked at home rather than in an office, and I never had any close friends. I might as well have been living right next to a waterfall, for all I could hear of other voices.

It was a year or two after Martin's death before a change came over me, and when it did, I couldn't be sure that it was any of my doing—it may have been less voluntary, more biological, than I supposed at the time. Happiness had gone through me like a ray of sunlight, like a spike nailing me in place, passing from the top of my head through my backbone and my heels to the center of the earth, but unhappiness seemed to settle down on me in a lateral direction like a fog, making me spread out toward other people, blurring my edges in a common exhalation of mists and sighs.

Nowadays, when I think about my mother, I wonder if it could be a hormonal development that altered me, maybe a response triggered by my mother's aging or my own, a late-life form of lactation, in which I had a vague sense of pressure that meant my body was getting ready to produce a fluid I didn't know I had in me and wouldn't necessarily put to good use. After all, I'd menstruated thirteen times a year for thirty-seven years by that time, and produced only three children. My breasts filled up with milk, but then I took pills that dried up the flow, so that I never saw it while I fed my babies out of bottles. Producing fluids in response to hormones hadn't necessarily profited me or my family.

I can only say that not too long after Martin's death, I became aware that within the next few years I'd probably face the death of a mother with whom I could not remember spending a peaceful afternoon. At that time, the questions that had worried me for so many years suddenly turned out to be questions there was no point in asking any more. Did it matter that I'd never done anything right in my life, so far as she was concerned? Did it matter that she'd never praised me? Did it matter whether we loved each other, or even whether she liked me or I liked her? There was a bond deeper than liking or not-liking between us. Our bond was death.

A child needs parents to give birth to him and nurture him. But why do parents need a child? To support him when he's old. To take care of him. But my mother lives on Park Avenue and has a housekeeper to take care of her.

No, something more than that is required: We need to mourn our parents. When I say mourn, I don't mean that I'd miss this woman and the aggravation we caused each other. I mean we need to see the parent whole at last, free of the emotional pratfalls of liking and not-liking. In short, the child must remember the parent—which means put back together the parts, or members, that have only been seen separately until that point. It's impossible to re-member, or even recognize, what you've never seen.

If a parent gives birth to a child, then a child returns the act, if not the favor, by giving death to a parent, a whole and proper existence after death, which is the function and challenge of mourning. The child creates the posthumous parent, and if there can be a stillbirth that leads to nothing but the garbage pail at one end of the cycle, then I suppose there can equally well be a stilldeath—in fact, they must occur by the millions. What we may need is a fertility clinic aimed at after-death existence.

This line of inquiry seemed important to me for my own sake rather than my mother's. No woman is grown up until her mother dies, I've heard other women say. The question was, what sort of person might I grow up to be, sometime in my fifties, and what part of me would remain a defensive, prickly, half-loved half child?

But quite a lot of time had to pass before these questions occurred to me. I can't tell whether they would have occurred to me at all, or occurred with the same intensity, if Martin had been with me. I can only say for sure that during the twenty-eight years that I lived with Martin, and for a year or two afterward, I irritated Marion and was irritated by her as seldom as possible, except for one visit a week and a more or less regular, more than less grudging late-afternoon phone call, made at an hour when my errands were finished but my evening with the family hadn't begun yet. Unfortunately, that was the hour when she took her shot of Scotch, which stimulated her dissatisfaction with her life in general and her daughter in particular as much as it did the circulation in her feet.

When Martin went into the hospital, I wanted less to do with Marion than ever before. I couldn't bear to see the expression on her face that meant she'd been right all along, as I'd soon find out for myself. Happiness was only a phase that people outgrow, like puppy love or a passion for sailboats, while reality meant sitting alone in a bedroom with cigarettes and Scotch and an injured kneecap and chronic emphysema—which wasn't helped by the cigarettes—waiting for a daughter who hadn't come to visit in the past three weeks.

She was sitting there and waiting to catch me.

"LOOKS as if it's clouding over." The doorman of my mother's apartment building is a wisp of a man dressed in a brown uniform with the address of the house stitched in gold on his breast pocket. "They said rain this evening." In years of service to this building, he has learned that female tenants feel entitled to sympathetic comments about the weather, whatever it may be, rain, sun or change (change is what causes colds or flu) whenever they go outdoors on foot.

"Still, it's nice to see daylight at this hour," I answered provocatively. An elevator man stepped forward, a strapping young fellow with an Irish face as round and pale as an untoasted English muffin, the remains of a look of country freshness about him. The elevators were converted to self-service years ago, so his job was to carry the shopping bag that held Martin's dirty pajamas, which I was taking home to wash.

I'd come back to my village. At that moment, I was standing four blocks south of the house where I lived with my parents until the day I was married, when I moved a block and a half east toward Third Avenue, where rents were cheaper. Meanwhile, my grandmother lived in the apartment that my mother owns now. In this village on the Upper East Side, no more than a dozen streets north to south and four or five avenues east to west, I'd wheeled my bicycle, my two-wheel roller skates (who else owned two-wheel skates?), my Silver Cross baby carriage—gray, restrained, without fringe, like the awnings of these upper Park Avenue apartment houses—Karen's stroller, Ted's tricycle, the shopping cart in which I lugged groceries up the hill from the A & P.

My heels clicked on the marble floor of the lobby. The elevator man's crepe soles squeaked. Except for a single window, never opened, that faced a patch of service court, the light in the lobby was electric, burning night and day in Nesle's sconces. Through this air that knows no seasons, air that has grown gray and old without being changed but without losing its quality either, like tarnished silver, we marched together toward the rear.

NOT too many people in the city do what my mother does these days—leave their apartment doors unlocked.

She doesn't do it because it contains nothing she values. Far from it. The truth is that she can't believe any world exists outside her apartment, and what doesn't exist can't hurt her, while any evils that have power to harm her are in the apartment already, laid away in the linen closet with the embroidered guest towels and the twelve-foot-long lace tablecloth, no doubt, waiting to be used.

"Pooh!" she used to say in her healthier years, to burglaries. The childish sound gave an irritating edge to her fearlessness.

"Don't make me more nervous," she says nowadays. "What do you expect me to do about it?" This particular afternoon she's bound to add "Don't you think I have enough to worry about?"

Danger has never been what worries her, in any case. I'll say this much for my mother in her younger days: She responded better to emergencies than to parties, and better to parties than to everyday life, which put her at her best in a crisis; she allowed me to run bare-legged in an era when other little girls were forced to cover their knees with leggings or snow pants; and she let me ride a horse and later sail a boat without a qualm. Even now, if I'm out sailing through a thunderstorm, it doesn't dawn on her that I might drown. The fact that she's German-Jewish may have something to do with her indomitable but graceless nature.

The final point worth making is that she can still beat all of us, even Ted, at Scrabble. Her mind is at its cool and clever peak in games.

Knowing that the door must be unlocked, I rang the bell anyway. I thought about turning the knob, decided to wait, then changed my mind. At the last moment, the door was opened from both sides at once.

The smell of cigarettes overpowered me when I kissed her. "You're so late," she said. "I expected you an hour ago. I was worried something terrible happened to you."

My husband was in the hospital with terminal cancer. What did she mean by something terrible happening to me? I'd dented a fender? Or was she worried that I'd spend more time with him today than I would with her?

She was wearing a dress, which was a hopeful sign, even though it was a purple knit that I remembered from nine or ten years back, with a cheap gold metal belt and stains on the skirt. "Don't lock that door," she said. "How many times do I have to tell you?"

"It's not safe."

"You don't know our doormen and elevator men. They don't let anyone up without knowing who it is."

They take care of her, she means, as her parents and husband used to take care of her, with the difference that they're interchangeable;

if one of them dies or quits, someone else will take his place, and she won't even have to bother to learn the new name. Still, she's not wrong about the door. There's no real danger from the street to be locked out in this well-guarded building, in comparison to the danger from the other direction, of being locked in. What she's waiting for is the moment when she'll fall and break her hip, the way her mother did—when she'll have a stroke, maybe, or a decalcified bone will crumble from her body's own weight—when she'll be out of reach of a telephone, no doubt, and her cries will be muffled by the thickness of the walls and Sylvia will have gone off to her class at Hunter. Marion's only hope for help is that someone may be able to open the front door and reach her.

Living in constant dread, she no longer knows that dread is what she feels. Her eyes have adapted to night vision. Death lives inside the apartment. Help lives outside the apartment, and wears the building's uniform. A daughter who lives in Westchester has no right to criticize.

"Where do you want to sit?" We crossed the living room, which was lit by nothing but a desk lamp. Forty feet away, a row of windows faced south across the rooftops, where flocks of pigeons must be whirling like streamers in the sky in this hour before roosting, the tops of their wings bright in the setting sun. But the shades, which were drawn to the sills, blocked out the view.

In the bedroom, the shades were at least raised halfway. Marion dropped into a lounge chair with a matching footstool, which was covered in pink vinyl as thick as automobile upholstery. "Tell me everything!" she demanded. "Let me have it. Shoot!" Her hair has more black than gray in it, a handsome pepper-and-salt effect. The jaw that she thrust forward at me is square, which she deplores; her forehead is high and broad, which she deplores even more strongly. "Shoot!" is one of her favorite expressions.

She might have been talking to her mother, in one of the phone conversations between them that made up the background hum of my childhood: "Come on. Dish me the dirt. I've been waiting all morning." Or she might have been talking to me as a small child: "Let me have it. That's not all. That's not enough. You're holding back on me." "What goes?" she demanded now.

"What do you mean, 'what goes?'"

"At the hospital." She set her jaw in the expression that means "Don't worry. Whatever it is, I can take it."

"Martin'll be coming home soon."

"Why isn't he home now? It's like pulling teeth, to get anything out of you. Why can't you talk?"

"I'm trying to tell you. The liver function tests came back today. Normal. That's very good. In fact, that's wonderful." When I was sick as a child, I used to lie in my bedroom and listen to Marion on the phone in her room, as she spoke first to her mother and then to her friends, glorying in the drama of the latest thermometer reading, the fevered midnight call to the doctor. Antibiotics hadn't been discovered yet.

"Liver? You never told me he has cancer of the liver."

"He doesn't have cancer of the liver." Cancer in the colon doesn't kill a man quite as quickly as cancer that spreads to the liver. No one lives long without a functioning liver. "It's a test, I told you."

"That's too complicated for me. With you, everything's a secret. I don't even know what he's in there for." She blew out cigarette smoke in her frustration.

She wouldn't get me to speak the word I hadn't spoken to Martin yet. Call the devil by name, hear the clatter of his heels. "I told you. He's in there for chemotherapy, the first round. Five FU. After that, he goes back to the hospital one weekend a month for more."

"He isn't going to go back to work, I'm sure." In her tone, I heard the fear—the satisfaction—of an older person watching a younger person die, an unloved one witnessing what can happen to a loved one, who is just as vulnerable as if no one cared.

"Not until we come home from London." If she wanted me to be a widow because then the two of us would be in the same boat, manless together, I could almost have forgiven her. But she didn't want me for herself. She wanted my story, as she'd wanted it when I was a child, so that she could tell herself or her friends that the news was killing her, but all the same she was needed. Just as she'd always expected, she'd been called on, what else could she do, she'd have to step in at the last minute and take over.

"You don't mean to tell me you're going to travel with a sick man?"

"Not too far. Only London and the countryside." Where we spent our honeymoon, I failed to add. "A couple of stately homes. I'll get back in time to put my boat in the water."

Now I'd done it. "That *verdammter* sailboat of yours," she gasped. When outraged, she lapses into badly pronounced German, which she wrongly suspects is Yiddish, although German isn't a language that she ever learned. She was born in Manhattan and educated at a private school for girls. Her mother was born in Quincy, Illinois, on the banks of the Mississippi, not far from Mark Twain country, as she likes to drop offhand into conversations—not many Jewish families have their roots along the Mississippi—but German was her father's native language, and so it became the family's private code, or at least a few phrases of it did, which were far more redolent of feeling than ordinary speech. "Now I know you're crazy. Don't tell me you're going to race this summer."

I'd assumed I wouldn't. "Of course I will," I said. Without my husband, she meant. Going off with other men to crew for me on Sunday afternoons. "I'll miss the pre-season, that's all."

I'd ordered new sails in the fall, so that was taken care of. The bottom was in good condition. It was the backstay that was a problem. Adjustable turnbuckles had been authorized by class rules over the winter, but the fittings that were available were either too small or too big and heavy for my boat, so I'd have to put something together. Every year, every racing class on the Sound grew more sophisticated in its competition. The rule in racing, as in everything else, was keep up or drop out.

Martin had never liked any sport—he had no intention of working unless he got paid for it, he said—but he disliked sailing above all others, because he ran the risk of being becalmed or soaked or chilled, with nothing he could do about it except put on a sweaty vinyl foul-weather jacket that smelled like an old enema bag. He saw no point in putting himself at the mercy of nature, knowing that nature wasn't inclined to mercy, so long as he was given any choice. Nevertheless, he'd encouraged me to own a boat for the past twenty years, if that's what I liked, and to race it and beat others or get beaten, as I deserved. Was I to believe that all those Sundays, while I was tacking around the buoys, he was deliberately building me up against a time that he knew all too well might be coming toward us?

"All I know is I never once went out on a weekend without my husband," Marion said. "Not once. In thirty-six years. Can you think of a single time I left him?"

No. But he left you. Many times. The first time when I was a year old. The last time for good. "So what does that have to do with getting along with each other?"

"That terrible summer house he rented in Vermont. Your father couldn't chase away a raccoon—I had to go outdoors in my nightgown and do it. Or change a fuse. No one is as helpless as that man. When we traveled, every night I had to wash out his socks for him." Her words broke off and her lips worked, as she paused to wonder with what sort of grace his second wife washes socks, changes fuses. "Your father's coming north soon?"

"No. Why should he?"

"Excuse *me*!" She recoiled with an exaggerated flutter of hands, as if I was about to slap her face. "I thought he might want to see his son-in-law."

"And what would Martin think, if Dad came all the way up from Florida, when we just visited him and Sally three months ago?" She wanted to know whether Martin knew that he was dying. "Anyway, I told you that when he finishes this round of treatment, we're going to London."

"Well, your father always faints when he visits a hospital anyway," she added, considerably mollified to hear that he wasn't about to come near me.

FOUR generations of women lived in our family at one time.

My mother had a stormy marriage and one daughter. My grandmother had a loveless marriage and one daughter. My great-grandmother was cherished by the ladies of Quincy for her good humor, light and lovely as her walnut torte, but no one had anything to say about her husband, beyond the fact that he was a silent man. She had two children, however, fourteen months apart, and she loved her beautiful boy, Norvin, who helled around the countryside in a buggy when he was a teenager, trying to kill turkeys with his buggy whip for sport.

"Isn't it a pity," I can hear the ladies of Quincy remark as they passed down the street, the hems of their dresses rustling the dry leaves, "that the boy had to be the one with those heavenly golden curls?"

But it was dark-haired, kinky-haired Fanny, aged sixteen, who taught herself double-entry bookkeeping when the widow moved to New York with her two children, and it was Fanny, even more surprisingly, who wore the highest collars and most elegant hats of her set, and turned herself into a beauty with not much more raw material than her intelligence and the way she carried her shoulders. It was Fanny who shortened her name to Fan—Fanny was a name for horses, she announced—and married the hawk-faced young man with the sort of virtues that make money, a man who promised not only to make a home for her mother and brother but also to give his unemployed brother-in-law a job for the rest of his life as part of the bargain. How many lives would have been altered, I wonder, if the girl had been the one in the family to be favored with those golden curls?

Who carved the meat in the household? A chain of women stepped to the head of the table, one by one.

My grandmother carved in her house, standing above the roast prime ribs of beef on Friday nights. My mother carved in her house, after discussing her menu with her mother on the telephone in the morning and again late in the afternoon and reporting on its fate the next day. And I too, I must say—I stood at the head of our dining-room table and carved the meat, serving Martin as I did the children.

But who ate the meat is another question.

Not I, in my mother's home. I wouldn't eat a thing, not if I could help it. With my high chair facing the wall, so that there'd be no chance of distraction, not even if I heard the sound of the elevator bringing my father home, I fought the spoon that moved relentlessly toward my mouth, forcing its way between my teeth, which only scraped the top off the load and left the bowl of the spoon still freighted. After supper, I vomited.

"You're lucky," the cook said. "I knew a girl who did that; she had to eat her own vomit."

That was the way in which I refused to give in to my mother and take my place in line behind my great-grandmother, my grandmother and my mother in the chain of women. When I talk about my mother this way, it's hard to remember that I'm talking about a girl who was barely in her twenties.

When Marion was seventeen, she met my father at a resort hotel in New Hampshire, where she was taken by her parents to spend July and August. He was eleven years older than she was, the handsomest fellow in the place, looking just like the silent-movie star Jack Holt, everyone agreed, with his dark mustache and his plus fours and his pastel-colored argyle sweaters. What's more, he was a lawyer in practice for himself, who also owned a Manhattan apartment house with the help of the banks, while the other males at the hotel were boys with acne and uncertain futures and parents who footed their bills.

"Sure," she says, "I'd stand up your father every time. I'd tell him that I'd meet him on the golf course at nine in the morning, and I'd be there all right, but with another fellow, and we'd go sailing past him. Well, I only told him that I'd *see* him there. And I saw him, didn't I?" Flirtations had a stagy quality, like a Cotton Club revue, in those days when every fellow had to have a come-on, followed by a good line washed down with a hip flask, and every girl had to have a snappy comeback. No one ever defeated Marion in a contest of pizzazz.

The voice of the twenties can still be heard coming out of her mouth, like a player piano grinding away in an empty bar. "Did you stay out late last night?" she used to ask me hopefully when I was single, and went right on asking me until the night when Martin went into the hospital. I'd disappoint her every time, by naming a boring hour like midnight. She always knew her daughter had no style. "That restaurant you went to, is that where the swells go nowadays?" If just once I could tell her that there were drunks stretched from one end of the living-room floor to the other, or that someone ripped off my chiffon dress and used it in Salome's Dance, she might be satisfied for a little while, or some distracted traveler inside her soul, dressed up for the captain's dinner on the last night on board ship, might think she'd gotten her money's worth out of her ticket.

All the same, when I watch Marion "put on her face," when I watch her rub rouge on her cheekbones with a puff worn as thin as a shoe lining, or spit on her dried-up cake of mascara to dampen it, or pull a lock of hair into a dip to hide her intelligent forehead, reproducing a look that belongs in the twenties—as I suppose all of us women wear the face of the period when we were happiest—I have a vision of a woman born in the wrong time or the wrong place, or at least in the wrong family.

What would I have thought of her, I sometimes wonder (but not when I'm with her; I'm never that charitable when I'm with her) if I'd been raised on the Israeli frontier while she patroled the fence around our fields with a gun? Would I have criticized her because she never uses night cream, much less a lighted makeup mirror, but still wears purple lipstick (she has never heard of owning more than one color) that she buys at the five-and-ten? She has no more sense of sexual strategy than a nun, no more concept of dressing to please a man. But what would she have looked like to me, and who would she have been, if she'd been born forty years earlier and become the bookkeeper who supported the family? Or if she'd been born forty years later, like Karen, and gotten her M.B.A. and gone to work in a brokerage firm or investment banking house, where her formidable head for figures would have been aligned with her passion for money?

Instead, she went to fashion school for a year after high school and got married at nineteen. That same year, she was offered a job working at home in her free time, going to fashion shows and then sketching the clothes from memory for a manufacturer.

"No wife of mine is going to work," my father said, as he installed her in an apartment in the building he owned, along with a Belgian tapestry he bought as a wedding present, a European cook, and, eight-and-a-half months later, a baby nurse. There were no other offers in her life. Nothing else happened to her for the next thirty-six years, except her husband's sporadic departures from home.

"Why did your parents let you do it?" I cry out once in a while. "A girl of nineteen, marrying a man of thirty? He had to write your senior term paper for you."

She shrugs. Her parents were never wrong. "I couldn't have been easy for them. I suppose I was a handful."

"And his family was Russian, besides."

"That's for sure."

"I thought your family wouldn't even let you talk to Russian Jews." I've gratified her and betrayed her at the same time—or betrayed her parents—by bringing up this subject.

"My father made him give up his real estate deals anyway, made him stick to law, before we were allowed to marry. My father saw to that, you can bet. P.D.Q." The notion that she might have become much richer if her husband had stayed in real estate only validates her father's wisdom. In Marion's eyes, very rich and very poor are conditions equally to be dreaded.

"What do you think happened?" I telephoned Martin one day. My voice was fluty with the knowledge that there was more drama going on at home for once than at his office. Martin handled matrimonial matters from time to time, but I would have called him anyway. "After thirty-six years of marriage, my father got up from the breakfast table and put down his napkin and walked out of the house. What's more, this time I think he means it. After thirty-six years. What should I say?"

"I'd say he gave the thing a fair try," Martin answered.

Actually, I said nothing. In my mother's view, that meant that I was on the side she'd known I was on all along. Who else could have bought the set of dishes for my father's new apartment that her friends had been in such a hurry to tell her about?

She put up no fight when my father wanted to go to Mexico to get his divorce. She, who raged at the grocer around the corner and accused him of being a thief because he had the gall to charge ten cents more for corn flakes than the supermarket did, now settled for practically no alimony, since she had inherited enough money from her parents to live on.

"Do you think I'm doing the right thing?" she asked me.

"I think you're incredibly generous." I wasn't at all sure I'd have shown the same spirit in her place.

"I hear he's marrying a widow," Marion said a few months later. "Very rich." My father's two wives are within a few months of each other in age, as if Victor, who was sixty-seven years old when he remarried, had a taste for domestic wine of a certain vintage.

"I wouldn't say Sally's rich." My tone turned vague as soon as Marion's turned pointed.

"I suppose he'll retire and live on her first husband's money, from Atlanta." She said this proudly, to show that in this first season of her divorce, their mutual friends still called and told her news, if only to get a reaction out of her that then became news of its own.

"Far as I know, she doesn't have that much. And a son to raise besides." If I overdid my role, she'd have Sally grabbing my father to get a meal ticket for herself and college tuition for her son.

"If only I were a widow!" Marion cries passionately from time to time. To be divorced, in her eyes, means to be fired, or at least forced to resign, from the only job she ever had. To be a widow means to get condolence notes by the hundred and memorial contributions for her favorite charity, where eventually a bronze plaque would list her husband's name along with the other husbands who are not only undeniably chaste at last, but firmly planted and bound to stay where they belong.

My father and Sally have been married for fifteen years at this point. Not long ago they moved to the west coast of Florida. "A condominium right on the beach, overlooking the Gulf—with its own swimming pool—that's what I hear. Don't worry, I hear everything," Marion said, giving away the fact that she doesn't hear much by saying "condominium" rather than "condo." "How that man gets his money beats me."

She knows that Martin and I visited my father in February. "They didn't have to buy an apartment. They rented one. And in Florida saying they have a swimming pool is like saying they have indoor plumbing."

"So it's a rental building!" she said in triumphant scorn.

"No, it's a condo." I doubt that she believed me, but I'm not generous enough to give her scraps of information that I don't have to give. Of all the people in their building (which is on the beach, just as she said), my father and Sally alone didn't have to buy an apartment for a couple of hundred thousand dollars, which they don't have, but were able to rent at a bargain rate from a widow who has been an invalid for years in a northern city. Maintenance and repairs were included in the deal.

"I don't get it." Marion shook her head. "In this building, the board of directors wouldn't let you lease. Or sublease. You can't even lend your apartment to your own children if you're not there."

I sighed. "I don't know how they managed it." I only know that Sally has the sublime instinct for comfort, which to her always means her man's comfort, of a cat locating a radiator grille on a snowy day.

"Nicely decorated?"

"They took it furnished. Sort of Schrafft's Spanish. With tassels." Which Sally removed. As Sally slipcovered the couch, and draped the end tables in matching fabric, and installed multiple heads with a needle spray in the shower, because my father really appreciates his shower, and put salted pecans—not peanuts but Georgia pecans, slightly warmed because she knows her stepdaughter likes them that way—in the crystal urn that's the sole reminder, along with her pineapple-pattern Baccarat glasses, of the style in which she used to entertain during her Atlanta period.

Sally used her own small inheritance to feather this nest. Gentile women think first of their husband's comfort and pleasure and second of their children's, I've noticed (Sally is Gentile), while with Jewish women, the priorities work the other way round: The children come first. No, my mother would contradict me. The mother comes first. In either case, attention, anxiety, money flow vertically, in line with the blood, in Jewish families and horizontally, like the occupants of the marriage bed, in Gentile families. "One thing I'll say about my son," Sally says about her grown-up son who lives in Dallas, "I never gave him a dime from the day he got out of college. And I never will."

"You've unraveled the secret of perfect happiness," I tell my father. "You've discovered the philosophers' stone. All you have to do is find yourself a Jewish mother but a Gentile wife."

Of course, I couldn't tell Marion any of this, any more than I could tell her that Sally joined the local women's division of the United Jewish Appeal as soon as she moved in, and has already been chosen as co-chairwoman of their benefit luncheon next winter, which is bound to be a sellout. There's no one as beloved by Jews, especially Jewish women, as a beautiful Gentile woman with silver-colored pageboy hair and pearls.

MY FATHER cocked his finger at me as if it were a cap pistol, and made a popping sound with his lips, which was the routine he used to go through when I was a child. "Are we taking a walk this morning, young lady?" he asked, precisely because he knew the answer, but wanted to hear me tell him of my own free will. It was February. Martin and I were visiting my father and Sally in Florida for the first time, but Martin was still asleep in the guest bedroom.

Every Sunday morning when I was small, my father used to take me down Park Avenue, dressed in his English walking suit, no less: dark striped trousers with a pearl-gray flannel vest and a dark jacket with a cornflower in the buttonhole, a cornflower because he was well aware of what that shade of blue did for the color of his eyes. It was impossible for him to walk for more than a couple of blocks without stopping to chat with someone he knew, or at least to tip his hat to people he knew by sight because they followed the same highly respectable route down the avenue at the same hour every week that we did. Occasionally, I suspect, he tipped his Homburg to strangers who looked like the sort of people he might have met sometime in the past and now forgotten (he never forgot anyone), because it was safer to disconcert a hundred strangers than to overlook one acquaintance, however remote. Shouldn't anyone be flattered, in any case, to be greeted by such a distinguished figure?

As far as I was concerned, he might have been born dressed that way, in the walking suit and the gray flannel spats whose beady black buttons he fastened over his shoes with a buttonhook; the spats matched the pearl-gray vest and striped silk tie. But that's not the way it was. We hardly ever talked about the past at home, my father's or anyone else's. "Whose business is it?" my mother demanded. All I knew was that he was a poor boy from the Bronx, the youngest of five children and the only boy, the long-awaited crown prince of the family, superseding all others. Not until I was grown did I learn from an aunt one day that my paternal grandfather had been a Russian furrier named Max Pilo, or Pillo, which was undoubtedly short for some less-pronounceable name that had been cut down to manageable size.

On the day that my grandparents arrived at Ellis Island, still in their teens but married and carrying an infant in their arms, a customs official told them that there were only three first-class Jewish names in America: Cohen, Levy and Goldstein. Which did they want? They couldn't believe their luck. Family names had been introduced only a short time before, first in Germany and then in Russia and Poland, and in many villages officials had to be bribed to register prime quality, high-sounding names like Rosenbaum (Rose Tree) or Gold-man or Silver-man. But here was this mighty figure, the guardian of the gates himself, wearing leather shoes as lightweight and pointed as a nobleman's, offering to give them any name they wanted, even the finest of all. Who wanted to be turned into a Cohen or Levy, which were the names of the ancient priests of Israel? What did priests know, with their mumble-jumble superstitions and their dirty beards? Could they even make a decent living? Max Pilo hadn't scrupulously stayed away from temple and eaten ham every Yom Kippur simply in order to be transformed into an hereditary priest the moment he set foot in the Land of Opportunity—but Goldstein, the stone of gold, a name like that had a ring to it. Such a name could only be an auspicious omen.

By the time that my father was in college, he practiced a little alchemy and refined his Goldstein down to Gould. "You know what? I've never heard my real name," I said one day.

"What's the difference?" he countered cheerfully. "You'll get married and change it soon, anyway."

"Don't you ever tell anyone that story," my mother added.

The boy was tall, he was broad-shouldered, he played touch football, and, with his invariable luck, when he was fourteen he broke his nose in a game, which added the final fillip of Gentile charm to his good looks. He was a hero in a story by Horatio Alger. Out of the Bronx he floated in a magic bubble, just as his mother and sisters had always known he would do, borne along by his two great talents: making friends and cultivating style. In high school, he joined a club known as the Washington Irving Society, which deliberately set out to remove traces of the outer boroughs and add elegance to its members' speech. By the time that I was old enough to remember what he said, he was using fancy words very much the way he flourished his silver-handled cane on our Sunday walks, which had nothing to do with helping him up and down curbs. It ill behooved him to indulge in flattery toward any man, he said, but that's exactly what he did all the same.

This much I saw for myself or figured out later on: My father's widowed mother doted on him. His four sisters barely reached to the top of his vest. He went to college for only two years before he went to law school, night session, and worked during the day as a clerk in a law office, while serving summonses for a dollar apiece on the side. Friends were his only resource. Looks and geniality were his talents, the way other young men had a nose for torts or a head for the intricacies of taxes.

The parents of his fraternity brothers patronized the collection agency he ran in his spare hours—and why not? The young law student was tall. He was handsome, although not as handsome as he became a few years later, when his hungry, assiduous look filled in. He was smooth-spoken, the toastmaster of first choice at weddings and fraternity dinners. Above all, the young man's prospects looked good, and most of these parents had at least one daughter at home who could use a fine Jewish husband like that. He did nothing to discourage their interest in his career. After law school, those fraternity brothers and their families turned into his clients, just as his secretaries later turned into his mistresses. His sisters, on the other hand, turned into Bronx housewives whom my mother never invited to the house except on state occasions like my graduation, when they brought much finer presents than anyone else. This was only fitting, since they were really too poor to have been included.

In later years, my father joined the Manhattan Club, which was known in New York politics at that time as The Powerhouse, the chief source of legal patronage, conveniently located just down the block from the Appellate Division of the New York Supreme Court. There his way was made agreeable by his knack of knowing whom to know. Judges and Tammany chiefs, who were themselves the products of Irish or Italian slums, regarded him as their bosom buddy, even if—or possibly because—he wouldn't match them drink for drink. His practice was largely a surrogate's court practice. The Surrogate of New York happened to be his best friend.

In turn, he thought of his benefactors as princes, and loved them for what they did for him. Flattery and favors were his natural climate, as mistrust and diminishment were my mother's.

It occurs to me how little anybody ever changes. Walking alongside the golf course opposite his house, my father moved in strength and pleasure, just as he had done along Park Avenue when I was a child. On this February morning, he was dressed in his modern walking suit: an apricot-and-white striped Lacoste T-shirt that I'd given him, worn now as a silent compliment to me, white shorts (his legs still straight and shapely), white wool socks, white running shoes and a floppy white cotton sun hat, so that he looked like an exceptionally clean, well-brought-up little boy. His hair and mustache were dark; he was still tall; his gait was as firm as ever.

Every once in a while an egret rose from the grounds of the golf course on our right and flapped in the air like a demented golf ball. My father waved at a jogger. He also waved at the truck drivers as they went by, partly because it's his nature to be genial, but also because he believes that a friendly wave makes them a bit more careful about slowing down when they pass him, which isn't insignificant for a walker who can't wear his hearing aid outdoors because of background noise from the wind.

When we reached the guard booth in front of his building, he stopped to greet the guard, as he always stops, no matter how many times a day he and Sally walk or drive in and out of the house. Not to keep track of who's on duty on a given day, not to know the man in the booth by his first name—more terrible yet, not to have the man recognize their car when they drive up, before he recognizes them—would strike my father as an irreparable loss of dignity and pleasure on both sides. He feels the same way about restaurant owners, the man behind the desk in the building lobby, the nurses in his doctor's office. In his own way, he keeps alive the primitive spirit that invests every place and human activity with a tutelary deity that must be fed and flattered.

"Horace, I'd like you to meet my daughter, Joan," my father said. "My lee-tle daughter, Joan-ie." At that instant, he was so moved by the fact that Horace could not only see with his own eyes that this tenant has a daughter, but witness the fact that this daughter flies all the way down from New York to take a morning walk with her father, that he had to stop talking long enough to wipe a trickle of spittle from the side of his mouth with a folded tissue.

"Now, you must've figgered that I was fixing to tell Mrs. Gould that you went walking with a pretty young lady this morning." Horace wore a broad-brimmed brown Mountie hat above a tan uniform with epaulets and a metal badge that said "Protection Services." His face was the same color as his shirt; his white sideburns extended to the bottom of his earlobes. When he stepped out of the booth to talk to us, he cupped his cigarette inside his palm as if protecting it from a mountain wind. "Well now, tell me, folks. Did I keep the rain away for you today, like I promised?"

"You sure did, Horace. And you're going to take care of that little matter for us again tomorrow?"

"I made a promise, didn't I? 'Till your daughter leaves,' I said. Never went back on my word yet." A tenant's car halted to be admitted. Horace saluted and raised the switch gate. Then he patted the rear bumper as the car drove through, the way he might have patted a horse's rump. "It's been a real pleasure meeting you, Jo-Anne. You come back to us real soon, you hear now? I can see you get your good looks from your mother's side of the family, not your father's."

Of course he supposed that Sally was my mother. His use of my first name, even if it wasn't quite correct, made it clear that he addressed my father as Mr. Gould only out of respect for his age, not because of his status as tenant. While we spoke, my father's smile hung in the air behind us like a caterpillar suspended on a silken thread, twitching a little to this side or that side as if in response to currents of air, tremulous not from weakness but from the effort to contain his rapture at this hour when the whole neighborhood can see that indeed he has a daughter, every bit as loving as he claims.

"Greetings and salutations!" he called out a few minutes later to a man who came jogging off the beach. "How are you, Senator?"

" 'Morning, Judge," answered the neighbor, a retired manufacturer of surgical supplies from Cincinnati. "You're looking distinguished this morning."

"You taking a breather from those budget talks in Washington?" my father asked. "I'm counting on you to lower that deficit, you hear me?" But no, it turns out that the senator is pooped from jogging up the beach to Pelican Cay and back, when he isn't anything like as young as he used to be. "Why, you're a pup," my father answered. "I'm surprised your mother lets you go out on the beach by yourself."

"I'm an old man," the neighbor protested. "Can't do six miles a day like I used to."

"To me, you're a pup. Care to know how old I am?" My father paused before adding his punch line, his whammeroo. "I'm eighty-three," he said, with becoming modesty, even though it wasn't quite true; he wouldn't be eighty-three for another three weeks.

The senator's delight was real. The regularity and length of my father's walk, the joy that he takes in his daily swim—the poor boy from the Bronx who never learned to swim as a child and still can't really swim, but who pats the water to placate it with his palm, and half laughs, half gasps out of the upper portion of his mouth while he does the sidestroke, two or three laps—the care with which he puts martini glasses in the freezer to chill before filling them, the way that he speaks of his wife as his bride—all these details are significant to his neighbors. They see him as portents of their own futures. They cherish him the way they cherish their livers.

"Lord love you!" the surgical equipment manufacturer exclaimed as we said good-bye. "Don't sit on too many sodomy cases now, will you, Judge?"

At that moment, as we prepared to go up to the apartment, where Sally would have a lunch of homemade soup and salmon salad on warm rolls waiting for us, the two men loved each other. But if, by some mischance, that neighbor should have a heart attack or a stroke or become senile—why, that would be too bad, but that's another story. My father won't visit the hospital; he won't go to the funeral either, if there should happen to be one.

This is part of his charm. In another month, if that same neighbor pulls through an operation against the odds and returns to the beach, my father will call out in all sincerity, "I've never seen you looking better, Senator," meaning "I never saw you while you were looking worse," and the invalid will be grateful for this edited reality in which he has never been seen as weak or threatened. The two of them will walk the sand together as if happiness were their private club.

A man doesn't show up in white shorts and crew socks and excellent health and spirits after eighty-three years as a result of suffering unnecessarily on behalf of others.

"Y O U K N O W what happened to my marriage, don't you?" Marion asks me every so often. Her tone makes it clear that she's been conquered by nothing less than the unconquerable, by the same forces that make food prices go up every month and make every object laid down on her bedspread instead of being put on top of the bureau where it belongs, even a pocketbook or magazine, wear out the threads by a microscopic amount.

"You know why your father walked out on me? I'll tell you why. If you must know." Her chin puckers until it looks like a fig. "His biggest client died. Arthur Fine dropped dead of a heart attack one afternoon, and there went your father's law practice. Right down the drain. His crony, Burt, had already retired as a judge—the old sot, used to tell me 'Just bruise the ice in my glass, will you?'—so there was no more political patronage either. Your father's nerves cracked. Just like that. He retired right afterward, didn't he?"

I have to hand it to her. She knows how to chew up the fact of her abandonment and transform it into something more digestible, into her chief source of nourishment these days, the way that trapped explorers are supposed to chew up their shoe leather and live on its juices.

"Well, his new wife is welcome to him," Marion adds, thrusting away the empty air. "Good riddance. There's only one thing I want to know."

"What's that?"

"Who's picking out his socks?"

"What?"

"You didn't see them at Ted's graduation? The color of them? And falling down besides? And his pants falling down because he wasn't wearing a belt?"

"I was looking at other things."

"I suppose she picks out his clothes."

There's silence between us, which I intend to mean that of course Sally picks out his clothes, she ought to, she's been his wife for fifteen years now. "Don't talk to me about men," Marion says, as if I've tried. "They make me want to vomit. Who wants to marry an old man, be an old man's nurse and wash his socks?"

Socks play a curiously large part in her thinking, it seems to me, those phallic bags that slip inside a pair of slippers, those silky condoms that are emptied of their contents at night and washed and hung up to dry over the shower rod in the bathroom. My father's socks, any man's socks.

I put on my coat and scarf as soon as we got up from the table, and picked up my shopping bag. "You're going home so early?" Marion asked.

"I'm going back to the hospital."

"At this hour?" She peered into my face as I bent to kiss her good-bye. "You're sure everything's all right?" She shook her head to show that she knew when she was beaten. She knew she wasn't going to get any more out of me for the night. "I hate to see you drive home so late," she added as I rang for the elevator.

"I do it all the time." On my way to the lobby, I wasn't sure if I had said that to reassure her or to make the point that it was only her house that I left early. With Martin, I planned to stay late.

HE WAS lying in bed when I came in, watching television on a set suspended from the ceiling of his hospital room.

"What've you got there? *All in the Family*?" I never remembered Martin watching a program like that before. Weekday evenings were for work, either at home or at the office. Weekend evenings were for going out or having friends come in to visit. Bed was for sleep, for work, for department store catalogues, for sex, once in a while for a television movie. For sickness. Never for a sitcom.

Apparently Edith Bunker had answered an ad from a couple who said they wanted to make new friends, a wife gussied up in a black lace dress and curls, who'd brought Edith per-*fume*, and a husband who'd brought a box of cigars for Archie. The visitors themselves neither drank nor smoked. "Then what do you do for fun?" Archie wanted to know. The audience roared. They'd guessed the answer to that one.

I took off my blazer and boots and stretched out on the bed next to Martin, while the visitors, who turned out to be former Harvest Moon winners, demonstrated the foxtrot for Archie. "They're trophy winners, you know," Edith proudly told a neighbor in her kitchen.

"Edith, I got to tell you, they're here to change partners—but *not* for dancing."

"C'm here, Edith," Archie called from the living room. "This guy's an expert. Maybe you'll learn something."

The studio audience laughed, and so did we. I heard a sound I'd never heard from the two of us before, not the explosion that paid tribute to Martin's one-liners, which was something between a gasp of astonishment and a bark, but, for the Bunkers, loose and easy exhalations, ears pulled back and mouths left open, waiting for more. Edith was forced to stand there, popeyed, while she registered what the rest of us had known for fifteen minutes already, that her guests were intent on wife-swapping.

We'd never been free enough to lie and float like this, in a pool of chuckles splashing down from a spot between the ceiling and the wall. Even in our pleasures we'd always been busy. Now there was nothing more to do. Lightweight and buoyant and negligible as children, we rose and fell on bubbles of laughter. Wife swappers, of course. We could have told Edith that.

At lunchtime that day, I'd met Martin's doctor, Ephraim Bentwick, near the doctors' dining room, and asked him some of the questions I'd been waiting to ask him. It would be more accurate to say that Bentwick was one of Martin's doctors. He wasn't the man who had diagnosed anemia back in October and wanted to run further tests. That had been our local suburban doctor, who took care of Martin's sore throats and flu, but as soon as Martin heard that this might be something more serious, he'd taken himself to New York, to the biggest name in medicine he knew, Ephraim Bentwick himself, former chief of staff for internal medicine of this teaching hospital and still a legend within its walls.

Once a year for many years, Martin had gone to Doctor Bentwick's office, ostensibly for a complete checkup, but really to keep his lines of communication open against the day when a suburban doctor at a suburban hospital wouldn't be good enough to deal with what ailed him. In this sense, Martin was a true New Yorker: He believed that anything could be improved through the use of money and effort, provided that these were applied early enough and at a high enough level of expertise, whether the trouble lay with his children's crooked teeth, his associates' writing style or the odds that he might go on living.

"I'm saving you for my terminal illness," he told Bentwick on each annual visit. Sure enough, it was Bentwick who had admitted him to the hospital three weeks ago.

"What about the X rays you took back in October?" I asked in the corridor. "Seven months ago."

Ah, yes, Bentwick said. The X rays. He was glad to have run into me. As it happened, he'd sent for those X rays only the day before and taken another good look at them.

He was tall and lean and as long in the shank as a Norman crusader. His hair was white; his skin was pinkish-white, like fine marble. I could see him laid out in effigy on a thirteenth-century tomb in the church of the Inner Temple, holding a sword like a cross in his hand, with chain mail curled in ringlets like wet fur along his arms and legs, and beneath his helmet a pair of bold, victorious and uncaring eyes.

I must bear in mind how many factors could affect the reliability of X rays, he said. There were all grades of advance preparation. A bit of retained fecal matter could look like a tumor, or *vice versa*. The barium could clump instead of laying a smooth coat on the intestinal wall, or it could run back into the small intestine and block the view. The rectosigmoid could be coiled; the cecum, up near the appendix, could be curled. Unfortunately the colon isn't a pipe, but rather resembles a hank of ribbon thrown into a drawer, a ribbon that can be thinner, fatter, loopier, ptosed, festooned this way or that way as it flops around in the interior currents of barium or air.

Bentwick's voice was saddened by the mortal constraints that were laid upon his art. "Now that I look the films over again, it seems to me there's a faint cloud—not really a cloud, but a smudge, even less than a smudge—in the corner of one of them that could have been—nothing." He gave me a charming smile, which meant that there was no need for him to have told me any of this. I could never have found it out for myself. The two of us were superior to either reproaches or excuses, his smile implied.

Outside the cafeteria door there was a puddle of vomit. Someone had thoughtfully placed a chair over it. Clusters of people, barely reaching to Bentwick's shoulder, diverged to pass the two of us, still standing in the middle of the corridor, then diverged again for the chair, then stopped and blocked the doorway of the cafeteria while they read the specials on the bulletin board. Roast beef, two veg., $2.85. Too cheap to be good. This was no country for tourists.

"Of course it's vastly easier to see something, or suppose you see something, when you take a second look after you've been inside and know what's there."

"And the blood count?" I asked. I was no longer as ignorant as I used to be. I'd bought *The Merck Manual* and read the parts that I might have read seven months earlier. Tenth edition, page 597: "Anemias due to gastrointestinal cancer are much more common than primary anemias, and medical treatment of anemia without investigation for a source of blood loss is an extremely serious error." After the neighborhood doctor discovered the anemia, Martin began taking iron pills on his own initiative, which made him feel better, but he went to see Bentwick anyway, who performed another blood test and confirmed the low hematocrit.

"Yes. The anemia." Here was a man who could afford anything he needed in this hospital, including his mistakes. "Quite right. I certainly meant to have your husband come back to the office in a month or so for another blood count." I could picture this man in tennis whites at Hilton Head, or in white broadcloth pajamas, brushing his teeth with powder, as easily as I could picture him in his hospital coat, so polished with starch that the pocket was welded to the fabric. "But you know how these things go. One becomes so forgetful at my age."

Bobbing his head and shoulders to say good-bye, the way he must have been taught in prep school fifty-odd years ago, he moved down the hall, his white hair shining with righteousness. From his serenity, I took the promise that he wouldn't hold his mistake against me. He'd be there when we needed him, he'd see to it that Martin suffered no pain. In the final reckoning, that was the secret of his power.

Twenty-eight years is a long, long time that vanishes in an instant when a cloud on an X-ray film obscures the sun. The cloud is recognized at once, we've been waiting for it all along. It's the sunlight that gleamed on the leaves in the morning and early afternoon that's forgotten as fast as the air chills, while we pack up the blanket and thermos and prepare to leave the hill.

If the technician who took the X rays seven months earlier had been a bit more painstaking about the preparation of the bowel, or if he'd had better luck that day . . . if the bowel happened to flop that way instead of flopping this way at the critical instant, or if the barium had clotted less and coated more, Martin might have been saved. If the radiologist who read the films had been observant enough to spot the cloud which was no bigger than the smear of a thumbprint, at a time when it could have been nothing, but turned out not to be nothing . . . or if Bentwick himself had scrutinized the films in the first place the way that he scrutinized the films in the second place, Martin might have been saved. If Martin hadn't been deluded into assuming that the most eminent doctor was necessarily the most careful doctor, which was the only error in judgment that I know of that he made in his life . . . or if he'd stayed with the neighborhood man who was champing to investigate the anemia further, because he was well aware of Martin's history and that of his family, and had his strong suspicions where the trouble lay . . . or even if Martin had used either man exclusively, so that one doctor or the other felt the full burden of his patient's confidence pressing on him until he took suitable action, his life might have been saved. If Bentwick hadn't been distracted by the forgetfulness he joked about, or maybe by the many honors hung around his neck . . . or if he'd simply been away on vacation in Europe for three or four weeks at the time, so that Martin would have been forced to find someone else, Martin's life might have been saved.

Granting all this, if Martin hadn't bought himself a bottle of iron pills, which exactly fitted his idea that if two pills a day were good for him, four pills a day must be better, and if I hadn't urged him to take the iron because it made him feel so much stronger, even if it masked his anemia for months . . . if I hadn't slighted his symptoms because I knew that he was a hypochondriac, and anyway, my mother's blood count was frequently lower than his, without any explanation that her doctor could find, and nobody paid all that much attention to her . . . or if I had simply read that page in *The Merck Manual* in October instead of in April, I believe that Martin not only might, but probably would, have been saved. That serious error, according to the *Manual,* turned out to be a grave error, so to speak.

On the television, Black Lace was explaining herself forlornly to the Bunkers. "You see, it didn't mean a thing. It was like two cars. The washing machine and dryer. Our marriage was drowning. Swapping saved us."

Archie was a panda, his eyes squinting in astonishment, his mouth pursed into a circle. Edith was a koala bear. Her mouth hung open in an oval, her eyebrows shot up under her carefully crimped hair. "I think I'd rather have drowned." She looked straight at Martin as she spoke. She knew he'd love that line.

He adored women on the far side of middle age, who wore their hair tightly crimped and spoke their minds and remained unbudgeable in their opinions; he much preferred them to girls. It was too bad. He would have loved me more, not less, by the time I got to be old and doughty.

Chapter 3

"WHAT are the plans for Christmas?" Marion asked me two Decembers later. "Are the Berkmans coming?"

Cissy Berkman is—Cissy was—Martin's cousin. She and Stan have spent Christmas at our house for the past ten or twelve years, ever since their daughter, Louise, who's their only child, went to Israel for her junior year abroad and never came home. We used to spend the holiday together chiefly because we're such a small family—Martin, Cissy, my mother and I are all only children—but also because Cissy, unlike Stan, is a German Jew, and we German Jews adopted the German Christmas with our particular secular frenzy, turning it into a test of affection for everyone involved.

In any case, the Berkmans can't stop their custom now of coming to see me. They're terribly responsive to moral obligations, which is what I've turned into in their eyes.

"Give yourself a year," my friends advised me out of no knowledge of their own, as if I could give it or else not give it, the decision was up to me. "You'll see, you'll feel better." That was two years ago last week.

I should have known that Martin would choose to go out with the sun. He had to pick the darkest season and the darkest week of that season, the week of the solstice, a time when the earth tips toward its farthest star, when its axis lets out a groan that only the animals can hear, while our climate hangs in the balance. One more person leaning in the wrong direction, that's all that's needed to send us toppling into the void, irrelevant and irredeemable as we know ourselves to be.

No, Martin would never have died in the middle of the day or in spring or summer, any more than he would have left the terrace on a sunny afternoon after setting up his deck chair, his box of Kleenex, his suntan cream and briefcase and the outdoor speaker for his stereo, his yellow pads and telephone, not to mention his electric fan with its extension cord and the pitcher of iced tea.

"I don't think you ought to drink this stuff," I said during that final summer. "Made from that mix with Sucaryl. Don't you read the newspaper?"

"It's not fattening," he answered, rubbing the hair that sweated over the elastic top of his bathing trunks. Our homemade iced tea had sugar in it. "Anyway, what harm can it do? I have cancer already." That was the only time I ever heard him use the word. He baked like a gingerbread man, then padded into the kitchen, pigeon-toed in his floppy espadrilles worn down on the sides, waddling a bit as men do who never get enough exercise, to fetch fruit salad and cottage cheese for himself, along with ice cubes that he dropped into Ralph's bowl of water.

No, he would never have stepped indoors while there was sunlight outside. I like to think that he left me as he would have checked out of a Nantucket beach hotel after three days of rain, saying, Who needs this? Who wants it? I can be much more comfortable in my own home.

"H O W do you think I'm going to get up to the country?" Marion asked. "It's the worst day in the year to travel. You think there are going to be taxis on Christmas? Let me tell you something, I'm not taking that jitney service that drives you to hell's half acre and back, with no springs in the back seat. And charges twenty dollars for the privilege." She wanted to find out how anxious I was to have her with us. "I think the Berkmans are the *most* charming couple," she added accusingly, as if I'd said I didn't want them.

Marion adores them not because they're charming and intelligent and attentive to her, all of which they are, but because Stan is a doctor—more than that, he's what Marion would call the biggest man in his field, which happens to be hematology. A bear of a man, well over six feet tall, he looks like a Russian woodcutter stomping through the forest, or one of those icemen I remember from my youth, with leather aprons on their backs, who used to reach out with their tongs and sling blocks of ice over their shoulders and heave their way up the front steps of tenement houses. Just to touch Stan's hand makes me feel stronger.

He runs a private practice, which could be multiplied several times over if he wished, but he's also a professor at Yale-New Haven Hospital, which begs him every few years to become chief of his department or else take over as dean of something or other. He collects chairmanships of scientific and governmental committees the way other men collect golf trophies as rewards for skill and practice. What's more, he's punctual. The Berkmans drove all the way down from New Haven, but they arrived before the taxi that I'd sent to fetch Marion from the city, along with the two young couples, Ted and Felicia, Karen and Kurt. The driver was willing to work on Christmas in consideration of a little extra consideration.

Up the path the Berkmans came like Jack and Jill, each carrying a shopping bag from the Yale Co-op in one hand, with Stan gripping Cissy's free elbow to make sure she didn't slip on the ice. When I touched their cheeks, I felt the surface of their faces frosted with cold as a result of the walk from the curb to the door, but the curly collar of Stan's sheepskin jacket held in the heat of the car. These days I have so few contacts with bodies that my own flesh is abnormally wide-awake.

"How nice." I added the contents of their bags to the pile at the foot of the tree. Already I could see that they'd brought a package for Gitte, the Danish girl who lives with us and helps with the housework while she goes to college.

"These fabulous ornaments," said Cissy. I was more pleased than I ought to be. Cissy works as a volunteer docent at the British Art Center in New Haven and runs the Art Council's annual fund-raising dance, which she refers to as "the ball." When I visit the Berkman house for dinner once a year or so, I don't meet other doctors, even medical school faculty, but Yale professors of this or that, even a Sterling professor or two, last time a sculptor from Guilford married to a civil rights lawyer, along with a psychiatrist, an expert on guilt, who was writing a book about penitential practices in medieval monasteries.

The Berkman house, which isn't actually in New Haven but perched on a cliff in Branford overlooking Short Beach, is a marvel to me, a Victorian castle with a turret shaped like an ice-cream cone dipped in pistachio-colored copper. Stan, the son of Russian immigrants, never owned an overcoat that no one else had worn before him until he was taken into the army during World War II. He's frank in his astonishment at finding himself in such a setting these days, but I've noticed that he goes out of his way to point out the house's drawbacks, as if he doesn't want to deceive us, even through silence, into giving him credit for more than he deserves. Have we noticed that the timbers on the underside of the roof are rotting? Do we have any idea how tough it is to find workmen who can give beams a rustic finish these days? A similar house down the road has just been turned into a halfway house for addicts, that's how hard it is to keep up these old monstrosities. All the same, when guests come to dinner and finally figure out how to twist the pre-electric doorbell, he likes to be caught playing his favorite toy, his pump organ—Bach's Toccata and Fugue in D Minor suits him—while the last rays of the sun hit the tall metal pipes in front of him that look like the nibs of a giant's penholder.

It's not only the size of the rooms or the height of the ceilings I envy. It's not the entrance hall that's bigger than my living room. I envy the hardships that the Berkmans have undertaken, the sort of character it takes to cope with a place so old and authentic that it makes my house seem suburban and boring (it makes me seem suburban and boring) by comparison. When I visit them in summer, I can feel the warped wooden floors ripple through the soles of my sandals. The porcelain toilets, with vines embossed on the bowls, are so high that my feet barely reach the floor. I can tell from the pokers that stand next to their many fireplaces that they use them often and burn nothing but real wood.

And what do I offer the Berkmans in return, to bring them all the way down from Branford? A pair of club chairs trimmed in braid to match the rug, and a fire made of pressed logs that I bought in the supermarket and burn behind a façade of a few real chunks.

No, today at least I offer them a tree. My grandfather, Carl, who came from Nuremburg, which is the center of the German Christmas industry, specialized in tree ornaments made of Bohemian glass. When blindness forced him out of business half a century ago, my mother took over his sample line.

"Isn't this one marvelous?" Cissy said, examining a pale-pink and yellow clown. "I had a toy just like it when I was little. A roly-poly, I think I called it." Two things redeem me in Cissy's eyes, for the evening at least: my widowhood and my Christmas tree ornaments. "They're so much lovelier than if they were red and green."

We were married around the same time. As a matter of fact, Martin's aunts and uncles gave us joint engagement dinners, which made it awkward when Cissy's first marriage ended after a year in a bitter divorce. By the time she met Stan, Martin's family had focused their attention on Ted, who was learning to talk. "Did you know that they sell these ornaments in antique stores nowadays?" she asked. "They've become collectors' items."

Two, her tone said. My husband and I came up this hill together hand in hand. Jack and Jill. We are two, and we will go home two, but you will stay here alone. You are one, and yet you have trimmed this tree, which may be more than I could have done in your place, but we don't know that, do we? so we mustn't assume that my character is inadequate. What hardship has done for you, it might do for me as well.

"Pete did the real work this year. He got out the lights and tested them and hung them on the tree." Two.

"He must be big by now." One.

"Unfortunately, he's not. Don't mention it. His size is still a sore point." Two, two, two.

"You mean he hasn't reached his growth spurt yet, that's all. Wait until he's really into his teens. Those are always the ones who turn out to be tallest, didn't you know? Watch and see."

I turned toward Stan, who resembled Ralph (who was out in the yard at the moment) in the way that he kept his distance from the tree, apprehensive of what his bulk might do if he wasn't watching. The heel of his hand was as thick as the trunk.

"I had Pete's wristbones X-rayed, because he insisted. His pediatrician said that he's perfectly normal. But I think he wants to be Wilt Chamberlain when he grows up."

Now I know why I decorated this tree and placed it so that the lights shine through the porch windows and up the road banked with rhododendron. I understand why I stacked presents at the base, visible to any delivery man who comes into the house, and why I hung Woolworth candy canes on it that nobody is going to eat. I have a child, I call out to the neighborhood exultantly—not as little a one as I pretend, I grant you; a teenager, turned thirteen last month, but unarguably still a child, still an inhabitant of my house—and tinsel and bubble lights and Atari are my portion, and downstairs in the cellar the gerbils live in their plastic cage, unaware that I've surprised Peter and bought them a new room, known as the Fun Parlor, for what's called their Gerbil-ding this year.

"Good looking as he is, I wouldn't worry about him," Cissy said, as Ralph broke into a frenzy of barking in the yard, which told us that the taxi had arrived, bringing Marion and the others.

Ted carried his grandmother's pocketbook and shopping bag. Felicia helped her climb the stairs to the front door. Once inside, it was Stan who removed Marion's coat and took away her cane, then handed her the walker that Ted fetched from the car, and escorted her to one of the club chairs. This was the signal that it was all right to let Ralph in the back door, now that he could no longer knock Marion off her feet, and also that it was high time for Pete to come downstairs and greet everyone.

I needn't have worried so much about the way Marion would look in front of the Berkmans. Her hair was set; she was wearing a handsome dress with a jacket—I think it was the outfit she bought for Karen's wedding—and if the gold pin and earrings were a bit too much in combination with the metal of her eyeglass frames, that was understandable.

"Three generations," Cis said, making it clear that she'd never had such luck. Her own mother, to whom she was devoted, died while she was in her teens. She clasped her hands as we grouped ourselves in a semicircle around the fireplace, except for Peter, who dashed down to the basement, and Ted, who was busy making drinks. "Aren't you the lucky ones?" In her silk shirt and a quilted vest, with antique watch chains around her neck, which is the touch I'd never have thought of, she looked not much older than Felicia or Karen.

Felicia perched on the arm of Marion's club chair and massaged the back of Marion's shoulders and neck with her thumbs. "Do you know what I brought up here to show you?" she asked. "The canvas for the tapestry pillow I'm making. I'll bet you don't believe I'm ever going to get that pillow finished, now be honest, do you?" Marion could feel Felicia's admiration for the ferocity of old age as it passed through her thumbs. "Would I be a pest if I asked you to help me later with the colors?"

Ted interrupted the serving of drinks in order to sit on the floor and make Ralph sit next to him to be calmed down, so that he would stop swishing his tail so dangerously close to the tree in his excitement. Meanwhile, Peter returned from the chemistry lab he'd set up in a basement closet, to show his grandmother what he'd bought with the Christmas money I'd advanced on her behalf.

"It's a ring stand."

"A what?"

"A ring stand. See, over here I put the beaker."

At this moment, Gitte came in to have a drink with us. Ted got up from the floor, after cautioning Ralph to keep a grip on himself, and brought an extra chair from the dining room, but something about the present arrangement failed to suit him. "Let me give you this straight-backed chair, Marion," he said to his grandmother, who has no trouble with her back. "It's higher. I think you'll be more comfortable." It was clear to me that she didn't want to move, but, putting two hands under her armpits, Ted practically lifted her out of one chair and into the other, furiously ruffled. Before she had an opportunity to move back, he handed her a drink and a plate with some cheese and crackers, while Gitte took the chair that had just been vacated.

"Over here I put the beaker. Or whatever," Peter said. "And the Bunsen burner goes down here. That's a kind of flame."

"I know what a Bunsen burner is, thank you."

"Well, I take my beaker, and I heat it over the—"

"Kitchen stove." Marion is quicker on the draw than he is. "And that thing cost eight dollars?"

"Well, look at it. It's very well made, and it's adjustable. This ring slides up and down."

"I should just supply the Russian army for that price." I recognized the answer as her father's. "But that isn't all the money I gave you."

"I bought chemicals, too."

"And what can you do with those?"

Peter glistened. She didn't know it, but he was about to overwhelm her. "I can make anything on earth I want."

"Anything on earth? All right, then. Make gold," she said. "That gets a pretty good price these days, I'm told. Eight hundred dollars an ounce."

"Six hundred," Kurt corrected. Kurt is always accurate. He never exaggerates like the rest of us, perhaps because his vision was trained on the level by prairies rather than by the exaggerated ups and downs of skyscrapers. Starting from a two-room schoolhouse in Iowa, in a family where his mother baked his birthday cake in the shape of a heart every year and colored it pink with food dye, he went on to Amherst and Harvard Law School on scholarships, while practically no one else in his town had even heard of those places. Now he's the star mergers-and-acquisitions associate of a leading law firm. His shoes come from Bally. His ready-made, three-piece suits look custom-made on his figure. His prematurely gray hair puffs out around his face in relaxed Congregational waves—he's a strikingly handsome man—making him look like a

New Yorker ad for V.S.O.P. cognac or the full-color advantages of private banking.

"Well, I can't exactly make gold. I mean I can. That is, I could. If I had some gold salts."

"Gold what?"

"Salts. Gold sulfate, or maybe gold nitrate."

"Oh. I see." Marion drew out her vowels and shot a glance at Stan, to make sure that he was listening. "But I thought you told me that you could make anything."

"Your grandmother's pretty sharp, you've got to admit," Stan said genially, as he got up to light Marion's cigarette.

"Filthy habit. I should go back to Smokenders and give this up."

"What are you making, anyway?" Stan turned to Peter. Beneath his courteous attention he strikes me as a sad man who gives off a sense that he wishes he were doing something with his life other than what he does. Maybe he wishes he had a son.

"Well, chlorine for one thing."

"What's that you say?" Ted burst into the conversation.

"I said chlorine."

"Hey, that's terrific! Chlorine, you say? I like that. I tell you what we'll do. We'll get you some empty plastic jugs. All you do is add water and you can bottle your own Clorox." Peter doubled up with laughter and relief. "You can set up a stand in front of the house and sell it to the neighbors, the way other kids, the dummies, sell lemonade." Ted's voice had a timbre different from any I'd heard from him before. "Get your ice-cold fresh Clorox. Step right up, folks. Nickel a glass."

It was the word "nickel" that gave me the clue. He was playing his father's role for his brother's sake, and the effort gave his words, beneath their bluster, a special sweetness. "Wait. Wait a moment. Was that chlorine you said?" Ted flourished his arms in the air like a lunatic. "The stuff that if a test tube of it breaks, they empty out the whole train, block the roads, clear the countryside?"

Pete was exalted, in view of his family, straight to the heavens. "Sure. It's what they used in World War I for poison gas."

"That's lovely," I said.

"And how do you get rid of it?" Stan wanted to know.

"Throw it over the hedge into the Perlmans' garden," Kurt chimed in.

I'd disappeared altogether from Peter's awareness. "Aw, I deal with stuff a lot more deadly than that," he said modestly.

Felicia brought over a scale drawing of her living room and expressed interest in Marion's opinion on the placement of chairs. "Personally, I can't *stand* catty-cornered," Marion said. In another half hour we drifted into the dining room, adjusting our pace to Marion's.

"Erythropoietin," Stan was saying to Kurt and Ted. "It's the kidney's job, but what we're trying to do, in cases of renal failure, is harness a secondary source, something we call the hepatic erythropoietic factor. From the regenerating liver. The way I look at it, the thrust of medicine for the next twenty years or so will be using the body to cure the body, or, even better, shaping or reshaping a body that will suffer from as few defects as possible."

"You mean quality control?" Kurt asked.

"Endogenous medicine, you might call it, in place of exogenous."

"Why don't you do some research for me?" I asked Stan, while seating Cissy at my right side in what used to be Martin's place.

"Research into what?"

"Spit."

"What?"

"Saliva. Spit."

"Oh, that's better. I thought for a minute you said something else," Ted interjected.

"No, I'm serious. What do you do if you cut your finger? You stick it in your mouth. And what do you do if the baby gets hurt?

You say 'Let Mommy kiss the spot.' But you don't kiss it, you hold your lips against it. And what does an animal do if he has a sore? He licks it with his tongue."

"Interesting." Stan murmured something about an enzyme found in saliva which may indeed kill germs, but he muffled his information in such a way as to let me feel that I was making a distinguished contribution to science. Cissy ignored us. Abstract speculation wasn't her line.

"I so much want you to come to New Haven and have dinner with us," she said, as she helped herself to the duck stuffed with prunes and apples and potatoes caramelized in sugar that Gitte had prepared. "Of course I could never cook duck the way Gitte does."

"It's a law in Denmark that you eat duck and *brunede kartofler* on Christmas Eve. But we're blasphemous. We're eating them on Christmas Day."

"I didn't tell you. We've had a rather poor autumn. I haven't kept in touch with anybody." The undertone of self-pity in her voice might mean that she wished she knew a beautiful young Dane who'd cook duck for her.

"I wouldn't buy chemicals from a toy store," Peter argued with his brother and brother-in-law in disgust. "I order them from a mail-order chemical supply house."

"Don't I know it?" My ear was attuned to this young one. "I had to sign a release so he could buy sulfuric acid. If he blows up the whole county, the company is guiltless."

"I wouldn't tell you about it now," Cissy continued serenely, "except that I wouldn't want you to think we've been neglecting you. I know how sensitive you are."

Stan, it seemed, had suffered stabs and tremors in his heart. "I didn't know a thing," I said. I was as appalled as she meant me to be by my inattention a minute earlier, but also by the distance we'd traveled since we last met. No, she wouldn't have confided in me sooner. I recognized the rightness of her aversion, and in my sympathy for that aversion, our feelings met for the first time. She wanted to tell me about her troubles, outpoint me as it were, and yet she didn't want to tell me about them, not me of all people, and most certainly not while eating my food. The disease from which I suffer might prove to be catching.

"What could you have done about it, after all?" she asked, in her most self-righteous tone.

Had she ever sat this way before, I wondered, two women shoulder to shoulder at a table without a man in between? The nearness of our flesh as we picked up knives, wrenched ducks apart, lifted our glasses, was suddenly as disturbing as if we were kissing.

Five or six years ago, Martin and I had speculated whether her marriage might be in trouble. Her face had looked pinched; a dinner party was canceled; she'd spent two weeks without Stan on a museum-sponsored tour of England. Either Stan was having an affair— he had plenty of opportunities, God knows, as what successful doctor doesn't, much less a doctor who travels around the country for seminars and serves on committees that have evening meetings?—or else he was pouring too much energy into his work. It was about the time that their daughter, Louise, announced that she was renouncing her American citizenship and would speak and write only Hebrew from then on.

"You know I'll drive up to keep the two of you company any time you want," I offered.

"No need." Cissy spoke briskly. "Stan's back on a full work schedule by now. Too full. I mean, I've made up my mind that the doctor has told him what's right for him, and I've said my say, and I'm not going to argue with him about it one minute more. However he wants it, that's the way it's going to be." She turned toward Kurt, who was seated at her right, but he was no use, he was chatting across the table with Ted about wines. "I want you to understand why I'm not in a position to entertain right now. I'm not neglecting you. That's the only reason I brought the matter up."

I heard a tone in her voice that was like the brandied peach we were eating—its sting nothing that the young fruit might have envisioned.

T W O, I repeat. Only two possibilities for any of us. Either we die first or we live alone, and although we claim, while we're young, that we'd choose the former, the truth is that no one remains unmoved by the lump detected in the shower where there shouldn't be any lump, the flower of blood that blooms and expands in the toilet bowl one morning. For a while, we're married—Karen and Kurt, Felicia and Ted, Cissy and Stan—or else we're single, divorced, widowed—Gitte, Marion, me—in which case we wait for the members of the first group to join us. Cissy is the oldest female in her division. It comes out much the same in the end. The men at the table worry about problems of survival; the women worry about survivorship.

Stan laid down his fork and blanketed Marion's thin hand with his own as he leaned over to examine her eyelids, his face, flat and broad as the steppes of Russia, hovering close to hers. A woman could get lost in the expanses of such a face. "So dry and sticky all the time," Marion said, rubbing one eye with her free hand. "And I can't read at all any more. But not at all."

"I'm in a word contest," Peter announced at the other end of the table, to what he'd recently learned to call his siblings. "Sweepstakes. It costs a dollar to enter. I can win five thousand, but the people who run it make money anyway."

"You do the scientific words and I'll do the literary ones and we'll split the winnings fifty-fifty, how about that?" Felicia offered. Cissy turned and listened with the rapt smile of a woman who doesn't care much for other people's children.

How would she manage without Stan, I wondered? She had just gotten her master's degree in art history when Louise was born, "and we young mothers didn't think it was right to work in those days," she always adds. In the early years of their marriage they lived in New York and she took courses at NYU, while Stan built up his profitable hematology practice—"blood money" Martin called it, which never amused either of the Berkmans—but by the time Louise was in high school and Cissy had a part-time job at a museum, Stan was ready to move to New Haven. By this stage of their lives, they travel too often for her to consider another job.

"On the second round, the words are harder. Only seventy percent of the people pass." Peter frowned in an effort to show how canny and calculating he is.

Which would she miss, I wondered, Stan as a person or the life she leads?—a question that I'm sure she'd find outrageous. Did she hold him responsible (I suspect she did) for the fact that here she sat, middle-aged and unemployed, her degree out of date, her daughter an exile in a foreign land? And at this point, Stan threatened to make a widow of her.

"Dear heart, you know I'm not a real doctor, I'm only a hematologist," Stan said, as he pulled down Marion's lower eyelids one at a time and peered over their rims.

The Berkmans' friends may not be limited to doctors, but it's his reputation or position or both that attracts them all the same, not that a good-looking, intelligent wife ever hurt a professional man. Still, Cissy's intelligence without Stan's power behind it loses its point.

What's more, the house in Branford, that marvelous old monster, is a frame for a man of Stan's size, with every doorway and bathtub scaled to a man's shoulders, with every doorknob meant for a man's fist, with storm windows that need a man to lift them, and with the garage in a separate building, so that packages have to be lugged across a gravel path. The house was designed for a man, a big one at that, with an income to match his size. How will Cissy pay the bills if Stan's an invalid, much less dead? The wood shingles perpetually need a new coat of stain, which has to be applied by brush, not roller, for full penetration, Stan tells us. The painters' bill alone last year would have supported a widow for six months. Comfort is cheap, she must have discovered by now; it's charm that costs a fortune to keep up. Without Stan, it's conceivable that her life may become no more tasteful and authentic than anyone else's.

"And by the fourth round—"

"You invent perpetual motion," said Kurt. Ted laughed. Peter laughed too, in order to cover up his mistake in plodding along where grown men leap. This is what delights him, the hoots and howls of the world of men.

Stan finished with Marion's eyes, but instead of picking up his fork again, he let his hand rest on top of her forearm.

All things travel in threes. To be old and alone is to be sick. To be old and sick is to be alone. But all the same, I sat and worried whether my mother was taking advantage of Stan by cadging free advice from him.

A year ago at Christmastime, Karen came up and congratulated me. "Congratulations? For what?"

"For surviving the high-risk period." For a year after the death of a spouse, she told me (she picks up these statistics on her job) the survivor has a chance much greater than normal of developing a major illness. The bruised peach rots first, it seems.

The thought of a peach led my eyes to Ted, who was busy slipping bits of fruit off his plate for Ralph. The collie's nose reached on top of the table and lay next to Ted's dish.

"What am I supposed to do? He's crazy for peaches. Though he wishes you wouldn't serve them brandied."

"Get that dog out of here. He smells bad," Peter demanded, now that he'd noticed Ralph's presence.

"Ralph's not a dog," Felicia said. "We lie down and take our naps together on the den couch and he keeps me warm. He's my afghan." She liked to nap at my house.

I couldn't be sure that Felicia and Ted weren't baiting Cissy, who doesn't like dogs. But why does Peter object to Ralph? I bought him as a present for Martin when Peter was three years old, just about the time when we might have considered having another child, but this last baby of the family has his own chronology; Ralph has passed adolescence and middle age and entered old age while Pete is still a boy. Pete may think that he has seen enough death in the family already.

Stan snapped his fingers to summon Ralph to his side of the table, and talked to him in a way that made it clear that this was some sort of muted reproach to Cissy, but he didn't touch him. Maybe he wanted to keep his hands clean in case Marion needed them. When the cake was passed, he placed a slice on her plate.

From this moment on, Marion wasn't as alone in the world as she'd been an hour ago, or if she was still alone, at least she was no longer powerless. To know a doctor socially, a doctor so important that he can pick up a telephone at any hour any day of the week and reach others who are also the biggest men in their fields, is to be back in the ranks of people who count. If anything were to happen to her right now, while she sat at this table, he would take care of her as easily as he put the slice of cake on her plate. Merely sitting next to him made his intercession less necessary, as if he were a human St. Christopher medal. "You know my daughter's cousin, Stanley Berkman?" she'll say casually to the next specialist she visits. "Yes, the big blood specialist from Yale. I find him the *most* charming man."

Eventually we got up from the table and advanced to the gifts we'd so ungreedily left lying under the tree.

"Did I tell you what I used to do to my Uncle Norvin when I was a girl?" Marion asked. "Oh, I was a devil, I don't know how my mother stood it with me." Her face grew vivid. The Berkmans and Felicia murmured encouragement. "She must have had her hands full, I can tell you that, all of us living together in one apartment. Before Christmas, I used to take some of his own socks out of his drawer and wrap them in a box, and give them to him all over again. That's how stupid he was, he never knew the difference." She smiled with pleasure as Stan helped her get her walker and piloted her around Ralph, who lay in the doorway to make sure that no one could come or go without giving him his due attention. "How my father put up with him in business I'll never know. He'd yell his guts out, and still Norvin didn't learn. Oh, my father was a genius in business. Any competitor would tell you that."

N O W I know what memory looks like.

There it is, sitting over there near the wall: my mother, Marion, winding the gift ribbons round and round her hand, making them into little coils, and smoothing and refolding the papers so that she can reuse them, because holidays come back every year, while the stuff that was inside those packages, which she never coveted anyway, evaporates out of the living room into our bureau drawers, into two car trunks, into the hall closet (but secretly, later on) ready for United Parcel—Mr. Ups, the children used to call him—to pick up in the weeks that follow. And by the time that Mr. Ups has collected the last package to be returned for credit, and the stuffed fruit the Berkmans brought us has been eaten, and the tree has been dragged to the curb and driven away in the bulk refuse collection for the month of January, she'll be right after all. Nothing will be left of the holiday but what she herself has saved, the once-used—even twice-used—wrappings, stored and retrievable, identifiable but not memorable.

H O W anxious they are to leave me, Peter not least, even though he wants to go no farther than his own room to play with his Atari, his big present of the year, which he got this morning, a fact that explains his immoderate patience at the dinner table. The wine has worn off. The tongues are weary from too much praising. Faces are turned away from the circle around the fireplace, turned toward New York, Connecticut, Atari. Bed.

Most of us suspect that the Christmas we've been watching hasn't been the real one, or only one aspect of the real one, the part we're willing to show one another, except for Marion perhaps, who's twitching in her chair and breathing hard and puffing out air between her teeth, like a swimmer struggling to get back to shore against an ebb current. What does she know about the scene she's just been part of, about the pearl earrings I gave Karen, for instance? "Beautiful!" she exclaimed, when Karen opened the box. "Put them away quick before your mother steals them." There was no way she could know that the earrings were mine in the first place, any more than she'd know I also bought Karen a corduroy coat that we picked out together a couple of weeks ago. But then I've no way of knowing about the secret gifts the young husbands gave their wives, and the other way round, in private that morning, or maybe they've planned to give them later tonight. In public we gave each other plenty, but not so much that we'd shock either Marion or the Berkmans, who suspect that I buy my way into my family's affection. And how do I know what the Berkmans said to each other about how much to spend on our gifts, for that matter?

"What's this?" Marion had asked, when I handed her a box an hour earlier.

"Open it and look for yourself." It was a robe, peach colored and fuzzy as a peach on a summer afternoon.

"Beautiful! Do you have any idea how many robes I have? Three. How many can I use?"

"With cigarette holes in them."

"So? I'll burn this one too." She reached for the tag that was attached to the cuff with a safety pin, but I'd gotten there first. This tag showed only the manufacturer's name and the fiber content. I'd cut off the price ticket that was stitched through the velour with a plastic string, and I'd put the robe in an old gift box I'd squirreled away in the cellar closet, so that it would be impossible for her to return it, even if she could get out to a store, and even if she knew which store to go to.

REVISION is what I need, re-vision, another level of possibility for this scene.

Here's what I yearn for: just once in my life to see myself with a box resting on my arms as if it were a platter, my fingers curled around the far edge, holding it out toward a woman whose face lights up—this one time, anyway—with astonishment as much as with love. "What beautiful wrapping!" she exclaims, while she undoes the ribbons as carefully as she'd undo a baby's cap strings. As soon as she makes out the contents, she leans over the package at an absurd angle, because of its bulk, and, putting her arms around my shoulders, she kisses me, first on one cheek and then the other, while I begin to cry for no reason at all.

SO WHICH of the two of us is the ungenerous one?

I am.

I refuse to give my mother anything she really wants. Even at the last minute, after the box is open, I could change her gift if I want to, I could hand her pleasure if I choose. All I have to do is open my mouth and tell her that the robe doesn't come from Saks or Bloomingdale's, which is what she's afraid of, or even from Alexander's, which might relieve her, but from someplace better, from a discount house that's cheaper than Alexander's, and even at this discount house I bought it marked down—all this is true—to a third of its original cost, because of a small hole in the sleeve, which I've darned. (My mother, who can't boil an egg, taught me to French darn when I was little. Mending holes, conducting salvage operations, must be closer to her temperament than providing nourishment.) If I said this, she might—I say, might—have accepted the present and even found satisfaction in it.

But I'm not kind enough for this. I require too much in return. I never change: I want to force some acknowledgment of my generosity on her, at the same time that I wait for her to recognize the nonrejectable nature of my love and bow down in front of it. I want love for the price of a discounted bathrobe. Be the mother of a grown-up woman with a will and a hunger of her own, I demand. Imagine that I spent more on you than I did—what difference would it make if I spent three or four times as much, if that's what I wanted to do?—because I'm no longer subject to your commands, or your economies either. Imagine that I bought this gift with a love purer than I feel. Open your arms wide, just once, in pleasure if you can't manage admiration, the way you should have opened them, but probably didn't, when I brought home a picture I drew for you at school.

My mother's own gifts were cash as usual, handed out in holiday envelopes from the savings bank, bearing each person's name except for the Berkmans. "Just like the doorman's," said Peter, but then turned ecstatic the moment he opened his envelope.

"This is in place of a Christmas card," she said apologetically when she handed one to Gitte, which meant that the gift was ten dollars.

Ted slipped his envelope to me in secret. At first I didn't understand why. Then I realized that Marion had given him fifty dollars instead of the hundred that she gave to each of the other adult children, Kurt and Felicia being treated the same as her grandchildren. "I love you anyway," her card read. Of course. I'd forgotten that she was furious because she hadn't heard from him in weeks. When I told her that he was in Tokyo on business part of the time, her anger doubled at the thought that he could have gone so far away without calling her to say good-bye.

Money is a language that we speak within our family, a coded interchange across the generations, the way that lovers in other days used to speak a language of flowers. Since no one pays attention to Marion's voice any longer, no matter how often or how bitterly she repeats herself, she resorts to this silent dialect, marked by slurs, gradations, subtleties, even terms of endearment, that no one interrupts.

Ted answered in her own tongue. His thanks were reserved enough to make it clear that he earns a handsome salary of his own these days; her message was received, but at the same time recognized as an attention-getting device, like a swearword used by a child.

ENOUGH, enough. We were sick of the games we'd been playing. There was a bitter aftertaste in our mouths following too much forced sweetness, as if we'd been eating litchi nuts.

The Berkmans were tactful enough not to mention that they had an hour-and-a-quarter drive ahead of them, and Cissy doesn't drive. "We'll be in touch in February," Cissy said, as she put on her coat. "Next month Stan's delivering a paper at a convention in Acapulco." She wrinkled her nose to make it clear that this wasn't her idea of a place to visit. "After that, we hope to go to the Galápagos. Depending." She and I kissed within our mistrust, understanding each other the way no one else in our families understood us at that moment.

Marion came out of the bathroom, breathing heavily. At the top of the stairs leading to the front door, I handed her her cane in place of her walker. I was taking her to New York along with the two young couples and their packages. Everyone but Peter felt the burden of an impending trip.

"I'll drive," Ted said, as we got into the station wagon.

"Never mind. I'd rather."

"Move over. You have to drive home." I squeezed into the front seat between my son and my mother, with Kurt, Karen and Felicia in the back.

"You served much too much food," Marion said, which I recognized as thanks.

"I'll cut through Beech so you can see the displays in the Italian front yards there," Ted said to Kurt and Felicia. "Ever see a lifesize nativity, three camels with wise men, twelve wooden soldiers and a clutch of snowmen, all lit up by a couple of thousand-watt floodlights, on a lawn the size of a Ping-Pong table?"

"Every year they add something new," I said, overwhelmed by gratitude because he no longer found the suburbs boring. "You going to the office tomorrow?"

"What else? Our busiest time, end of the year. Hey, who do you suppose is in our office this weekend?" he asked his brother-in-law, his spirits rising as the wagon headed back to his own city, his apartment, his work.

"Who?"

"Phil. And you know why?"

"Bartwink made him work? That maniac?"

"His group is in the middle of a deal with the Ar-Bee people. So all of a sudden Bartwink announces 'Yes, of course we're prepared to produce the papers over the weekend. We'll have them ready for signature Monday.' Didn't even care that it was Christmas. Not a reason in the world for it."

"Except that Bartwink is crazy."

"He wanted to show off, that's all. So Phil got stuck." The brothers-in-law sounded like schoolboys laughing at their teachers, knowing everyone in common even though they work at different firms.

Scraps of talk about their offices brought gusts of air from the country I used to live in. "You remember Ezra Lazarus?" I asked. "Used to come into a negotiation that started at dinnertime, and say 'Before we settle down to work, so we're not disturbed, gentlemen, let me take your breakfast orders.'"

My interruption was ridiculous. How could they remember a lawyer who was invalided out of the firm while Ted was still in high school, long before any of us had met Kurt? The word "gentlemen" must have grated on their ears, now that half of the first-year associates (I have to remind myself not to say "first-year men") are female. And what do I mean anyway, when I say "the firm"? I mean Martin's firm. Which is not the same as Ted's firm. Or Kurt's firm. Every sentence that I speak dates me in their ears. Diminishes me.

The brothers-in-law remained silent for a moment, pretending to search their memories for the long-vanished Ezra Lazarus.

"I think you're rude," Marion said to Ted, although her glance included me. "I can't understand a word you're talking about." She turned to me. "You bought a gift for me to give Sylvia? Poor slob." Anyone who works for her, any black person in particular, is a pathetic creature in her eyes, in need of charity. The week before, she'd pressed me to invite the poor slob for Christmas dinner, as if this young and beautiful black woman with a mother in the Bronx, several sisters in various parts of the country and at least one boyfriend that I know about couldn't find any better way to spend her holiday. "What did you say you bought?"

"A sweater. I put it in your shopping bag, gift wrapped."

"A sweater? I'll bet she has a dozen sweaters. But that's all right. I want to pay you." She's capable of feeling pity and envy at the same time. "What size did you say?"

"Small."

"Small? Are you crazy? She's a size fourteen at least."

She has known Sylvia only since she herself shrank. "Mother, Sylvia and I are the same size."

"You don't use your eyes very carefully."

"Anyway, don't worry about it. If it doesn't fit, she can return it. That's why I bought it at Bloomingdale's."

Ted was talking over his shoulder to the three young ones in back, not about the office now, but about plans for New Year's Eve.

"Did you see Gitte come into the living room and sit herself down like a queen? And never get up once to help at the table?" Marion asked me.

Ted became silent.

"And pour herself wine! *Umberufen!*"

"And why shouldn't she?" There was gravel in Ted's voice. "We were having a Christmas party."

I floated the way I used to float between my mother and father when they quarreled, keeping myself from drifting toward either side.

"She's not one of the family yet. Am I right?"

I knew I shouldn't answer. "She's the one person in the family who doesn't leave home."

"Well, just tell me this, did she take the best chair in the living room? Or didn't she?"

"She didn't take it. Ted moved her into it."

"Ted! Has to be a big shot. Move everyone around, tell them what to do."

"I put her right where I wanted her," Ted said, in a voice that should have warned her by its softness.

"Why?"

"So that she and I, and not Stan, would be sitting opposite you."

Again, "Why?"

"If you must know"—her favorite phrase curved and turned around and flung back at her head—"because you were sitting with your legs wide apart."

"Oh, God."

"With everything on view."

She collapsed against the door of the car. She shrank to the size of a child that sucks its thumb. "I should never be allowed to go out, not any more. This is it for me. Forever."

For the moment, at least, she meant it.

I PLAYED the radio to keep myself awake on the drive home, Corelli's Christmas Concerto on WNCN. When I turned from the street into my driveway, the bushes were struck by the glare of the headlights as I parked on the gravel, then wiped out as the lights switched off, then struck again, but softly, as the station-wagon door opened. Under the sodium lamp across the street, a bare forsythia bush was awash with yellow light, its twigs and buds finely drawn, as if it were dreaming of its bloom.

So here we were at last, the two of us, just as I'd known we'd find each other all along, the house and I. It's strange how our romance has deepened in the years since Martin's death.

I opened the door. The living room glittered at me in a way that it never glitters during the daytime, mysterious sparks of light leaping out of the glass over the big picture on the far wall and glinting off the lacquer cabinet. Through the dining-room window, I saw two red eyeballs glaring from beyond my garden, the electric eyes of my neighbor's burglar alarm, where in summertime his bright-blue bug zapper crackles through the trees.

By degrees the house fitted itself around me, growing warmer every minute, like a fur coat put on over bare arms after the lining loses its initial chill. In the kitchen, Ralph awoke and creaked to his feet reluctantly, knowing that he was about to be put out in the backyard. Hurrying to clean up the mess that I'd left behind, I threw out the torn gift wrappings, but stored the ribbons and decorations my mother had salvaged, then opened the door to let Ralph back in for the night. A Christmas tree, its lights still blinking in my neighbor's window, jumped abruptly closer to me in the darkness.

As I climbed the stairs to the bedroom, I kept to the outside of each tread so as not to wear out the carpet in the center, postponing the day when I'd have to buy a new one. Upstairs, there was a bathtub to fill and lie in as long as I liked, a tape player to turn on, hand lotion to pump from a bottle, a pile of books waiting their turn. Without stopping to hang up my clothes, I switched on the electric blanket so that the bed would be warm by the time I got into it.

Here it was then, the last and most subtle seduction of all, and the fact that I recognized my danger would do nothing to save me. Women don't love men, my blanket tried to tell me, or don't love them as much as they think they do, or love them only for a few hours at a time. Women love sex, children and homes; women love electric blankets, which keep them warm without bothering them during the day. Men are the means, more or less desired, to those thoroughly desirable ends.

I felt myself succumb to the passions of the spinster. Home. Comfort. Security. Order. Predictability. Predictability is the lure. Freedom from change, unless I say the word "change." (And if I am the one who says the word "change," then how can it be change?) Any other lover I can get rid of when I choose, if convinced that I face a relationship as limited, and in its own way as demeaning, as this one, but not this lover, this house, or if I do, it will only be to replace it with another, much the same in its habits.

The irony is that I wasn't very fond of this house while Martin was alive, and certainly I wasn't the sort of homemaker he would have wanted. Was it because I thought we were still young, and secretly I hoped that some day there'd be another house, a handsomer one, or at least a more authentic one, like the Berkmans', maybe? Or was it because I didn't need to care about walls and furniture so long as I had Martin with me? Vain and pretentious as we human beings are, we claim to love other human beings, but I suspect that only angels are capable of such love. The rest of us love circumstances.

Well, middle age has its own form of passion. The questions are stilled. The future has arrived. There'll be no better house for me. How fortunate I'll be if there'll be none worse. I know a lot of marriages that survive on weaker ground.

Like all romances, this love affair of mine runs on money, although it's the single subject that I'm not allowed to talk about to decent people—the Berkmans, for instance—as if it were something shameful or unreal. It's real, all right. Cissy Berkman and I agree on that. We women need money the same way that we need sex—not a lot of it, but a steady supply, just enough so we can fall asleep at night.

Chapter 4

"Y<small>OU'LL</small> be sure to get here early?" Karen asked for the second time in one phone call. "Kurt and I want to make sure you're here before Ted and Felicia."

"Of course I'll come early," I protested. She knows that I often show up late and frantic. "I'll pick up Pete at school after hockey practice—maybe take him to visit Marion for half an hour first, as long as we're in the city. She's complaining she hasn't seen him since Christmas. But you don't get home from work until half-past five anyway."

It was the tail end of February. All night long, the wind shook the house, gusts of rain lashed it, the barometer threatened to fall out of its glass. Pete got up twice after midnight. I heard the splitting sound when his bedroom door opened, but didn't dare ask what was keeping him awake. Down in the kitchen, Ralph moaned through the small hours and dashed toward the front door and circled the floor again, his toenails clittering against the tiles. For a week now, he had refused to eat and had bitten clumps of fur out of his tail, which meant that somewhere in the neighborhood a bitch must be in heat.

Gale warnings, the weather radio said the next morning, from Watch Hill, Rhode Island to Manasquan, New Jersey, to twenty miles offshore, northwest winds thirty to thirty-five miles an hour, stronger in gusts. The dactyls flew in my face like spray.

HE MUST have gone back inside the lower school building to warm up, leaving me wondering whether I should stay where I was or get out of the car and hunt for him. It was ten minutes past four. After I'd finally gotten to sleep, I'd overslept. I'd been running late all day.

On both sides of the school's curved driveway, the cars lined up patient as camels, a female driver in each, the existence of this private suburban day school being predicated on a leisure class of mothers, willing to drive at all hours. Even now, an hour after classes ended, a dozen students sat on the stone wall that separated the school from the street. One of them opened a black leather case and took out a French horn, which he brandished at the others and threatened to play. A station-wagon door opened to take in two older girls, their silhouettes like dandelions in jeans and puffy ski jackets, their hair skinned back from their private school profiles; from the bottom of their double-zipper parkas, clumps of ski-lift tickets jangled against their pelvises like barbaric jewelry. The wagon they climbed into had a boat hitch on the rear bumper, covered up by a yellow tennis ball.

Through the car windows, which were shut tight against the weather, I couldn't catch what the students were saying, but it was clear to me that every one of them was part of a team, band, cast, chorus, club, editorial staff, science project, governing council—

maybe even part of some sequence of misbehavior and detention—never mind what, but woven so tightly into the fabric of the school that they didn't come home at dismissal time, but dangled their legs along the wall a whole hour later, like a fringe on the border of the day. I was a stranger to this part of school life. So was Pete. Usually he came home on the bus, but today he was staying late only because, as an eighth grader, he was forced to practice with his ice hockey squad. The best athletes in his grade had been skimmed off and segregated into teams already, with names like Peewee and Squirt, but the rest of them, including Pete, were jumbled into Squads A, B and C.

The older students were streaming out of the upper school building now. No matter how pushed we were for time, there was no way we could skip the visit that I'd promised my mother we'd make. It was bad enough that she wasn't included in the dinner the rest of us were having at Karen's—didn't know anything about it, I hoped.

Could Peter be standing in line to use the pay phone in the upper school building, to call home and see if by some slipup I was waiting for him there, or if he'd missed me and I'd left for New York already? When I stepped out of the car, I had to push the door open against the weight of the wind.

"See you Monday!" a girl in high-heeled boots called to two other girls, ignoring a boy who walked behind her. She took a few steps toward the student parking lot, pivoted and called out, "What's first class?"

"The front of the plane," the boy answered. I could see where Peter found his masters.

Standing in the path of these creatures in my shapeless blue storm coat, the hood pulled over my head because my hair frizzes in this weather, I felt conspicuous as a rock in the middle of a stream.

"Oxford," said a Botticelli blonde to a teacher who'd propped himself against a tree, his tweed jacket and craggy face blending with its trunk. "I'll be at Oxford. Isn't that wild?" She tipped her pelvis forward and her shoulders back; she rocked her body in a bow, first toward him and then away from him. Her books were cradled on her belly between them.

"You'll be all right?" For some reason, this man with his green book bag hung over his shoulder seemed concerned about her.

"Me? All right? Are you kidding? How could I be anything else?" Her tone sang out that he'd see nothing remotely in her league at home this weekend or anywhere else for that matter, nothing until he got back to school on Monday and saw her again, and what made him think he'd find anyone who came even close to her standard next year?

Catching sight of the dark hulk behind her, she turned around. "Are you looking for someone? Can I help?" The school prides itself on instilling good manners.

I WAS never young and easy like this. When I graduated from high school and went off to college, I was sixteen, the girl who wore a pink garter belt with long dangling elastics to hold up her stockings on weekends, while the others went barelegged in spectator pumps, or else painted their legs with tan liquid makeup and artistically drew seams up the backs with eyebrow pencils. Stockings had grown scarce; the war effort needed the silk for parachutes. During the week, I wore short-sleeve cotton shirts and pleated plaid skirts like a parochial school girl, made by a seamstress out of material that my mother bought on Grand Street. I wore saddle shoes with removable steel arches, because my mother had been told that my feet were weak. The others wore loafers but no socks, to save the bother of washing.

At night I secretly tied a hairnet around my head when I went to bed, to try to keep my hair from curling. The other girls had cascades of hair that fell over one eye, like Rita Hayworth, like Veronica Lake. When they slouched against a wall in their sloppy Joes and dipped their heads, those ripples warmed one breast and hid one eye, so that the left eye had no need to know what some boy's right hand was doing. I was fourteen and they were sixteen when I came into the school on a scholarship from an old-fashioned—in fact, archaic—grammar school, having skipped some grades along the way. No one told me the rules had changed; I wouldn't have known what to do about it if I'd been told. In class I waved my hand in the air when I knew the answer. Whenever a teacher spoke to me, I jumped to my feet and stood with my hands at my sides—careful not to let my fingertips lean on the desk—and I never said "yes" or "no," when asked a direct question, without adding the teacher's name. The others, just as bright, drew highly original cartoons in their notebooks, called the teachers by first name, read *The Nation* and *The New Republic,* went to nightclubs in the Village or marched in picket lines on weekends, and prided themselves on not knowing how to spell.

"Love nests," I said to my mother. "That's what they've got. They smoke, they drink. I know who goes all the way with who."

"Then that's the gang I want you to run with," she answered, as if anyone had given me the choice.

Nobody made fun of me. When I asked to sit at their table in the lunchroom, my classmates moved over amiably enough, but no one saved me a seat the next day, no one shared a secret with me. And no one told me not to fold my handkerchief into three neat triangles that poked up above the pocket of my cotton blouse, and not to match the handkerchief to my skirt, any more than they told me years later not to match the braid on my club chairs to the color of the rug.

"Thought I'd die if I had to wait another minute," the girls said, as they leaned against the building after school and inhaled the first deep breath from their cigarettes, while they waited for the English teacher to pick them up in his car and drive them to his house for a glass of sherry. When they leaned down to step into the car, their hair fell over their shoulders, their ropes of pearls hung straight as plumb lines, pointing to the center of the earth. What hurt me was that when the English teacher called on me in class, his hardest-working student, a faint haze of disdain unfocused his eyes.

In short, no one told me I was guilty of the single fault that nobody can forgive: I tried too hard. Over my skin there lay too nice a glaze that kept the burrs of human contact from sticking to me.

The girls who cross in front of my car to get to the student parking lot this afternoon are seventeen, eighteen years old, with the buttocks and car keys of women. I remain sixteen forever, because that's when I leave them and go off to college, where I'm the youngest again, and don't know what it feels like to French kiss, and never manage to catch up and become part of the glory group.

IF PETER didn't show up soon, it was going to be impossible to visit my mother, no matter what I'd promised.

A group of middle school children approached the waiting cars now, their faces familiar if not their names, which meant that they were probably eighth graders. These girls hunched their heads and shoulders over their books as if to keep them from being snatched, their hair hung slack across their jawbones, but already some of them moved differently from the way they did in September—like this one, who carried her books poised on her hip with the burdened, sideways grace of a fourteenth-century Madonna. The boys were shorter, rowdier, more clannish, except for one who came running toward my car, his chin tucked low.

"Did you get your ice hockey schedule for next week?" I greeted him.

"Not yet."

"What do you mean, not yet?" I came at him in gusts like the wind. "You know I have to make your orthodontist appointment." Peter never forgets anything. How could he have forgotten today of all days? "Then run to the field house and get it."

"It isn't posted."

"Not posted on Friday afternoon for next week?" Why was he the only boy with his ski jacket zipped up to his neck?

"You don't believe me?"

"That's right. I don't believe you."

"You're calling me a liar?" He scowled. He thrust his face forward. "You wanna bet a dollar?'

My voice grew fiercer. "Then how'm I supposed to make an appointment?"

What did he care about dental secretaries? He shrugged. "I'll ask next week."

"And the dentist is supposed to sit there and wait until you're kind enough to call? If the schedule's not posted, then I'll ask someone who knows." I turned toward the field house.

"Who're you going to ask?" He grew wild. "You're not allowed to go in there after sports."

"What do you mean, not allowed?"

"Don't you dare embarrass me! You'll see. Five dollars, I betcha."

I could tell. He took one look at the bulletin board, nervous at being there outside his time, and bolted. He never can find anything on his own for that matter, won't ask for help—can't ask—never knows his schedule. Doesn't even know the date. Oblivious. In a daze. Nothing like his classmates.

Late as we were, I hustled down the path, clutching my hood under my chin because the rain had begun again, with Peter trailing angrily at my heels.

But I was wrong. I even stuck my head into the office of the athletic director and asked, while Peter burst out of the building to escape such degradation, but the schedule wouldn't be finalized, in the director's phrase, until Monday.

"See! See!" My child jeered as we walked back to the car. "You had to embarrass me. You wouldn't believe me. You never believe me, you think I'm an idiot or something. That's five dollars you owe me. Five bucks. You know that?"

Two girls came up the path, swaying gently from side to side. " 'Bye Pete," they called out, fluent as birds. "Have a good weekend." A boy passed and greeted me by name. My own child didn't say a word, just scowled and slunk past everyone as if he came from some distant, more primitive tribe.

It wasn't his manners that enraged me, it was his determination to be unnoticed. When he acts so much punier than he is, I yearn to pluck him off the ground and hold him in the air, so that once and for all he'll find himself named and visible to everybody in the school. "Say good-bye to the girls," I called out to him, and this high treason, this wanton act of aggression on his own territory, threw him into a temper at once raging and sullen.

He ran into the car and slammed the door. "That's the last time you ever call for me," he said. "Ever." He sounded like his grandmother.

"It may be that."

"You think I care? You think I can't walk home? I like to walk home. Stay away from me. That's all I want." His hatred is real. It will never go away. At other times in his life it will give way to other feelings, but it will always lie underneath, ready to surface on short notice. His tongue stuck out of his mouth an inch. He could claim to be licking his lips.

I didn't slap him, but after I started the car and got away from the school grounds, I yelled, high grinding tones that didn't seem to be mine, and yet I knew them well. I couldn't stop. There must be some of my grandfather's craziness in me, I decided. Pete cringed at the side of the car and gasped.

Who was this woman with a cowering child? This hideous creature in her storm coat and hood and driving shoes, this howling witch? My ugliness enraged me further.

I never yelled at his father like this. In fact, I never yelled at Martin at all, not because he was perfect but because he was invulnerable. Any time that he chose, he could pick up and leave me, and nothing would happen except that I'd be destroyed. In every relationship between two people, I've noticed—and not only two lovers or spouses, but any two people—one leans further forward and the other leans further back, and the one who leans further forward is forever in danger of toppling over and falling into the void, while the one who leans back is in no danger at all, except of giving away more of his freedom of motion than he chooses. It's not the relation between the pair that's so important as the relation between each and the perpendicular.

I never yelled at Martin, because I couldn't afford to. Martin never yelled at me. He felt no need. Our friends supposed that we were faking our harmony, or that we didn't know how to communicate.

But this was my child who rode in the car beside me, my heart, my insides, who couldn't leave me any more than I could leave him. He'd been born because I needed him. Night and day, he lived in the glare of my gaze, which baffled him like a light kept burning in a cell. He was my prisoner, and he was afraid, and it was his fear that kept him my prisoner; it was his fear that I couldn't bear. All I longed for was to make happiness explode around his ears in a golden shower. All I wanted was to liberate him—liberate me—from the terrible knowledge of what I was doing to him and would undoubtedly do again another day unless he stopped me.

I was the mother, the monster mother. I was Medusa, Tiamat, Grendel's dam. I was the sea serpent rising from the sea. I was storm and chaos, spawning in water. I was the power that gives birth and drowns.

And who was he? He was Perseus, he was law and order, the new generation, the conqueror of chaos. He was the young sun-god with his fine sharp blade, who carried the future on his hip like a sword.

But no, my son wasn't grown-up yet, he didn't have the strength to take out his sword and lop off my head and make a new world out of my intestines and set both of us free. I was too demanding for him. He wasn't demanding enough for me.

As we drove in silence toward the highway, the right side of my body was aware of him, from my shoulder to my seat, with a depth, a sweetness of knowledge more piercing than love.

When we stopped for a light, another car drew up next to us with an older boy as passenger, his nose stuck into a book which he held no more than six inches away from his face. It wasn't an entirely pleasant face I saw, separated from me by two pieces of glass. It was good-looking all right, but swollen, as if the boy was overly juicy, but what caught my attention was the way he buried himself in his book.

His mother, who was driving, waited for the light to change, caught up in her own thoughts, as separate from him as if he'd already left home. Suddenly I recognized in her car the drama that I would never acknowledge in my own, that all of us leave our children and they leave us not once in a lifetime or even once in a while, but many times in a day, each time a fresh betrayal of the promise that I was making to myself once again. Forever, this time.

"What was new in school today?" I asked.

"Nothing."

"Nothing?" As we got near the toll booth, I fumbled in my wallet for exact change, but he made no move to help.

"I'm working on an invention," he said as we passed the second New Rochelle exit. "A sport hat that's cotton on the inside but Mylar on the outside. To reflect heat away from the head. I'm pretty sure I can get a patent on that."

Is it possible that all this happened because I was on my way to have dinner in New York with all three of my children, but my mother hadn't been included in the party?

"Do you want a Coca-Cola, Peter?" my mother asked. "No? Ginger ale? Cookies, then?" The soft drinks weren't Coca-Cola but the supermarket brand, he knew. The cookies were those the Berkmans had given her for Christmas.

Marion was asleep in her reclining chair when we came in, wrapped in an old afghan but also dressed in a green velvet robe that I didn't remember seeing before, *The New York Times* crossword puzzle lying on her lap. A television set was splashing the five o'clock news in the lollipop colors of a major network just beyond her feet. I noticed that Reagan was wearing his eyeglasses more often now that he was president.

She stirred. "I didn't mean to wake you," I said. It wasn't true, of course. Not more than half an hour was left for the visit. "Do you mind if I turn off the sound?"

"Go ahead." Half asleep, she flapped her hand disconsolately, as if accustomed to losing whatever she'd wanted, then straightened up as I brushed my cheek against hers. "You drove all the way down here in weather like this? And brought Peter?"

"How else could we get to see you?" For once, her hair was becomingly brushed. It was possible that Christmas had shocked both of us into a new awareness of each other. "That's a beautiful robe you're wearing. The collar and cuffs are real lace?"

"A present from the girls." The girls were the women with whom she used to play cards, who gave presents as a group, the way they pooled their bridge losses into a kitty to treat themselves to dinner every few months.

"For your birthday?" How long had it been since she was a regular member of that card group—ten years, maybe? They only exchanged gifts for major birthdays, which meant that it couldn't have been later than her sixty-fifth. It never crossed my mind that she might have bought the robe for herself.

"Not my birthday. When I moved from 1185, I think." Buildings on Park and Fifth avenues are known by their numbers; buildings on cross streets and lesser avenues are known by the number of the street. She moved into this apartment right after her mother died, which was fifteen years ago, and yet the robe looked brand-new. Was this the point I was supposed to catch—that while I was wasting my money buying her a robe for Christmas, she had one hanging untouched in her closet all the time, much handsomer than the one I'd bought?

CHARM bracelets ran in the family, but while my grandmother's carried only antique seals, my mother's had various ornaments hung on it. One Christmas, my father gave her a gold disk etched with a picture of the New York skyline, the windows lighted with diamond chips. Marion took it out of the box. She dangled it between her thumb and forefinger, her nails shiny red reflectors like the tree ornaments behind her. "Isn't this the charm that Trifari copied for five dollars?" she wanted to know.

She was right, of course, which was what irritated me—not only that she was ungrateful, but that she was right. My father could be both extravagant and obtuse where she was concerned. At least she still cared, I tell myself now. If she criticized one charm, that implied that there was another she'd have been willing to accept. These days she's purged of desire; she's a wraith plucking at her robe, as if to remind herself what it's made of—unless the desire to show me that she doesn't need a robe from me counts as desire.

But why do I keep referring to him as "my father" and call her "Marion," when she's the one I hunger to be close to?

MARION lit a cigarette, even though the ashtray resting on top of the battered crossword puzzle dictionary was full. "It was a handsome gift," I conceded, granting the point that once upon a time she had four friends who valued her a robe's worth.

"Thank God I have friends," she used to say in the old days, chiefly after she no longer had them, by which she meant her playing companions, who arrived at the apartment in sets of four, like place mats, to play the game best suited to their talents. The smart ones came for bridge. No older than Karen is now when I first remember them, these women—none of whom had finished college and only one or two of whom had ever worked, and that strictly because they needed the money—were either childless or at most the mother of one child, who invariably turned out to be a daughter. As soon as they came through the door, these young women turned rapacious, tricky, combative, secretive, censorious, above all dogmatic, all for a tenth of a cent a point. They never took time out to eat until the game was over.

Standing behind my mother's chair, I'd hear the thud of the deck being cut on the felt card-table cover, and the whir as the halves were interleaved by her thumbs. Then I'd watch her fingers curve with inexpressible grace, their lacquered tips arrayed against the back of the deck, as the semicircles of cards fell into the nest of her hands with the long, soft rustle and gentle yielding and settling down of cooped-up birds. At such moments I yearned to grow up and be as clever as she was.

In another era, the game was mah-jongg, which might have been imported to show off the enameled nails and cocktail rings and golden charm bracelets that clicked and clacked against the tiles, setting up a clatter from their wrists to their fingertips. "Three bam," the women said fiercely. Or "Three crack." "Crackerjack," was the finest epithet one player could use to describe another, carrying with it the snap of their games.

But what happened? When did those Wednesday and Friday bridge games diminish to one a week, and then that one only on a standby basis, when a regular player was sick or vacationing? And who worked up the courage to tell Marion she was no longer wanted, except on the few occasions when she was wanted? How did they hide the fact—or maybe they didn't bother to try—that the game was thriving without her?

"Silk velvet," she said.

"Then it has to be dry cleaned." The words were out. I hadn't meant to trap her. The robe I gave her is machine washable. "But it's very becoming. You should wear it more often."

"For whom? For the back elevator man?" Two bridge games shrank to a single gin game, which shrank in turn to something simpler, a child's game really, called Spite and Malice, played once in a blue moon when some woman drops in for old times' sake, carrying a shopping bag to show how many errands she has done today or how many she still has to do, so that she's forced to go home early because she's either busy or exhausted. "My friends are sick," my mother tells me. "Or their husbands are sick or dying. Who goes out on the streets any more?"

"What can I give you to eat, Peter?" she wants to know now.

"Nothing."

"No cookies? There may be some hard candy in the living room."

"No, thank you."

"No, thank you? What kind of company are you? I don't think you're very nice—all you say is 'no.'" Wary of anger this afternoon, Peter sits on the edge of the dressing-table stool, his eyelids lowered halfway. "What do you have new to tell me?"

"Pete's taking up cross-country running in school this spring. He wants to go on a mountain-climbing expedition this summer instead of going to camp."

"As if he isn't thin enough."

"I'll bet he can give you words for your crossword puzzle. Especially in science. Did you tell Marion you got an A on your science project?" He jumps at the invitation to take the newspaper from the lamp table. "Here, let me turn on the light."

I moved toward the overhead switch, but Marion winced and pulled the chain of the lamp next to her instead. The robe lost its congealed luster. "Come over here and read in the light. Marks. Pooh! Did you ever hear what my father did to me?" Peter had to hold off before tackling the puzzle. "I got eighties and nineties—this was the Calhoun School, very fine in those days—but that wasn't good enough to suit him. One month I came home, and my average was ninety-eight. 'If you can get ninety-eight, why can't you get a hundred?' he wanted to know. So the next month I worked like a dog. I decided to show him. And you know what happened?"

She glared at Peter as if confusing him with her father. "What happened?" he asked reluctantly.

"I got a hundred."

I picked up the cue. "You showed him. Then what did he say?"

"He said, 'If you can do it once, why can't you do it all the time?'" She locked her jaw. "So that was it. I never tried again."

Sylvia appeared with a shot glass of Scotch and a few crackers spread with cheese on a tray.

"No, thank you, nothing for me." I prayed that Marion wouldn't ask why the two of us were in town so late this afternoon and what we were doing for dinner. She shook her head in despair, but made no comment as she leaned forward and jutted out her lower lip to swallow a cracker whole.

Look up from the puzzle, Peter. Look. Did you see that? What you have just seen is the alligator snap of loneliness.

"Madeline Popper was here Monday."

"How wonderful." There was too much praise in my tone.

"Didn't stay half an hour. The way she buzzes around, she drives me crazy."

"She still working as a volunteer tutor in the schools?"

"I suppose so. She chases her own tail. She's lost so much weight lately, her neck looks like a pelican's."

"Why don't you invite her for lunch one day? Wouldn't that be nice?"

"And who's supposed to cook the lunch?" Marion heard what I didn't answer, that I'd bring in a frozen quiche from any of the gourmet shops in the neighborhood, or smoked salmon and bagels or roast beef and rolls from a delicatessen; I'd bring a casserole from home, I'd bring anything and everything, but I'd leave her no excuse for loneliness. I longed to stuff her refrigerator—the way I longed to stuff Peter's life—as desperately and randomly as she longed to empty it.

"Don't be crazy. We don't do that sort of thing any more." After a few minutes of drinking, she panted more noticeably. In the distance I heard the buzz of the house phone and the sound of Sylvia's voice when she answered it.

Marion stirred. She took her feet out of the afghan, so that I saw the robe full length. She turned to empty her ashtray into a large envelope that must have brought a stockholder's report in the mail but now served as an ash receptacle, while Sylvia entered the room to announce that Doctor Nordlinger was on his way up.

At that moment I understood that my mother never had me in mind when she put on the velvet robe with lace collar and cuffs and combed her hair. "Why don't you let Pete dump the ashes in the kitchen?" I suggested, to get him out of the room.

As it turned out, this wasn't the Doctor Nordlinger I knew, but his son, Jack, a curly-bearded young man about the age of Ted and Kurt.

"You've met my daughter, Karen?" Marion asked. "Give the doctor your chair." She expected me to leave the room, but no, the doctor wouldn't have that, he insisted that I mustn't disturb myself, this was more of a social call than a medical visit, anyway.

"I'm Joan, I'm not Karen," I said while he straddled the ottoman at Marion's feet as if it were a pony.

She cocked her head at him and frowned. "I thought you promised to get a haircut," she said with mock severity, pert as a teenager picking a quarrel for the fun of it.

"I will. I promise. Soon as I have half an hour." He seemed to enjoy her tone, as if some agreement kept them both in the late 1960s, when he was a harmless sort of hippie, still a student perhaps, his hair and beard foaming out of his head in a mass of curls. Leaning forward, he grasped Marion's wrists, to take her pulse, I supposed, but he didn't let go of them.

"You're going to have a drink with me today?"

"Do you know how many house calls I still have to make?" His tone assured her that he wasn't trying to avoid her, he was sorry to turn her down, like a man resisting seduction. Since he was wearing Frye hiking boots, I believed the excuse. He pulled down her lower eyelids, but seemed engrossed in studying her crumpled figure.

"What do you hear new about Doctor Schecter?"

"Nothing much. I don't really know him," he said with regret.

She blinked at the insult. He couldn't expect her to believe that a man in his position didn't know Doctor Schecter. "Forty years that man was my doctor. No. I'll correct that. He wasn't my doctor. He was my god." While he held her wrists, her body stiffened, as if to remind him that Nordlingers only took over her care after her real doctor was unavailable. "You must get news in the hospital."

"I hear he was a fine person."

"A god. That's what he was to me. He was a guest in this house *many* times."

I didn't tell her that Carolyn and Foster Schecter visited my father and Sally in Florida a year ago; what's more, not only visited them, but invited them to spend a weekend in turn as houseguests in Connecticut, an invitation that my father and Sally were too busy to accept. Marion glared at me in fury all the same, as if she could read my mind, her cheeks pumping in and out like bellows. "You're making Peter sit in the kitchen all alone?"

Jack Nordlinger intervened. "Is Doctor Schecter still alive?"

"Eighty-one pounds of flesh and a plastic bag. If you call that living."

The doctor hummed and held her feet, one in each palm. Her feet and legs are thin and elegant, with unpainted nails, the feet and legs of a girl.

"What can you do about her eyes?" I asked, while the doctor examined her nose and throat, in the tone of a child willfully misbehaving in front of company.

"Exactly what is supposed to be the matter with my eyes?" In the uprush of anger, Marion looked twenty years younger.

"Every time I talk to you on the phone, you complain about them. You tell me you can't see."

Turning to the doctor, she asked "Have you any idea how many eye doctors I've been to?"

"I sent you to Doctor Pratt."

"Don't mention his name to me." She pawed at her right eye like an animal with a wound. "What does it mean when I have pus there?" The doctor stiffened. Having struck home, she went on rubbing. "What's pus, anyway?"

"That's not a question I can answer, just like that." Leaning over, he examined her slowly, first the eye she was rubbing, then the other. "You don't have pus, in any case." There was anger as well as relief in his tone. Nettled by her accusation, he tried to regain his lightness of spirit, but viewed her now as a patient to be humored, not as the friend who invited him to have a drink a few minutes ago. "A tiny secretion in the corner. Remember the sandman, heh?"

"Should she see Doctor Pratt again?"

Marion twisted her shoulders to keep me out of the grown-up talk as completely as possible.

In the bedroom when I was little—it was my grandmother's bedroom that I mean, and my grandmother who sat in the chair against the window, my mother who took the chair at her feet—the two women bore each other company in the silky harem of the afternoons, closed in by a gauzy sky, taking off their dresses and unhooking their bras if the weather was hot so that they could dry off the hollow underneath their breasts with their handkerchiefs. Their floppy breasts—their spaniels' ears, they called them—rose and fell, rose and fell, in rhythm with the murmurs about C.H., my grandfather, who was the cross they had to bear, or The Pot, who was the Czechoslovakian cook, or *Das Kind,* who was me, although I wasn't supposed to understand, and all afternoon long my mother leaned toward her mother in perpetual tilt, keeping her back toward me, while her mother leaned back in her chair.

Within a few more minutes, Jack Nordlinger jollied Marion into better humor, like a cook whipping air into egg whites. He even made a deal with her, that if she'd come into his office for X rays and blood tests, he'd solve her other problems. When he got up to leave, I followed him to the front door.

"She pants for breath," I said offhand, as he pushed the elevator button. I didn't want to antagonize him by asking straight out whether she'd been tested for anemia.

"It's the depression that bothers me," he said. "The way she slumps in her chair as if someone has beaten her."

Beaten her? Marion as victim? While the young man talked about the new antidepressant he planned to send over here, his mood rose as if he'd taken his own prescription. "Of course, we ought to get her into the hospital for a sigmoidoscopy, if her condition's good enough."

"Sigmoidoscopy? What for?"

Now I'd embarrassed him. "Better find out if anything's going on there," he murmured.

Loss of weight, weakness, possible anemia. They could be signs of anything or nothing. Anyway, everyone knows that life expectancy in the elderly isn't materially affected by most types of cancer. Only the young die fast.

He pulled his gloves out of the pocket of his pea jacket.

"I hear you've got a new baby in your family," I said warmly.

For a moment there, he was worried that I might latch onto him just when he was ready to hurry off to the house calls that stood between him and his dinner, but now he saw that he was safe. He supplied the baby's statistics and accepted congratulations in return. By the time the elevator door opened, we smiled at each other like conspirators, one leaving and the other soon to follow, both of us hurrying toward our children through the twilight that airbrushes out our flaws and forgives them for the night.

But the minute that I closed the front door behind him, I was filled with a sense of haste. We'd been frittering away our time, Marion and I. I had to get her shabby old robe away from her—she'd have put it back on now that the doctor was gone, I was willing to bet on that. She had to go outdoors in decent weather with Sylvia, she had to offer her friends some lunch, she had to send her dying doctor a get-well card, and speak kindly to Sylvia for once, and even remember her daughter's name. She had to catch at the flying coattails of grace. But for whose sake did she do have to do all this, hers or mine?

Coming back into the bedroom, I needed to find an excuse for the time I'd spent talking to her doctor without her. "Jack's sending up some new medicine," I told her. "A mood elevator. You'll be dancing in the streets within a week."

She looked as if I'd struck her. "You call him Jack?" she whispered.

THE WIND was still raw. In the suburbs, weather is picturesque, seen from a warm spot behind a window or windshield. Out on the city streets, as in honest-to-God country, weather is real. People walk.

I know this uptown neighborhood, the city of women and children, the way a farmer's child knows the fields. Each building is a different height, a different color, but within a limited, contiguous range, like trees in a forest or rocks in a field, earthborn all of them, a city of brick: red brick, brown-red brick, rose-red face brick from Pennsylvania for the fronts of houses, tawny alley-cat brick for the rear courtyards where I played ball against the back wall when I was a child.

"Here's the school I went to for a year in second grade, Pete. This building here. And up that hill there's a garage that'll put air in your bicycle tires." We walked a few blocks north on Park Avenue. The buildings were splendid old ladies like my grandmother's friends, more or less the same age and height and stolid shape, a clique of friends, a "set" my grandmother would have called them, careful not to outdo one another and become conspicuous for style. One had a stone garland across the front; another had a balustrade necklace; over there a pair of Grecian urns stood like diamond clips on either side of a doorway.

"There's the house I lived in from the time I was ten until I was married. Every Saturday, an old Italian with a hurdy-gurdy played in the service court—over there, behind the iron gates."

"A hurdy-gurdy?"

"A hand organ. Not the kind that plays Bach. He played 'O Sole Mio' off-key. We threw pennies out the window. He picked them up and put them in his old felt hat. I always felt he couldn't afford a monkey to pick the pennies up for him." But he had the face of a monkey himself, and he took off his hat in a sweeping bow like a monkey, every time a few coins hit the concrete. As we passed the gate of the service court, I saw that there was a lock on it now. The sign over the back door still announced that this entrance was for Tradesmen, Deliveries and Domestics, but it was the door that we children used with our bicycles and the door my mother came through when she pulled her cart from the supermarket. A thought struck me. "I wonder what he did the rest of the week. I never thought about that."

"Pennies, huh? You must've been the last of the big spenders."

"Well, nickels maybe." Actually, I was sure it was pennies. I started to cross against the light, but Peter froze, like a creature from the woods, and looked for traffic in the wrong direction. "Hurry up, will you, Bambi? We're going to be late at Karen's." He laughed. He didn't mind that.

On Lexington, most of the shop windows were lighted for the night. The clutter of the hardware store dappled against my eyes. Inside the furrier's window, night and day, the time was a chill blue twilight, and the mannequins had penciled eyebrows from the 1920s. But Lexington was a lot fancier than it used to be when I lived there—who would have dreamed of a bookstore that sold nothing but cookbooks? The shoemaker was gone. In his place a take-out gourmet shop offered casserole of veal *chasseur* and French loaves tonight.

We turned the corner, and Karen's street swooped away from us, down to the East River a quarter of a mile distant, where a buoy was barely visible. The back of the legs got tired when pulling a shopping cart up this hill. "The Ruppert Brewery used to be down there, but the street was cobblestones in those days. There are still supposed to be tunnels underneath it leading to the river, so that barrels of beer could be rolled right from the brewery onto the barges."

"Tunnels?" I caught a glint in Peter's tone, which had nothing to do with cobblestones and horse-drawn brewery wagons. He was thinking of drug drops from offshore boats. He could supply the whole of New York that way. The whole east coast.

But the street no longer smelled like rotten apples from the brewer's mash, and when I looked at my watch I was appalled to see how late we were. How could I have forgotten that I was supposed to get here early? For the first time it occurred to me that Karen and Kurt might want to talk to me confidentially before Ted and Felicia arrived. Maybe the expense of furnishing the new apartment had been greater than they expected, and they could use a loan from me.

That made two of my children that I'd betrayed this afternoon.

SHORTLY before Thanksgiving, while she and Kurt were hunting for a place they could afford to buy—and I was happy because they were about to commit themselves to the New York area, instead of Atlanta or Houston, where young lawyers can afford to join tennis clubs—Karen telephoned one afternoon and asked me to look at an apartment with her, as I'd looked at several others that she'd considered. The price was fair. She gave me the address.

"I don't need to come," I told her.

"Why not?"

"I know the building. Go ahead and buy. You'll be happy there."

She'd picked the building where Martin and I had lived when we were married, the apartment house where Ted was born and she herself was conceived. Only real life gives in to such strokes of sentimentality. Fiction manages its affairs with better taste.

"You're nothing but a salmon going upstream to spawn," I said, when she told me she bought it.

It was our trousseau home. Such a thing still existed in those days, a three-and-a-half-room apartment rented two months before the wedding, to give my mother and the interior decorator time enough in which to work. My family paid for everything, from the wall-to-wall carpeting to the crystal chandelier, as my mother's family had done for her. By the time we came home from our honeymoon, monogrammed highball glasses were lined up in the bar; monogrammed turquoise hangers dangled in the hall closet; turquoise taffeta ribbons, with lead weights sewn in at one end and monograms cross-stitched at the other, kept the stacks of sheets and guest towels—which were also monogrammed—lined up in military formation in the linen closet. (But had I done as much as I could do for Karen and Kurt? Or had I done as much as I should, if not as much as I could, and how could I be sure?) It didn't matter whether Martin and I ever earned enough money to invite guests to use those highball glasses and huck towels. We'd been given our due. From that point on, we could only chip or dirty what had been rendered to us perfect.

As I hurried down the steps of the building, I found myself off balance; I wasn't the single self I imagined, even though this wasn't my first visit to the new apartment. I was too light. I missed the weight of a Silver Cross baby carriage that wobbled on supercilious springs and pulled me forward down the steps.

Going upstairs in the elevator, I could see Peter out of the corner of my eye, peering at himself in the mirror that hung on the back wall. With one hand he smoothed back his hair—I never saw him use that gesture before—and at the same time he dropped his lower jaw, only an inch, but that was enough. It lengthened the proportions of his face. It hollowed his cheeks and sucked his emotion back into himself, through the drooping mouth and half-closed eyes. At that moment, I saw him the way the girls we passed at school must have seen him, a young man, not a boy, who smoothed his hair and studied himself with remote and cautious pride, like an out-of-towner cruising through Times Square with a loaded wallet.

The moment that the apartment door opened and Karen appeared, Pete bubbled back to the surface and turned into a boy again.

I'D BROUGHT a change of clothes along. I wanted to go into the bathroom and wash, but Karen and Kurt were crowding me into a corner of their bedroom, giving me no privacy, which was strange when I was in such a hurry. "Have you got a towel?" I asked. Kurt was so close that the hairs on my arm brushed his shirt sleeve. What could I do but turn my back and strip off my blouse anyway?

And now Karen told me. I gasped, but I'm not sure it was a gasp of joy. It was a scoop of air, like the pants in the last stage of giving birth. It was beyond feeling. It was a need for oxygen. I'd been knocked out of the center of my world and needed a little time to find another place to stand, to reach a new under-standing.

Until this minute, I was the still point; they were the spokes. I was the maypole; they were the dancers. That was no longer true.

"Little mother," Kurt said, nuzzling her ear. That word meant Karen from now on. "Does she look old enough for junior high?"

"How soon do you think I'll have to wear maternity clothes?" Karen asked as I kissed her. "Do you think I ought to give up my job?" Her voice had the same tremor that it used to have when she moved across the courtyard from the middle school building to the upper school and worried whether she'd ever find the lunchroom.

I was trying to button my blouse. The fabric that covers the buttons jammed in the holes. My fingertips must be leaving stains.

"How long has it been?" Why was I surprised? They bought a two-bedroom apartment, after all. Salmons swim upstream.

"Four weeks from conception." Already she spoke a new language. "The test came back Wednesday."

Her willingness to tell me so soon touched me to the quick. My own mother must have told her mother, her other self, as soon as she was aware of her pregnancy—but how long did I wait before telling Marion? Two months, even three months of stingy silence? "Don't tell anyone else," I said. "Except family, of course. Makes the time seem too long." Tempts the gods, I meant. She'd tell everyone in her office the next morning. Counting on my fingers, I burst out "But that's the end of October." What other time could it be? Martin's birthday was October 26. His grandchild will be born on his birthday. His grandchild will be a boy, and his name will be Martin.

While I hugged Karen, I couldn't help looking over her shoulder at her night table, where there was a framed snapshot of her father that's supposed to be put away or laid face down whenever I come to visit, because I still can't stand pictures. This one was taken on October 26, at a party for the family, not only for Martin but for Ted and Peter as well, since the three birthdays fell within ten days of each other. There Martin sits in his new silk bathrobe, laughing, holding a drink—seven weeks remaining before the end—enjoying the jokes of his children (Karen and Kurt were engaged by that time), his belly swollen, but his belly doesn't show in the photo. "I'm pregnant," he explained, and in a sense he was right of course, he was carrying the death inside him to term. In the picture, he looks radiant as I'd never seen him before, as a pregnant woman looks radiant, his mouth open to speak, his face unlined, perhaps because of the excess fluid that was puffing him up, perhaps because he no longer had anything to worry about, not his office or his clients or his health or anything else, for that matter. He was doing whatever he could do. His life had been taken out of his hands. Dying is, among many other things, a vacation, a vacation from the cares and decisions of living, more than a vacation, a vacancy, a space where there hasn't been any space up to now. A space that makes room for something else.

Never before had Karen forgotten to put the picture away, but she was distracted tonight. Or maybe she wasn't, maybe she wanted her father with us at this moment. "Scorpios are the best," I said. "Stubborn. Impossible to handle. But the best."

"No, no. It won't be Scorpio. The doctor says the middle of October."

"Never mind him. You'll be late. You'll manage somehow." What doctor? Had she found an obstetrician so quickly? She never had a doctor until now whose name I didn't know. "Another male Scorpio. It's a good thing you're a Virgo, you'll be able to cope with him."

The house phone buzzed. A few minutes later, the bell rang and Peter opened the door for Ted and Felicia. "How about some light in here?" Ted boomed out. "You should've told us you were saving money. We could've each brought a flashlight."

Felicia was more beautiful and more attenuated than ever. "Such a pet of a room," she said, even though she'd seen it before, in a voice which made me wonder if she and Ted had quarreled on their way over here. She was in Ted's class in college, yet she's only six months older than Karen.

"You look knockout," I said of her raw silk skirt and shirt.

"You can get away with a nineteen-dollar dress if you wear a hundred-dollar pair of shoes," she taught me once. In her presence, Karen's living room seemed pretty-pretty. When Felicia sat down on the couch, her legs buckled at the knees like those of a unicorn in a tapestry.

"Later, you have to help me decide what to do about the bedroom," Karen said to her sister-in-law. "There's nothing in it but the stuff from Kurt's apartment."

"Better not ask me." Felicia laughed, tapping a cigarette out of her pack while Ted frowned. "I've had my dream bedroom planned for years." For days at a time, this young woman can't bear to answer the telephone. For nights at a time, she reads herself to sleep with *The Wind in the Willows.*

"What's in it?"

"A wrought-iron canopy bed. But the canopy is made of vines, and there are palms behind it—maybe a few budgerigars flying through the leaves—and a great grass bedspread, with a leopard cub curled up on it. Taking a nap. From a vine overhead a two-toed sloth is dangling. Actually, I can never remember which I want, the two-toed sloth or the three-toed sloth. One of them is nasty and smells bad. That's not the one I want. In the bathtub there's a seal—named Henry, of course."

"Why of course?"

"Because all seals are named Henry."

"What about a collie? Have you forgotten Ralph?" I tried to postpone the moment when she'd hear the news.

"I'll take ginger ale," Pete volunteered. Kurt was taking drink orders and filling them so quickly that it was clear he wanted us to have something in hand when the official announcement was made and a toast was in order.

"Forgotten Ralph? But you wouldn't count him in with the animals. Now would you?"

Half an hour later, after we'd heard the announcement and drunk our toast, and after Felicia had been missing for a while, I went into the bedroom and found her sitting on the edge of the bed, one leg wrapped first over and then under the other, her toes pointed, staring at the cable television, which was sending out nothing but geometric test patterns. It was the only light in the room. I sat down next to her and put an arm around her.

"Not yet," I said. "That's all. Not yet for you." The television shot concentric rings at us like something out of *Star Wars.* In the other room, her sister-in-law radiated the conviction that happiness is nothing more than a question of good management.

Not-yet and Nevermore went in to dinner together, which was long and deliberately merry, and then Ted and Kurt watched a rerun of *Notorious* on television, starring Cary Grant and Ingrid Bergman, but Peter insisted that he couldn't join them, he had to start his algebra homework. Felicia and I helped Karen clear the table.

Fifteen minutes later I went into the second bedroom, which Kurt used as a den, and stood behind Peter's chair and put my arms around his neck. "Karen's baby will be raised entirely on pizza and Coke," I said. Not to mention acceptance and joy. There's the mother you should have had, Peter. I rubbed my cheek along the fuzz and dip that led from the nape of his neck to the bony peak of his spine, while he bent his head over his homework, scrubbing away with his eraser, blessed with enough sense not to be overwhelmed by my evening remorse any more than he was overwhelmed by my afternoon anger. "How do you suppose Similac tastes mixed with Coke?" I was a generation older than when I came into this apartment, but I couldn't expect him to notice the difference.

"Karen was exactly the age you are now when I became pregnant with you. This won't be a den any more, you know. This room'll be your niece or nephew's nursery." His eyes looked as if they'd been erased and smeared as many times as the steps in his algebra problems. "Can't you stop working? You've got until Monday." I know that he can't stop. He knows that I care.

Leaving him to his homework, I went into the kitchen to help the two young couples with the dishes, after which Ted and Felicia went home. Karen, Kurt and I had a drink together. Kurt and I took brandy. Karen drank water.

At last I've discovered where the love of grandparents gets its force—not just from any mellowness of age or tenderness that comes to those of us who've known endings as well as beginnings, but from an emotion fiercer and less self-centered than any other: shame. Our children know the worst there is to know about us. Knowing it all, somehow they survive it all, and having survived, they are still willing to trust us to touch what they themselves hold dearest. It's the closest we can hope to come on earth to forgiveness.

When I went back into the second bedroom to get Peter, I found him stretched out on the floor, fast asleep like a little child. The bulk of him spread over the rug—suddenly he looked as big as Gulliver—convinced me that this was the last time I would see him in such a position.

BACK home, I borrowed Pete's biology book (we had nothing like it when I went to high school, or when I was pregnant either, much less when I was in eighth grade), and turned to the section on embryos, where I found a picture marked "Four weeks after conception." My grandchild was the size and shape and translucence of my cuticle tonight, but he had features already, blurred like a miniature snowman enduring a thaw, and he had a heart as big as his head that was growing outside his chest wall—so exposed, so vulnerable, I was afraid for him—like a red poppy on Veterans Day that he gallantly chose to wear to salute me.

Chapter 5

*D*URING the last summer that Martin was alive, clothes became a problem for us—his clothes I mean, not mine; we were having them altered at the tailor's shop in the village rather than buying them. It was impossible to buy any with the waistline Martin needed and still have them fit the rest of his body.

"Give me everything you can in the waistband," Martin directed, standing on a three-inch platform in front of a mirror, the tailor kneeling at his feet. I saw only the top of the tailor's head, but knew it was full of disapproval, as his mouth was full of pins.

"Give you an inch, maybe an inch and a half in the trousers," the tailor said, taking the pins from his mouth without looking up. "But it's going to show."

"Don't worry if it shows," I soothed him. "My husband keeps his jacket on in the office."

The tailor's shop is the oldest building on Water Street, over a hundred years old, or at least it's the only one that has never been modernized, keeping its lapstrake wooden planks and the hand-lettered sign over the door that informs us that "A. Pellitteri, Fine Tailor" does business here. An amber-colored plastic shield covers the windows all summer long, dyeing the air inside the shop the color of iced tea.

Over Mr. Pellitteri's head, a fluorescent bulb, his only modern touch, burned in spite of the summer sunshine, casting a shadowless light on his bald spot. He never looked straight ahead, not even when he greeted us. His eyes fell at once on the clothes in our hands, while behind the counter his wife went on pressing a pair of slacks.

Martin became sick in April. No, I should say he became sick the previous October, when the anemia was detected, or maybe I should say it happened years earlier, when the first cancer cell in his body began to replicate. The only thing I can say for sure is that he was operated on in April, he left the hospital in May, and we went to England for a couple of weeks in June, so that altogether he was away from his office for a little over two months, which was the first such break since he'd graduated from law school thirty-six years earlier. Now it was July. He was back at work, and the trousers had to be let out to accommodate a belly that was puffing up with fluid.

"I got to open up the back seam," the tailor sighed, oppressed by a job that wasn't going to come out right no matter how hard he worked. It was bound to look pieced together. Nonetheless, we knew that Mr. Pellitteri would find a good inch and a half in the trousers somehow. When Martin sat behind his desk in his office, talking on the phone with his swivel chair tipped back so far that his knees were as high as his head, he wouldn't look very different from any other lawyer, only a bit bigger in the belly than before.

"A R E H I S affairs in order?" the doctor asked me tactfully that summer. Of course they were in order. Martin's affairs were always in order. (In the last analysis, they were my affairs now anyway, not his.) He had enough money to take care of him for the rest of his life, which wouldn't extend beyond the calendar year in any case. For the period I thought of as "afterward," we had group life insurance which would take care of Peter and me, a lump sum that would pass outside the estate, tax free, since Martin had arranged matters so that it was I, not he, who paid the premiums and therefore owned the policy. Lawyers, like poets, do their most subtle and meaningful work in contemplation of death.

Then what was this man doing in his office all summer long, when he owned a house in Westchester with a Japanese maple crowning the rock garden, an ornamental plum tree, a patch of mint and a lawn sprinkler that sent out an arc of water in one direction, then raised itself to vertical and caught its breath a moment before letting the water droop from its own weight in the other direction? Along with the house, he owned the right to use a beach no bigger than his backyard, impossibly buggy at low tide on windless summer evenings, where our dinghy was tied up. He owned a complete set of Gilbert and Sullivan albums, an electric pants presser that worked while he slept, an aluminum-foil sun reflector, bottles of QT lotion that made him look tanned even when he wasn't, yogurt in the icebox and cake in the cakebox, and Ralph, seldom brushed, who lay on the earth underneath the Japanese maple most of the summer to keep cool, so that the light that passed through the leaves as if they were stained-glass windows made his fur shine red and gold. In the inventory Martin could also count three children, a car and a station wagon, a racing sailboat, a dinghy and a wife. Was sitting in an office the best use that a man could find for his time?

Probably not. But if he knew how to do something better, then he and most of his neighbors and friends should have been doing it since the age of fifty or so, by which point they'd accumulated enough money to live on.

The truth is that every man dies the way he lives, in the style of the year that he was born, and Martin was born in time to remember the crash of '29 and the Depression that followed. The worst thing that could happen to a man of his generation wasn't death; it was losing his job. No, there was one thing worse than that: it was having no work to do. Without work, a man was a ghost, a shade, holding out his begging bowl to those still fleshed out with the business of the world. He was an object of charity at the annual meeting held by the partners to divvy up percentages; he was a pet, a parasite within his own family; he was a reminder to friends of where, but for the grace of God, they might have gone by this time; he was many things Martin could mention, but he wasn't a man.

Anyway, what could be more engaging than what he was doing? How could an empty beach on a weekday compare to the three-ring circus he ran in his office? He was alive and working, wasn't he? Then why should anything change? While it's obvious that all of us spend our lives moving forward toward death, it's less obvious that there's no such thing as a dying man, not within the membership of the American Bar Association at any rate, any more than there's a person engaged in the act of being born.

"Thank you for the flowers—they brightened my room," he wrote to a friend from the hospital before the operation. "However, after forty-eight hours of castor oil and clear broth, I was so hungry that I ate them." Devouring was more this man's style than lying back and waiting to be devoured.

He didn't want to let go, not even to fly. He didn't want to be an enlightened spirit; he wanted to eat lunch at Le Madrigal. He wanted to hold on to his clients in his corner office, which is the way he comprehended his place in the world, the volume that his soul affected. A man whose telephone is ringing, whose desk calendar has every line filled in, has reason to believe that he's still alive.

Besides, as Martin might have said—assuming that he knew what I knew by that time—things might have gone wrong. He might have taken the proper step for a philosopher, quit work and given up his clients. And then, through some fluke, he might have gotten well after all. Instead, during that summer he went to the office every weekday, but one weekend out of every two or three he checked into Mount Sinai Hospital for chemotherapy, bringing his attaché case and yellow pads and office telephone directory with him.

On my second trip to the tailor, at the end of August, I came alone, carrying a bundle of Martin's suit trousers. An octopus of a monstera plant sprawled in the window, where the air was no longer the color of the freshly made iced tea of July, but cloudy and brown, like iced tea left to sit in the refrigerator too long.

"You've got to find us another inch, Mr. Pelletteri." The tailor's head sank into a deeper depression at the prospect of more work. His wife kept herself out of our conversation behind her ironing board.

"What for you let your husband gain so much weight, Missus?" he chided, stretching a waistband between his hands. "Don't you know that very bad for a man's heart?"

APRIL to December. Eight months it was taking us to produce a death.

This is what I didn't realize in the beginning: That death, like life, develops inside the body from a single cell, which might or might not embed itself in a site where it's possible to take nourishment and divide and grow more complex, as well as larger, until every part of the system is affected, if only to the slightest degree. And this is what else I didn't understand, that a man and woman must create a death between them and carry it to term, a good death, to use the old-fashioned expression, a death conscious of what it's doing if possible, but death in any case, a secret that the two of them preserve inviolable, even while it's obvious to the outside world.

"You've changed," Martin's optometrist said. "I've never seen you relax like this. Have you had a lobotomy recently?"

The belly swells. The growth grows. Never mind our paranoia. Cell division doesn't take place any more rapidly in cancer than it does in normal tissue, nor are the cells themselves very different in size or form. All creation begins in the same lumpish way, as undifferentiated tissue. And all the cells in our bodies contain genes that can be called proto-oncogenes; all are potentially cancerous. These proto-oncogenes may have evolved more than a billion years ago and played an important role in the physiology of single-celled organisms, the beginning of life. Apparently the message that they carry is crucial enough that evolution hasn't been allowed to slap them around with the rough hand that alters the rest of our genes, but has kept them intact, not only in us, but in all vertebrates. They are close to the origin of life, it seems. They are the survivors.

They are also death, of course, but that's only from our point of view.

SO HOW do we draw a distinction between growth as life and growth as death, when all growth is geometric? Our bodies increase their number of cells not only while we're inside the mother's womb, but until we're three or four years old. Being born takes a long time it seems, about as long as a college education, and, as in college, some parts of us develop later than others. After early childhood, cells may or may not replace themselves, depending on their type, but some go on replacing themselves even after the early stages of what we call death, since death too is more protracted than we've been led to believe, a matter of levels, a process or even a progress.

If embryonic cells are grown in a laboratory dish, those that appear normal will go through a finite number of doublings—about fifty for fetal lung tissue, for instance. Even if the cell strain is frozen at sub-zero temperature after a certain number of doublings and then thawed out later, it will pick up its count where it left off and go on reproducing until it has ticked off its allotted sequence of fifty doublings, give or take a few, after which the strain will stop reproducing and stop functioning. In short, it will age and die.

But cancer cells are different from all others in this respect: They never stop reproducing. In effect, they refuse to grow up. If given enough space and food, it seems they can go on forever—there are strains that have grown in laboratories for over forty years now, doubling their population every twenty-four hours, as healthy as ever from their own point of view. Immune from weakness and change, they act as if they alone, of all life forms, never fell from a golden age of immortality; as if they alone, like perpetual adolescents, are prepared to keep on going after the rest of us creatures, the civilized and inhibited, the decently behaved members of society, have vanished from earth.

So we discover what we've known all along: Chaos is immortal. Only order grows and dies.

WHAT do you think you're doing now? Martin interrupts me. Making a hero out of cancer?

No, of course not. I'm trying to be fair.

You mean you're doing what you always do, he accuses me. Taking the part of an outsider, any outsider, against your own family.

I NEVER saw a summer as beautiful as that one. I don't mean there weren't other summers just as beautiful—I'm sure there were—I mean what I say, that my eyes weren't open to see the others in the same way. Suffering is, in the last analysis, a sharper way of seeing.

At five every morning, the automatic sprinklers in the front lawn woke up with a clang and stuck their heads aboveground. At eight, the gardeners parked their trucks on the roads of Shad Point and pulled the rip cords of their machines that kicked like motorcycles and roared like jet engines; they were gone by ten. One day, without my being aware of it, the man who cut our grass lopped the dead branch off the white azalea bush.

At midnight, sitting alone on a deck chair in the backyard, I heard the katydids, with their three-toned call, Ka-ty-DID, overriding the noise of the crickets. A steady plashing sound, like a small brook, came from my neighbor's attic fan.

July and August. Summer hung up there in the tops of the trees. There was only one way the season could go from that point on, but not much we could do about it, except the little things we'd always meant to do: pick out a Sunday school for Peter, for instance, and announce Karen's engagement, although the wedding itself would have to be postponed. She'd waited too long.

I'd never been much interested in maintenance and order before—Martin had always had to prod me—but that season I called in the plumber, the roofer, who had to replace some gutters as well as cracked slates, even the mason, to reset the flagstones on the front walk that had been a hazard for years. We ordered storm windows for the living room and a new oil burner that would reduce heating costs in future winters. It was a great season for the men who serviced our house. Together, Martin and I went to White Plains and bought more clothes for me than I'd ever bought at one time in my life, and for once I took pleasure in the pleasure it was giving him.

It was strange how Martin and Karen discovered each other that summer. Ted was easy for a father to know, a natural-born winner of prizes and our firstborn to boot, who ruptured the membrane of our experience and left nothing for his siblings to do but follow in his track. By this time he was a lawyer, not with his father's firm, it's true, since there's a rule against that in what they call the "better shops" downtown, but with another firm that was just as big, just as good. The two men tossed legal phrases back and forth to each other that summer with the same pleasure in their mutual skill with which other fathers and sons sent Frisbees sailing through the summer air.

As for Peter—Peter, of course, was the baby.

But Karen was a girl, which wasn't easy for a man born right after

World War I, who never had a sister, to understand. Little girls didn't argue or mess or break things, but they had arms that snapped off if you didn't put their sweaters on the right way. Girls whined, objected to dirt, had to be taken indoors to pee, knew the price of everything, looked at you through slit eyes but withheld their criticism and eventually eloped with a gas station attendant, if you didn't watch out. His daughter didn't elope with a gas station attendant, but she didn't ask for his advice on how to conduct her life, either. When she went to college, she majored in Greek and Latin, which seemed like the other accessories we'd paid for—riding lessons, a long Dynel wig, which was known as a fall at that period, Javanese dancing, a rope of pearls—luminous and elegant, but not much use.

Her degree was wonderful, he said. Now she was well qualified to sell pencils on the steps of the Public Library. Did she intend to make classics her career? Certainly not. Good. Then she could take secretarial training and become an executive secretary, which was the back door to corporate power. He was accustomed to managing young associates, it was his greatest talent, but this time he'd found one who didn't choose to be managed. No, she didn't care for his idea. She'd decided she'd rather have a secretary than be one. What then? The cosmetics industry, maybe. She'd always been interested in mythology.

As it happened, she didn't go into the cosmetics industry. She went into an employment agency instead, and came out with a job as assistant administrative director of The Detwirth-Manning Institute (which was most particular about the use of the word "The" in the title), a private foundation devoted to economic thinking on the very loftiest level. Her chief assets were that she was tight with money, coolly efficient, uninterested in global economics and unimpressed by Nobel laureates.

When a man learns to recognize his daughter, a blossoming takes place on both sides, a swelling of his heart that corresponds to the swelling of her sexual power—I think of Cordelia, of Beauty who left home to live with a Beast—a moment of revelation that is entirely different from what happens when he recognizes his son. The daughter turns out to have been kind and loving, but strong-minded from the first sentence of the story. Unlike a son, her new maturity turns her father into something greater, not something less, than he was before.

And so that summer Karen brought stories of business life to her father every day, at home or in the hospital, the way that other people brought him bunches of flowers, and Martin responded not as a father but as a professional man who knew a thing or two about ERISA and pension-plan vesting himself.

ON A MONDAY morning in August, I picked Martin up at the hospital after his weekend of chemotherapy, but we didn't drive home, we drove down to Le Madrigal for lunch instead. A pair of associates waited in the corner banquette that was reserved for Martin whenever he wanted it.

"I spoke to Howie Taubman this morning," he said, unbuttoning his jacket, as if nothing else he'd done that day was of any interest, "but I don't expect him to get anywhere with the husband. If I were you, I'd start drafting the complaint and motion for temporary alimony."

The waiter came over for drink orders. Martin and the older associate didn't want anything. The younger associate ordered Campari and soda, newly popular that year, which showed us that he was sufficiently tough-minded to drink even if his superiors didn't, but smart enough to pick something suitable for the middle of the day. He swiveled all the way round in his chair to confront the waiter head on and make sure that his drink and appetizer were served at the same time.

"But don't say anything to the wife about it," Martin cautioned. "She can't seem to keep her mouth shut. Or anything else, for that matter."

"I don't understand why you never get a glass of water in this place unless you ask for it," the younger man said irritably. "How many years has it been since the water shortage ended?"

"Makes you order more Campari." The senior associate made a memo on his yellow pad of Martin's directive about the complaint and motion.

This was the favorite lunch spot for the high-power publishing industry, I'd been told. Editors brought agents here. Deals for subsidiary rights were struck across these tables. Writers were invited to such a place only if editors expected their books to earn considerable money or prestige for the house. When writers were asked where they'd been taken to lunch (and friends in the business would be sure to ask) it was enough of an accolade to murmur "Madrigal."

No one had ever taken me here—no one would ever take me here—except my husband.

"Looks like the Eau de Pinaud my barber used to keep on his shelf," Martin said, when the Campari and soda arrived. "Never mind. You're too young to know what I mean."

The captain came over to the table and addressed himself to Martin. "Our specialty today is fresh tuna, grilled with a julienne of basil and just the least touch of garlic." He whipped a memo pad and pen out of his pocket and began to sketch, as if words weren't nearly good enough for what he had to describe. "Then we have roast leg of veal, sliced very very thin"—the pad showed a roast with vertical strokes of ink shaving it down—"served with purée of carrots and lightly braised leeks." Leeks? People sat down and ordered leeks and tuna?

I read the menu line by line while the artist-captain ripped the veal off his pad and began another sketch. In any case, I wasn't supposed to be visible at a lunch like this, when Martin took out the younger lawyers—I was the giveaway that he and his suitcase needed to be driven home, so it was just as well to be absorbed in ordering my food while the men took their pick from the day's specials the captain described, without looking at the menu.

Martin opened his attaché case and laid some papers on the table. "Let's move on to the next problem," he was saying. "In this case, we've got a maximum recovery of two hundred thousand. Absolute maximum. He let Carravone stick a liquidated damages clause into the contract for that amount." The younger man looked as if he was about to interrupt. "Don't ask me why he consented, but he did, and now we're stuck with it."

The truth was that Martin wasn't a legal scholar, like some of his partners. He wasn't a great courtroom orator either, not like A.P.G., the chief litigator in the firm, who could play on jurors as if they were two rows of holes in a harmonica. Martin lacked the sublime self-confidence to make speeches in a courtroom without reading from his notes. He could never quite overlook the possibility of defeat.

"How much is the counterclaim?" the older associate asked. Thirty-two years old, he already had lines that stretched from his nostrils to his mouth. His curly hair crept down toward his eyebrows; his skin was dark, but not from suntan. It was the face of an anguished monkey. In the spring, he'd been passed over for partnership, which wasn't the same thing as saying he'd been rejected. The hovering finger hadn't picked him out, but it hadn't pointed to the door either; he'd come up for consideration again next year.

"Carravone claims that because of the breach of contract, he missed out on another deal, so the amount of counterclaim is what he'd have made on the missed deal. But that's hogwash, let's ignore it," Martin answered. "We ought to be able to get the counterclaim thrown out in court."

"Who can tell? With those lunatics on the bench?"

Martin and the older associate attacked their salad, while the younger man, secure in his cholesterol count, worked on eggplant beignets as a first course. Why should he care how much he ordered? The client was picking up the tab.

When the senior associate failed to make partner, it was Martin who had to break the news to him. What could be done? The poor fellow couldn't make himself more brilliant or more charismatic than he was. He couldn't even work any harder. Already he was billing three thousand hours a year, and some of the partners complained that that was the trouble. He was such a dull dog, that's why they'd voted against him, he was so dull he should've been a judge instead of a lawyer.

What did these people want from him, anyway? He'd been pushing his way up a ladder ever since he was nine or ten years old, beating out the competition, pushing as hard as he could. Now he was thirty-two, and his life might be permanently squashed out of shape in a conference room one Saturday morning in May, and there wasn't a thing he could do about it. He'd never even know who voted against him.

Of course he wouldn't be fired. He could stay at the firm indefinitely as a permanent associate, over-age in grade, a hybrid monster (the arrangement never seemed to last very long), neither a powerful old partner nor a pushy young associate, disowned by both sides. Or he could go to work someplace else with the firm's connivance, maybe to some less persnickety firm in another city. He wouldn't starve, but his children would go to schools that didn't teach lacrosse or Latin, where they'd meet and marry a different class of people, and when they were grown-up, they'd look at him with a different sort of appraisal in their eyes. His wife would be loyal and quite possibly tactful, but she'd find out all the same that some musk she'd undervalued at the time had evaporated from their bedroom air. And why? What was the magic dust that lay on some people's shoulders and apparently not on his?

It's possible for a man to be willing to sell his soul to get what he wants, I decided, and not to find any takers.

The three men were deeply involved in the Carravone case, with the senior associate jotting down notes on his pad. I reached across him to get the butter, so as not to interrupt.

Then who at the table could be considered happy? I asked myself. Could I swear that I'd been happy a year earlier, when Martin was healthy (though he wasn't healthy: the cancer was busy multiplying inside his colon where we couldn't see it), but my book had been rejected, and no editor took me to lunch anywhere, much less a place like this? There was no point in claiming that one sorrow was less worthy than another. That sort of distinction was reserved for angels.

Come to think of it, how could I be sure I wasn't happy at that moment? Martin had suffered no pain so far, only a stiff neck of sorts in April, and that didn't bother him now. Maybe I worried too much about living and dying, when the real distinction was between pain and no pain. A day might come when I'd look back at this lunch with nostalgia and regret.

"Let's say we go to trial and win the full two hundred. In his tax bracket, what's it worth to him? Half?"

"Less."

"Have you discussed with him how much a trial would cost?" Perky as a rabbit, the junior associate hoped the firm would be able to make him happy. He'd turned down a clerkship with the U.S. Court of Appeals for the Second Circuit to take this job, but if living in New York proved too much of a hassle, why, he'd move to Frisco or L.A. Or maybe he'd stay here a year or two and then take a flyer at the U.S. attorney's office. He'd have to see.

I'd never met him, but I'd met a couple of hundred like him, summer associates and first-year associates, during these past twenty-eight years. Every summer, I'd entertained the new crop—perennially the same age, but not the same disposition—at cookouts in our garden. Young lawyers were much more bumptious these days, more hostile too, full of contempt for the system that thought they were worth such outrageous salaries. They showed up at the house in taxis paid for by the firm. They were curious about meeting me; they wanted to find out if I was allowed to open my mouth, if I was cowed by this formidable partner I lived with, or if perhaps I was too dull to have anything to say in any case, a mind laid up in mothballs in the suburbs. The men went through the house to check out the number of bedrooms and quality of art they could expect to own if they decided to stick around long enough to go through the partnership gauntlet themselves. The women looked me over for signs of wear and tear. I added sugar and brandy to the sangría, because I'd promised Martin the evening would be a success.

"If it's going to cost us fifty to litigate, it'll cost Carravone fifty, too," this younger man said. "So why wouldn't the two of them be willing to settle for seventy-five? A hundred at the outside."

"That's not the point—what it'll cost to fight," the older man reproved him, tapping his breadstick on the table. If Martin lived until the spring meeting, this man might conceivably be made a partner. If not, not.

"Cost us, you mean," Martin said gloomily. "We've run up more than sixty thousand in time charges already, and you know what he's paid? Ten."

"So bill him," the young one said. "That'll make him settle."

"Not a chance. We'll never bill him for the rest, we'll have to swallow it. He's one of A.P.G.'s old buddies from Talmud Torah days."

"What you mean is we pick up the cost of winning the extra money for him. We might as well take the money out of our pockets and hand it to him."

"But maybe I'm giving in too easily. Settle for seventy-five on a case we ought to win hands down? We've thrown in a lot of time already. All we have to do is finish our trial preparation and make a short, sweet motion to throw out the counterclaim."

Maybe he was growing soft, he meant. Maybe he was losing his nerve. Cancer, or chemotherapy, or cancer plus chemotherapy these past three days might change what a man wanted to sink his teeth into, just as it made him pick fish today instead of the beef that he usually ordered.

On the other hand—and for Martin there was always another hand—he had no right to go to trial where it wasn't warranted, only to bolster his ego. "Hell. A.P.G. would go in there and hammer a spike through his balls," he added. "And he's seventy-nine."

The senior associate used a piece of roll to sop up the gravy from his beef and was relieved that the decision wasn't his.

The junior associate hacked at the second wing of his duck and made up his mind that if the case went to trial, he'd get off it by hook or by crook. This wasn't the kind of matter that brought a fast-tracker glory or even good contacts. He'd asked around. He was nobody's fool. He'd found out that this senior partner who expected him to sing for his supper, or rather his lunch (he'd be sure to diary every minute of time for the meal) had been sick, might get sicker—well, wasn't the best bet to get the next blockbuster that came into the office, the kind that made the newspapers, that was for sure.

The difference between the old lion and the cub wasn't in what they knew but in what they expected. At this moment, the cub was expecting the raspberries and crème Chantilly he'd ordered for dessert without even checking the menu. Martin had never in his life been free from qualms about his future, which was true about anyone who'd lived through the Depression. He'd been hired by a relatively obscure firm with twenty lawyers and watched it skyrocket. He'd joined the profession when it was small potatoes, and now it was lunch at Le Madrigal.

But would he be hired by that same firm if he was getting out of law school today? Even if he was hired, would he be made a partner—against competitors like this youngster (Note and Comment Editor of the *Yale Law Journal,* Phi Beta Kappa, *magna cum laude,* Order of the Coif), now polishing off his raspberries, who battened on mergers and acquisitions and antitrust and the other high-tech shenanigans that were so profitable these days? Martin had been lucky in choosing his era. He'd become a partner when the scale was more nearly human, but how much longer would his era last, even if he were well?

Anxiety had made Martin resonant, like the hollow space inside a bell. I hadn't realized it before, but this resonance must have been one of the reasons why I married him—for this bold, deep clamor as well as for this timbre of doubt, this sense of tragedy hidden at the heart of the bronze. I couldn't have married an unsuccessful man. But I couldn't have married a man who believed in his own success, either.

For the first time, while my husband flagged the waiter to bring the check, I understood that I loved him for the uncertainty he worked so hard to hide.

Neither of the associates had raised the question of whether Martin was strong enough to handle a trial. What did their silence mean? How much did they know? The bulletins about his health that he'd sent back to the office during the past four months had been as carefully phrased as dispatches from the battlefront, and for the same reasons. A problem had been detected. There'd been an operation. Memos, drafts, phone calls should be forwarded to his home. He was available for consultation by phone. He was on vacation. Associates should be warned, should be prepared: He'd be back soon.

All the same, since his return he wasn't as overworked as usual, which was at least as worrisome, and might be as diagnostic, as the lab reports, but, unlike them, couldn't be hidden from him by a well-meaning wife. Was it possible that his clients or his partners—or the associates, who had the instincts of young wolves and scented everything first—knew more than he did about his condition, had caught a whiff of weakness on the wind?

"I spoke to Bronson yesterday," the older associate reported happily. The two men loved each other. "He was slobbering with praise and gratitude for the result you got for him. He says there's no way money can pay you for what you did."

"I certainly hope he's not planning to use anything else," Martin answered, more pleased than he was willing to show, while he produced one last file to go with a second cup of tea. Only the junior associate had ordered dessert.

It was a quarter after two. Bills were brought to the tables on little pewter trays. We were still wrapped in the days of innocence, when men ate roast duck, or beef with gravy, or raspberries and whipped cream, and no one thought it necessary to pull the carbons out of charge slips and tear them up and drop the pieces into ashtrays.

"Anything else I can bring you?" the captain inquired.

"Matter of fact, I could use some Marlboros," the junior associate said, patting his pocket.

"And how are you fixed for suits?" Martin asked. Either the cub wasn't as sharp as he thought he was, because he didn't know that the old lion had swatted him, or else he was so sharp that he had no need to care about anyone else's opinion.

Once we left the restaurant, the August afternoon struck us full force. I put on my sunglasses; the men blinked. "Doing much sailing this summer?" the older associate, who'd known me for seven years, asked, looking at my upper arms, which were brown as turkey drumsticks hanging out of my sleeveless dress. His question was cautious.

"Of course I've been sailing. Why wouldn't I sail at this time of year?" He shifted uncomfortably. I'd been unfair. "You know how I am," I said more amiably. "Recuperating from Larchmont Race Week."

"You have the same boat?"

The sky was milky. In a race, this would be a day to hug the Long Island shore, not let any boat get further to the southwest than we were, and keep a sharp eye on the smokestacks there, so that if the smoke suddenly leaned in our direction instead of rising straight up, we'd know that the four o'clock sea breeze was on its way. The breeze would come from the southwest or maybe the west and then shift to two-ten, two-twenty, right past Execution Rock, possibly quite strong, and it would come in by four or a little after, with all this heat to lift the stagnant air and create a vacuum, or else it wouldn't come at all today.

"You didn't hear about Holy Week? Ask her how she did," Martin prompted.

"You sail together?" the young associate asked, startled. Until this point, I'd been invisible.

"Only one of us is crazy. I stay home," Martin said. "But she won silverware."

"Under grace and favor," I added, to return the compliment. I turned to the brash young man, who would never have the generosity of soul to give his wife, if he ever found one, anything he himself didn't want. "Why don't you recruit some new crew members for me? I've installed hiking straps this year."

Sailing wasn't a pastime that summer, it was a time outside of time, where I was nobody less than I'd been before. The contest was to see if I was still hanging together, if I could keep myself moving half a boat length ahead of my own inadequacy. There was a bruise on my upper arm, which may have been the reason that I'd worn a sleeveless dress.

"Crewing for you must be like working for your husband," the young man said.

"And what made you think we were different?" Because one of us happened to like battling the waves, while the other happened to hate it? Or because one of us was a suburban housewife?

But now Martin and I had told them everything we wanted them to know. The associates edged away crabwise, the senior man anxious to get back to his desk and his workload, the junior anxious to escape before someone he knew caught him in our company and supposed he'd been brown-nosing the management.

Martin waited until the two of them began walking toward Lexington before we turned in the other direction and headed for the garage over near Second Avenue. There was no need to emphasize the point, in front of them, that Martin's hours were lower that summer than they had been at any time since he was hired by the firm.

ONE of the burdens of love is the ability to see death through somebody else's eyes. For me, since I'm a sailor, death is a wave that breaks over my head and sweeps me under its curl, down where I can't breathe, and drowns me—or maybe it's the other way round, and because this is my image not only of death in general, but of my own death in particular, and because I've always been more afraid of water than of anything else, and because I don't swim well, I've taught myself to handle small boats.

I never asked Martin what death looked like to him, and yet I know. It wasn't a wave breaking over his head, which is an excess of energy, an excess beyond his control. Too much energy couldn't frighten Martin or overpower him; too little could. For him, death was nothingness, a blank. For him, death was a yellow pad with nothing written on it.

"HOW much d'you suppose I'll have to pay a nurse to come in by the day, eight-thirty to five-thirty?" Karen asked, as the two of us ate supper in her apartment one Thursday evening three summers later. That was how I found out that she intended to go on working after the baby was born.

I'd picked her up at the office after work, and we'd gone to the infant department in Bloomingdale's, where I thumbed my way through racks of fuzzy-footed garments, which looked longer than any baby could possibly be.

"Side snaps," I said. "Babies hate anything pulled over the head." Undershirts come in pink, blue and yellow as well as white these days. Some have teddy bears printed on them, but the most expensive ones, sold in boutiques, have pictures painted by artists, with matching underpants to go over the diapers.

There was always a stain on the right side of the neck of Peter's shirts, I remembered, where the milk trickled out of the corner of his mouth no matter what I did, while he lay pillowed on my left elbow.

Karen didn't argue, which must mean that her books on child care said the same thing, or the teacher of her parenting class at the 92nd Street Y, or her friends who were upperclassmen in motherhood.

I'd tried changing arms when I gave Peter a bottle, to even out the yellow-brown stains. It didn't work. My arms insisted that a baby had to be held against my left side. Was that so that he could feel the rhythm of my heart while he fed, or was it a question of keeping the dominant hand free to protect him? Do left-handed mothers feel the same imperative? Do fathers? Do little girls automatically pick up their dolls that way?

A neurobiologist has come up with a theory recently that, early in human evolution, mothers who held their infants in their left arms, where they were lulled by the sound of the heart, had tranquil babies who cried less and therefore didn't frighten away as much small game. As a result, these mothers were more successful at hurling rocks at rabbits and other food. They and their children fared better and passed along more of their genes, so that today the preponderance of the basically symmetrical human race is right-handed.

So many things that I'd never known about, or known about but never thought about, suddenly seemed to be regulated by miraculous powers whose conspiracy and dominion I'd never suspected.

"Don't bother with the three-month size," I said, as if she was in high school and I was telling her the points she could skip in writing her book report.

So, as of this evening, my future grandchild owned terrycloth stretch suits that took the place of long gowns with drawstrings at the bottom that bunched, wet and wrinkled, between a baby's legs;

a dozen Curity diapers, no more, and those only for burping, since paper diapers no longer leak, I'd been informed; a gingham crib bumper with matching sheets, made practical by those same non-leaking diapers. Everything was better than it used to be except cribs and playpens, and playpens aren't used much any more, she told me. Afterward we went back to her apartment to eat supper together.

"Let's start on the chicken salad. The corn needs another five minutes to cook." I'd brought dinner from home, enough for two nights, so that she wouldn't have to market and cook in the August heat, but I'd added corn from the farm stand on the Boston Post Road, to avoid duplicating the picnic suppers I'd catered three summers ago. "My feet hurt. I should've worn sneakers," I said.

"You want a pair of slippers?" Karen asked. I'd taken off my shoes and laid one foot across my knee, so that I could press my thumb against the spot where my metatarsal hurt. Behind our voices, the air conditioner set into the kitchen wall sent out a mist of sound with a burble in the back of its throat, not unlike the crickets in my backyard. Karen's kitchen wallpaper is blue and white, her china is blue and white, as are her place mats. My kitchen is blue and white, too.

I find this congruence moving, the way I find it moving that she keeps Triscuits and Lipton's chicken-noodle soup and Pepperidge Farm cookies and corn flakes in her grocery cabinet in roughly the same proportions that I keep them in mine; I'm touched that I can lay my hands on her Baggies and dish towels without even looking for them. It wouldn't matter to me if someone said that we look alike, which we don't, although we tend to walk and talk alike and give the same impression from a distance. That sort of inheritance seems mechanical to me, but her purchase of a curved grapefruit knife that's a replica of mine, her use of tongs to take the corncobs out of the water, strike me as an affirmation of the household in which she was brought up. On the other hand, I'm not in the least bothered—as a matter of fact, I find it stimulating—that Ted has nothing much in his refrigerator but balsamic vinegar, raspberry vinegar and diet orange soda pop.

"When you and Ted were little, I had what was called a bathinette in the living room—we had the D line apartment with only one bedroom, remember?—a folding rubber tub that stood on high legs. I filled it with a pail of water from the bathroom, and when bathtime was over, a long rubber tube, like an enema bag, drained the water back into the pail. The top flipped down to make a dressing table."

On the first afternoon that the baby nurse was off, Ted lay naked on the lid of the bathinette a yard above the ground, only inches from the diaper pins stuck into its pocket. When he was about to cry, his eyebrows knotted and changed color, turning purple before the rest of his face did. I begged his forgiveness in advance for all the mistakes I was about to make. I'd neither treat nor mistreat any second child the way I treated or mistreated him.

"We had to change an infant's clothes every couple of hours, because the rubber pants in those days gave them a rash. Rubber pants were only for lap time. Anyway, they dripped through the legholes, and after you washed them often enough, they turned crackly and lost their color." And when they lost it, no matter what color they'd been to begin with, they faded into the mournful shades of aging hydrangeas, and rustled with a papery sound like hydrangeas drying in the autumn wind. "My God. You know what?"

"What?"

"I sound like Marion."

"What does she know about rubber pants? Anyway, she never took care of you herself." Karen is quick to defend me against the charge that I'm anything like my mother.

"She's always telling me how she suffered because she had to take me downstairs in my carriage—in the morning, yet—while the nurse was busy washing and ironing my dresses." Ted was the baby who slept the sleep of the passionate, a purple stain on his left eyelid like a plum-tree leaf, visible only when the eye was closed, that might have been a bruise left behind by the forceps.

"That reminds me. Do you suppose I could put a stackable washing machine and dryer in here?"

"In this kitchen?"

"Are you kidding? In the storage closet. Trouble is, it's not very close to a plumbing connection, and I'd lose my only place for storage."

"Besides, it'd cost a fortune. You'd never get the money back when you sell the apartment."

"Well, how do you like the idea of a nurse going down to the laundry room in the basement, carrying an infant in one hand and a sack of dirty clothes in the other?" Her voice, which had grown querulous, turned softer again. "Maybe the answer is to use the clothes and throw them away."

I stood up and walked over to the stove to get the corn. "None for me," Karen said. Come to think of it, she'd never liked it since those years in her teens when the kernels got stuck inside her braces. She'd worn those braces until she was eighteen.

"You aren't trying to keep your weight down, are you? Look at your arms and legs. You'll wind up even more underweight after the baby is born than you were before. You want iced tea or Coke?" Taking down the heaviest glass I could find, I stuck a metal spoon in it.

"Neither. I've told you and told you. No caffeine." So far, she'd drunk only water. "What are you looking for?"

"Never mind. I found the tea bags. You've got both Constant Comment and peppermint." My favorite kinds. But she'd already stood up to help me.

Six-and-a-half months pregnant, she was no bigger than many women who weren't carrying a child, only obscurely bulging beneath her navy-blue smock with its puffed sleeves and Peter Pan collar. Her face, thin as ever, was slightly oily and broken out, although not as bad as it had been for the past few months; the pores on her nose could be seen distinctly. Her hormones were churning. Without warning, she'd reverted to the unvarnished and thrilling looks of her teens, when she was still a duckling, her father said, who hadn't yet turned into a swan.

Her hair had lost its luster (her father's hair had lost its luster and changed color that last summer, as if it had oxidized; the growth of a foreign body seems to create a need for brilliantine) just as her bones had lost their pertness. Which is to say that she looked marvelous. She was bored with the merely beautiful. She'd passed beyond that.

"We can bring the two-twenty line in from here. When we put in the washing machine and dryer."

"Thank God you air conditioned this kitchen." I dropped a tea bag into a glass with a Planet of the Apes picture on it, a giveaway from Burger King or McDonald's.

"What choice did we have? This is going to be the baby's playroom as well as the kitchen."

"Sit down. I can help myself. You look tired."

"Well, I'm not."

"How can you help being tired if you're working and keeping house and pregnant? And shopping in the evenings besides?"

"When would you like me to do my shopping?"

"I can get you anything else the baby needs in Westchester, if you'll let me know what you want."

At every stage of my life, my mother told me I was doing too much, I was wearing myself out, I was going to have a nervous breakdown one of these days, and for what, for whom, what did I think I was doing? Did I think anyone was going to thank me for it? Didn't I think my children would call me Mother just the same? Or did I need money so desperately that I was forced to work? Well, in that case, if I was so hard up, she'd have to give it to me.

"Your water's boiling," Karen said.

I understood Marion better now. She was paying the tribute that age and idleness pay to youth and vigor. "You know what I'll get you? A whistling tea kettle, so you'll know when the water's ready."

No. I was only beginning to understand my mother. Every time that I came to see her, when she told me that I looked tired, or looked thin, and I bristled as Karen was bristling at this minute—because there was nothing the matter with me, it was only a reflection of her bitterness that there were more demands on my time than on hers—she meant that she'd been sitting in her chair all afternoon long, expecting a visit from her daughter, when in through the door walked a middle-aged woman.

"Why shouldn't you look tired? I didn't mean to criticize." I poured boiling water over the tea bags and filled up the glass with ice cubes and listened to them pop. Luckily, the glass didn't crack. Not until she has a daughter of her own will Karen find out what tenderness her drawn look aroused in me. I wanted to carry her to bed in my arms, the way I used to carry her as a little girl, when she fell asleep behind the living-room sofa, her nap time overlooked because she was the smallest and least-demanding member of the family. Which meant that she was the member best able to fend for herself.

I wanted to tell her that at this minute she looked tired of the rest of the world. Including me.

THEIR bellies swelled, Martin's and Karen's. Their bodies became what they'd been all along, but what the rest of us hadn't noticed: calendars.

An embryo is a foreign body. If a woman's immune system—if Karen's immune system—rejects the foreign growth, the result is a miscarriage, death for the embryo. A cancer cell is a foreign body, carrying antigens on its surface different from those on normal cells. If the body rejects it, as we must assume it does the vast majority of the time, the result is life. The most fundamental knowledge, carried in our flesh, is this distinction between self and not-self, and yet a woman's body overrides her own knowledge and allows a parasite to survive inside her womb. Right from the beginning, we make allowances for our children that we wouldn't dream of making for the rest of the world.

J U L Y , August, September. Martin and I carried our future destinies, our new roles, in his belly that summer, which was our anti-honeymoon in a way. On an anti-honeymoon, you don't go away together; you stay where you are and try to find out who you are when you aren't each other.

We went out fairly often in the evenings, the usual round of office parties for summer associates and neighborhood barbecues, during one of the last seasons when charcoal-broiled steak and salt on the corn on the cob were considered desirable, and when good hostesses had the exterminator spray the garden against mosquitoes on the afternoon before company came.

One evening, when we were going out to dinner in the city, I made a mistake about the address and we had to walk twenty extra blocks, the trousers of Martin's best-fitting suit fastened with a safety pin because, despite Mr. Pellitteri's valiant efforts, the button wouldn't reach the buttonhole. That didn't bother him. But I bothered him later on in the evening, when I came up behind the couch where he was sitting and ruffled his hair with my hand. In twenty-eight years I'd never managed to moderate either my love or my dread of losing him, and this was a hard time for me to learn.

Here was a man who hated islands, who refused to stay at hotels surrounded by beaches, where there was one ferry a day to the mainland and no way to escape in between. How had he managed to survive all those years of marriage to a woman so unsure of herself that she would have been destroyed by his desertion? Where might he have gone, I asked myself afterward, when the question could be asked, if he'd felt free to leave the island? In any case, the question was moot by that summer. Terminal illness meant that the ferry service had been canceled. Not suspended, but canceled. The first loss a man suffers, when he knows he's about to die, isn't loss of strength but loss of options.

Pregnancy was also an island, of course, but Karen and Kurt had no desire to get away from it.

"THE FERGUSONS have one of those houses up in Connecticut somewhere, you know I never know where, the kind of house that they send you an engraving of on their Christmas card," Karen said while I drank my tea, which was cold but diluted at the top of the glass, where slivers of ice remained, strong but lukewarm down below. "With an Irish setter. Well, one of the guests was the most gorgeous blond I ever saw, some client's brand new wife, long, straight hair, a perfect nose. Tall as Felicia. She used to be a magazine cover girl, I found out later. She and her husband left early, and the rest of us started talking about how beautiful she was. 'Isn't that a coincidence?' I said. 'That's exactly what I look like when I'm not pregnant.' "

I laughed with satisfaction, as if she'd made an improbable return in tennis. She'd proved herself her husband's equal. "Kurt was pleased," she admitted. No sense pretending that these little scenes don't count.

"Still, I liked being pregnant," I insisted. "Looking grotesque in the last months, no matter what I wore. There was freedom in looking awful." Maybe I'll wind up like Marion, free of the need to dress up for the back elevator man. "It was like being at camp."

"You forget. I hated camp. No bubble bath."

"I can understand why the Arabs want their dancing girls thin but their wives fat." Karen had stopped eating. "Hey, you haven't eaten half your chicken salad. And no corn and no cake." She would accuse me of nagging her to eat again.

"I'll have the rest as a snack before I go to bed." When her mother wouldn't be around to scrutinize her plate. She stood up and carried her dishes toward the sink, leaving the rest of my meal in front of me. "You didn't answer my question. How much do you suppose I'll have to pay a nurse?"

I couldn't sit still and watch her work. Not sure what to do, I brought my plate and glass to the dishwasher and then walked over to the stove. Her kitchen was so narrow that I had trouble sliding past her without brushing her buttocks. "I don't know. I never hired anyone like that. But up in the country we pay thirty a day. Sometimes forty." Why did I say "up in the country," as if I live in the Northern Woods?

"What? How would you know? Who do you know who pays that? With a newborn baby?"

So the moment came and went, and after all my warnings to myself, I saw it only after it had passed, the moment when some intricate balance of need and approval shifted its weight between us. The balance shifted at the instant when her question, which was never meant to be heard as a question, was answered by my answer which was no answer at all, only a habit of handing down decisions or opinions to my children from above, because I couldn't bear to be silent in front of them. This time, I hadn't even been listening. I'd failed to pick up the clue when she said "How much do you suppose?" that she wasn't asking for the product of my experience, which couldn't be relevant, as she knew all too well. She was delivering the prologue before telling me about her visits to several friends who were new mothers, and now I'd spoiled everything, both by deflecting her story into argument and by making her, or at least her friends, sound wildly extravagant.

"I mean what would you know about that? In New York City?"

"You're right. I don't even know a practical nurse except Sylvia, and she's not experienced with infants. Anyway, it's different when you hire someone by the day and you're not providing room and board and telephone and all that." We both heard in my voice the simple fact that she could live without my good opinion of her more easily than I could live without her good opinion of me. "Also there's carfare and travel time to think about. You want me to wash out this pot, or leave the corn in case Kurt wants some with his supper when he gets home?" I peered into the big aluminum pot that I'd handed over to her long ago, when I moved up to stainless steel. It's the old spaghetti kettle that I used to use to sterilize baby bottles in their rack.

"You really think he's going to sit down and eat corn on the cob at midnight?" Had her voice changed in the past few minutes, or had it changed long ago, and my perception had only now caught up with the fact? She always had a tendency to whine, but this wasn't the pitch at which I heard the "Oh, Mo-ther" of adolescence, the emphasis heavy on the last syllable, which meant nothing more than that she was tugging at the leash, she wanted her freedom. Now the emphasis fell early in the sentence, on the word "really," a warning before she made her point, and her tone was like the Tuffy pot-scrubbing sponge on top of her sink, smooth and absorbent on one side but abrasive on the other. What it meant, among other things, was that she could get irked by my stupidity if I wasn't careful. It meant that she was the keeper of the treasure from this point on, and there'd be no access to it except through her consent.

The tongs with which I lifted three ears of corn out of my old pot and into the garbage were exactly the same kind, although not the same tongs—I've kept the originals—with which in other days I lifted nipples from a saucepan of boiling water. Was I the daughter who made fun of my mother and grandmother for owning the same items, each copying the other, so that their kitchens and linen closets and clothes closets repeated their household goods in different colors, the way that their phone conversations picked up and varied and elaborated each other's phrases?

"Chances are he won't want anything to eat by the time he gets home. He has something sent in from the cafeteria if he doesn't go out for dinner. Anyway, he's putting on too much weight."

"Ted gets so many meals from Chinatown that he's going to wind up with almond-shaped eyes. Did I tell you my idea for the perfect Yuppie Christmas present? A silver-plated container to hold take-out Chinese food. Monogrammed, a dollar fifty extra."

We were ready to begin again—we will always be ready to begin again—chastened by our recognition of whatever it was that had shifted its weight between us. With more details than necessary, Karen laid out for me the problems of her working friends' lives. They hire high-minded Jamaican women for exorbitant salaries, who try to toilet train a one-year-old child, I was told. Or they find a twenty-year-old political activist who has just had an abortion, and they call her a nanny. Or they use day-care centers, where the babies pass colds from one to another and back again but learn to socialize early.

"I thought babies under six months old couldn't catch cold," I said. While she talked, I carried the pot, which I considered too heavy for her, over to the sink.

"I'm not sure about this whole thing. I'll give it a try."

"Having a baby?"

"Keeping a job. If I find a miracle woman to take care of the baby, that's fine, but otherwise I'll chuck it. You never worked while we were little."

I couldn't accept the gift. "But I did."

"You wrote at home. That's different."

"Don't fool yourself. I wasn't always with you. Not by a long shot. And when I was, believe me I was no sweet pea." Pizza and Coke and kindness, that's what her child will be reared on. "Think what a job would have meant to Marion. And to me, if she'd been allowed to work. It might have been the saving of me." Trying not to splash, I leaned over the sink to pour the milky water out of the pot, releasing a cloud of steam that smelled of grass, like the sweet, damp breath of a cow. Karen drew back a few inches. "There are all kinds of creative ways to be a terrible parent."

With the water emptied out of it, the inside of the pot revealed a dark-brown ridge of median high water, and lighter, less certain, but bluer ridges for the spring tides and neap tides of thirty summers' worth of corn on the cob and stewed peaches, thirty winters' worth of spaghetti, each meal depositing a film of salts that discolored the metal, each meal followed by a scouring pad that circled around the sides and left the surface as striated by the family's geologic ages as a cliff. Once the pot was empty, there was no place to lay it down except on top of the stove.

"Why don't you put away the stuff that ought to go into the refrigerator first?" Karen suggested. "I mean, there's no room for two people to work at a sink at the same time." By dumping the corn water on top of her, I'd interrupted the motions with which she'd been moving dishes from the counter on her left into the dishwasher on her right. Had I imagined that sitting at the head of a dining-room table has any significance? No, it's standing in front of a sink that matters. She was occupying the command post now, while I could only be scraper and putter-away in her household. Not even dryer. The dishwasher had taken over that job, destroying the former neat pairing of domesticity.

"I'll have enough chicken salad for sandwiches in the office all week."

"By the way, when you market next week, remember I won't be here for supper on Thursday. Pete's coming home from camp. I have to go to the airport to get him." It wasn't camp, of course, it was a wilderness expedition that he'd picked out himself, but it soothed me to use the anachronistic word.

"Have you heard from him?"

"Naturally. Doesn't he always write just before he gets on the plane?"

"What did he say?"

"I told him I'd kill him if he wrote one more Sierra Club description of forests and altitudes. I want to hear something about the people he's with."

"Ooh-h." Karen puckered her lips and crooned on behalf of her younger brother, who was being picked on by his mother because he wouldn't shorten his focus to look at the other teenagers in the group, for fear of seeing how much bigger and hairier they were.

"He says the scenery in Olympic National Park is purely ineffable. Those are his words. Also, he's come through a lot of F and D situations these past few weeks."

"F and D?"

"Thank God you asked. He put in an asterisk. Fall and Die."

Karen laughed. The phone rang. It was Kurt, calling from the office. Seizing my opportunity, I rinsed the cereal bowls left lying in the sink from breakfast, corn flakes tough as leather sticking to the bottoms, and washed the big plastic container that I'd brought from home filled with chicken salad.

"You've done it again," Karen sighed after she hung up the receiver.

"Done what?"

"Left the strainer out of the sink." She dropped it on top of the drain.

I stared at it. "I forgot. I've lost the habit."

"I know. And now you'll tell me it's because you're used to having a Disposall. That's what you say every time." Her tone was light, to show that she meant what she said but could only say it because she was my daughter. "And I'll tell you that we're not allowed to have a Disposall in the city. And you'll say that's too bad. And I'll say a sink trap is just that, it traps food, and the food sits down there until it rots. And you'll say that's right, you forgot."

"That's right. I forgot."

If there's one thing that irritates me more than anything else about my mother, it's exactly this, her predictability. Whatever I say or do, I know what she'll say or do in return, a pong for every ping, with never a plink or a plash. I take this to be the first symptom of approaching death, with its hardening of the responses, sluggish circulation of sympathies, cataracts forming over the memory and imagination.

So it has begun to happen to me. But not quite. Or not quite yet. The difference between us is that my mother doesn't have Karen for a daughter. Karen understands me, which means that she loves me, but doesn't mean that she loves me less because I can no longer surprise her. (But why should my daughter love her mother, who never loved her own mother, or at least never faced up to the fact if she did?) I can afford to be ungrateful to everyone except the person who teaches me something.

How long a time it has taken me to discover what I've been doing all these years. I've been raising the mother I always wanted to have.

Chapter 6

"WHAT was new today?"

"Nothing special." My mother was on the phone. What could I tell her was new? The bathroom sink was leaking? The plumber said it might be impossible to fix it, it was so old, so I might have to get a new one? That would have been pretty good, but I didn't think of it in time.

"What?"

"I just came back from market," I said.

"What did you say?"

From the window I could see the first little propellers from the maple tree lying on the flagstone walk. Most of them were still green, but some had already turned brown.

"Nothing much. Tomorrow morning I have an early appointment at school with Pete's adviser." Why did I always point out to her how rushed I was, how early I'd have to get up in the morning?

"Talk louder. I can't hear you." Her voice was slurred. Had she had too much Scotch this afternoon? I held the receiver with my shoulder while I slid back the screen and released a fly caught between the mesh and the glass.

"Bea was here." She whispered.

"How nice!"

"She buzzes around so."

"Well, I guess that's how she keeps her spirits up."

"You've got to hand it to her. She's smart. She found a tax form in an envelope. But it said 'None.'"

"Wait! Federal or state?"

"What? Can't hear you."

"Federal or state? I just paid your federal."

"Can't hear you."

"Then turn that damn television off and you'll hear me."

"There's no television on." No anger either.

"I said I paid the third installment on your federal tax the other day."

"Then state."

"Remember, we weren't sure if you paid the June installment twice? I've written to the tax bureau. Don't do anything meanwhile."

"I don't know. I can't any more." I picked up my mail and began throwing ads in the trash basket.

"You have a date tonight?"

"Mother, this is Monday. Why would I have a date?"

"I don't know. I just thought."

"I'll be doing bills. I'll be right here. Matter of fact, I'm going to send in my tax installment too." I made an effort. "Good thing you reminded me."

"For nineteen eighty-one. Isn't that right? That's what we're doing?"

"Of course."

"We paid for last year?"

"That's right, Mother." I heard a different tone in my voice.

"Well, you're busy. I won't keep you. Thank you for calling." She'd thanked me.

But I hadn't called her. She'd called me. That's what I found unsettling.

WHAT happened to my mother sometime in the night after her telephone call—or maybe it was happening while we were still on the phone—was a stroke, which I should have suspected except that it's always inconvenient to think of our parents as mortal, and not only mortal but just plain vulnerable.

When I got to her apartment the next day in response to a phone call from Sylvia, she was crumpled against the side of her pink plastic lounge chair. She couldn't hear out of one ear; her words were slurred together; she was nine-tenths asleep and her right arm and hand wouldn't work, but she'd propped a cigarette between two fingers of the useless hand, and she brought her mouth to its level by resting her chin on her wrist. Her lips puckered into a circle, like a giraffe lipping a clump of leaves. Then she forgot what she was doing and the cigarette dropped from her hand. The fabric of her robe showed a hole with a rapidly widening black circle around it. I had to go into the bathroom for a glass of water and throw it on her lap.

"She'll have to go into the hospital," Jack Nordlinger had said, when I telephoned him at his office. He'd already been in to see her by that time.

"Why? What can you do for her there? You know how she hates the place."

"We might have to aspirate her lungs."

In the end, the doctor agreed to try it my way, which was her way too for once. I called a medical supply house and rented a hospital bed with rails, a tray table, a commode, a walker, all of which arrived promptly. The furniture in her room had to be rearranged to accommodate the extra bed, I had to dig up her Medicare number for the charge slip, but nothing was a problem. I was shining with energy and decision. In fact, I was never more sure of myself than while I gave orders to the men who carried in the bed, and hunted up an extension cord for the reading lamp that had to be moved, then dashed into the kitchen, where Sylvia was sitting frozen on a step stool, gripping the telephone as if ready to scream for help. She'd have to get to work and find us an extra nurse, or else the doctor would find one for us, I told her. It would be out of the question to leave my mother alone for five minutes. Sylvia caught my energy—I don't know whether she was terrified of losing her patient or her job—but meanwhile I'd thought of something else: We were going to need an intercom. As soon as we had my mother settled in her new bed with the side rails drawn up to make a crib, I'd dash to the Radio Shack on Lexington and buy one.

But why this explosion of energy? I asked myself. Was I drunk on goodwill, because I'd succeeded, with so little trouble, in doing for her what we all pray that somebody will be on hand to do for us one day—that is, make it possible to stay in our own homes when it counts?

No, there was something left over from childhood in the ardor with which I rattled and shook the situation to see what comfort I might have left out. When I was little, there were times when she let me get her pocketbook ready for her before she went out for the evening. I'd pick a handkerchief from her bureau drawer to match her dress and check her compact to make sure there was powder in it; I wouldn't forget her cigarettes or her lighter or mad money. Well, now my day of devotion had come for sure. The daughter who'd never been able to do anything right in her life was making good at last.

I asked the men from Keefe & Keefe to shove her bed with its curlicue headboard out of the way to make room for the steel rails of the hospital bed, and then, between us, Sylvia and I got my mother into it and straightened out her body with a mutual heave. For a minute she opened her eyes and looked around the room. "Look at the Big Boss," she whispered scornfully.

I know, I know, I wanted to answer. I was beginning to suspect whose daughter I was. Pray God that we should never have to submit.

The Big Boss. The skipper. Well, what was so bad about that, if I was full of energy because I'm always at my best in a storm—hadn't I just found out where I inherited that trait?—but at my worst when I have to sit in a bedroom with nothing to do? In any case, I'd finally found something I could do for her, which wasn't the worst possible expression of love.

"You know what she say to me this morning?" Sylvia asked before leaving the room. "She say her mother following her around the room all night. I say 'Where your mother?' and she say 'Out in Queens, in the cemetery, but she following me around. She telling me the time is come to join her.'" I answered that I'd sit in the room until I was sure she was asleep, and then I'd go down Lexington and buy an intercom.

When was the last time I tried to do anything for my mother? I asked myself. Oh, it was easy enough to buy her a discounted bathrobe she didn't want, or a package of Bic pens or an intercom, on no better justification than that she could use them, while it was clear to her that her apartment, which was an extension of her body, was so chock-full already that it was impossible to squeeze another thing into it. The attempt would threaten her life; it would block her up, the way it would block her up to eat her meals unless she could get rid of some of the matter caked in her bowels, have a really good movement for once, but her daughter didn't care about that, either. Wouldn't even listen to her talk about it.

It had been a long time since I'd sat in this room and been quiet.

Maybe it had been a lifetime. I couldn't remember such a break before. When I sat still, I did nothing right or wrong.

But when had I done anything as ordinary as touch her? I saw her one afternoon a week for two hours, which meant that I had to make only one trip to Lexington Avenue to feed the parking meter. Our cheekbones grazed once in each direction—ten seconds for hello, and another ten or fifteen for good-bye. Her grandchildren saw her every month or two, and pecked her faster. The only person who touched her with intent and regularity was Sylvia, who at least put a hand under her armpit when she got in or out of the bathtub or up and down from the toilet, even if she was paid to do it. Also her doorman. Also her doctors. Especially her doctors. Most especially the young one, who kept his fingers around her wrist while he spoke, or laid his palm on the back of her neck or on her inner thigh. No wonder she loved him.

I moved closer to the bed. The truth was that this woman was like her father. She was in no sense a touching person, and so she was hardly ever touched. She was passionate, yes, but that was different. I could remember being thrown laughing on the bed and pounded with kisses and tussled with hugs, just as I could remember the smacking sounds that I heard through the wall between our bedrooms in a summer hotel in the mountains. I was willing to bet that once upon a time this girl had been a hot number, she must have had It, as her generation said, but quite predictably It was under-utilized like the rest of her talents, and curled in upon itself and became diseased. Every talent she had dug its way into her flesh like an ingrown toenail. In any case, she never found out about the layer, only a few cells thick, where two bodies brush skin against skin.

I'd never had this freedom to look around her room before, I'd never paid much attention to her furnishings, or considered the fact that Marion had picked these things out, any more than I would have thought that she'd picked out the tone of her voice.

If I had looked, I might have understood long ago, woman to

woman, what accounted for a mauve spread with four-inch fringe and a headboard made of wooden vines and tendrils painted silver, even without the giveaway of a brace of Italian cherubs nailed to the wall of the bathroom, the gold paint flaking off their creases of fat to reveal old wood. Cherubs aren't nailed to the wall of a bathroom by a woman who expects to have an orgasm, or by a woman who has forgotten about orgasms, either. A woman who has confidence in her own kindness, or in the probability of kindness being shown to her, doesn't need an empty porcelain powder box with porcelain roses on the lid, or a vase full of dusty beaded tulips. I was sitting in a 1920s boudoir, or rather the boudoir of a woman—a palpitating virgin, I almost said—waiting for a 1920s lover with Valentino hips to seduce her. It was a room that any man hated. The air was as inconsolable as the tufts of cotton she soaked in the dregs of perfume bottles and pinned inside her handkerchief box, where they gave off a travesty of the death of flowers.

(Sally's bedroom was blue and white and sunny, and dominated by my father's Barcalounger, but then the room didn't belong solely to Sally.)

There was one piece of furniture in Marion's room that was a man's piece, however, six drawers with a pair of doors in front of them, made to suit a man's height and convenience. This chifforobe, as my grandmother called it, belonged to my grandfather and then passed to her, and she brought it with her when she moved into this apartment. Inside those drawers, I know, are clumps of egret feathers snipped from old hats that seem too heavy for any birds to fly with, a speck of dried blood at the tip of each quill. In the top left-hand drawer is my grandfather's pocket account book, bound in wine-colored morocco, first page dated January 1, 1899, in which every penny he earned and spent was written down in copperplate script by this teenage immigrant: five dinners at his boardinghouse, eighty cents; barber, ten cents—but five dollars for a health examination by the German consul. There are padded glove boxes and underwear boxes with pins from vanished corsages stuck in their lids, and inside the boxes are gloves and slips bought thirty years ago, when my mother and grandmother bought the same thing in different colors, or bought similar things but always the finer, more expensive item for my grandmother. They were the same size, five foot seven, handsome strapping women. It was clear to me that I would never measure up to them.

Marion has caught me peering into these drawers from time to time. "Wait. You'll have a picnic in there one of these days when I'm dead," she says. Does she suppose that I can't understand the terrifying beauty of objects that have been worn, laundered, rolled up, moved from the front of the drawer to the back by hands no longer here, treasured as too good to use, invalided out as too old to use, but never thrown away because of the wrenching conclusions that would require? With good cause, she mistrusts the objects in these drawers. First they were her mother's, and now she considers them hers, but in all this time they've learned nothing about loyalty, no—no more than her daughter has. They'll outlast her. They'll pass down the line exactly where she thinks they'll pass, and they'll do it with the dreadful evenhandedness and indifference of things.

I walked over to the bed. I lifted my hand. Only her head was sticking out of the cover, cocked to one side, hiding the right cheek that looked hollower than the left today. The cover made it easier for me. A head doesn't look animal, not like an armpit or a neck. When I touched her arm under the blanket she stirred, as if even now I was bothering her.

"Nothing," I said. "I'm going out to buy something."

Then I sat down. She wouldn't dare grow feeble on me with things left unsettled between us. That would be cheating, and if she was nothing else, I knew from our Scrabble games she was a fighter to the end.

But what might happen, I wondered, if I could lean over and cuddle her—not what would happen to her, which in the last analysis was beyond my control, but what would happen to me, what door to my nature might spring open? Would all the lights in her apartment be switched on?

No. That was asking too much of me. Maybe I could sit on the edge of her bed, maybe even lean over and peck her, but that was the limit. There was no way I could lift my arms away from my sides. Why should I? When had she last petted me? Not smothered, but petted? Would my head have been buried in her clothes? I couldn't move. Habit is a feeling stronger than any feeling.

I stroked my children, of course, but that was nothing more than an instinct I shared with every female cat. I stroked my father too, granted, but that was partly sexual attraction and partly memory: His shoulders formed a natural saddle when he carried me through the apartment on my Royal Elephant Rides. I straddled him, as he lumbered from side to side like a noble Indian mount, then stooped to pass under a door frame, while his head, like the pommel of a saddle, pressed against my pelvis and his thighs shook from the strain of lowering and raising two bodies at the same time. His body always tended to tremble, in a most affecting way.

Strange that we've never been close like other mothers and daughters, Marion said over and over again when I was little, and went on saying when I was grown. Nothing like my mother and me. Oh, how that woman could laugh. Oh, but we had such fun together. I could never take you on a picnic, you wouldn't eat hard-boiled eggs, you were never any fun. I guess you must be strictly your father's daughter.

She was always the one who pointed these deficiencies out to me. Our history lay heavy between us.

But at another level, our history didn't matter at all. This wasn't a question of liking one another. That was something we could never manage to do, but it was irrelevant, the way it was irrelevant that I would never hang wooden cherubs on my walls. We would never manage to understand our feeling for one another—call it love, or don't call it love—except as a burden that we shared but couldn't carry any distance together, no matter how often we tried.

Our history didn't matter, because more than history lay between us. Biology lay between us, which was harder to argue with. Nature, that pitiless housekeeper, was in the room with us, canny and self-serving, callous and unsentimental, preventing me from being kind.

There I sat, programmed according to the ethologists, as every human is programmed in order to serve nature's ends, to respond affectionately to a particular silhouette, the short profile with bulging forehead and pug nose, the baby face in other words, rather than the face of maturity or age. We are compelled, without realizing it, to think that bunnies are cute but weasels are not, to find pandas and seals and porpoises appealing, but foxes and wolves deceitful; we are born to feel that the young of most species deserve our protection, at least after they grow their fur. The head develops before the face. We respond to the lack of a nose bone. That's all our vaunted tenderness amounts to.

Mother love originated among the birds, I've read, to permit the development of the young after they've hatched from the egg. The more self-sacrificing the love is and the longer it lasts, the higher the development of the species. It's as simple as that. Parental love can be seen as the essential tool of pedagogy. After the nestlings have been taught to fly, the purpose of mother love comes to an end.

In medieval bestiaries, the pelican—a bird appropriately enough, a symbol of love and self-sacrifice and therefore of Christ—is said to bear babies who slap their parents in the face with their wings while still in the nest. In retaliation, the parents strike back and kill them. (Oh, the temper, the outrage, just like mine, and just like mine the remorse, the suffering that follows!) Three days later the mother bird pierces her breast and lays herself across her young, pouring her blood over them until they come back to life. (What other scene do I play out with Peter every week?) In a starker version of the story, the pelican simply stabs her breast until she draws drops of blood, which is the food she uses to nourish her young.

But in later life, what are the young pelicans expected to do for the mother bird in return—in return for her blows, of course, as well as in return for her heart's blood? On this point, the bestiaries are silent. No one helps us. No one teaches us what we need to know. Life exists—life has always existed—in order to foster the generation that is coming up. Only now do we ask, for the first time, what new response our synapses must learn in order for the young to feel a need of their own to nurture the old.

Half a billion to a billion years of animal life have led up to this morning, when I sit in my mother's room, caught between my daughter who is carrying a child and my mother who is lying in her crib, with no one to tell me how and for whom to peck my feathers, or whether old birds as well as fledglings can be nursed at the pelican's breast; no one to model the new set of gestures that I need, or teach me a level of tenderness denied to other animals, some new moral development comparable to the invention of monotheism, or music, or romantic love, or sailing, or laughter, involving ever more intricate patterns of pleasure and pain.

I'll have to begin, no matter how feebly. Without teachers or models, I'll have to begin. I'll begin this minute, I'll take notes, I'll start by charting the signs of age I notice in myself. One side of my face, the left, the side I sleep on, is more wrinkled than the other and must be older than the right. All my secrets must sift through my brain to the left side of the bed and settle around that eye socket during the night. My eyebrows grow sparser. So does my pubic hair. Sparser and colorless, rather than gray, revealing everything when there's no longer anything worth concealing. My toenails grow so thick I can hardly cut the big ones. Soon I'll need an eyebrow pencil, and a chiropodist, too. If I can't learn to love the signs of age in myself, how can I learn to love them in anyone else, and if I can't see age as a lightening of flesh and spirit from their burdens, then how can I see death as anything but an end? And what am I doing sitting in my mother's bedroom with *New York* magazine in my hand, reading the picture captions, when I know that there's something my mother has to get from me, and until I give it to her, she won't be able to die in the right way?

Whatever it may be, it's not the statement that I love her, nothing so simple. She knows I love her. I suspect that the knowledge only increases her pain. It's something more carefully hidden, but what it is I can't imagine.

But there's also something I want from her, or rather want to say to her, but can't manage, it's too hard for me. Mom. That's the word. Mommy. When I talk to her, I call her Marion, or I don't use her name at all, or at best—and only once in a long while, almost always from a distance when I'm calling for her attention, not when we're in the same room, much less kissing each other hello or good-bye—"Mother." My mother, I say to other people. Marion, I say to the children. I don't have a mom.

And there's something I wait to hear. My name. Joan. Even "dear," if that's not too much to wait for. If she uses a name at all, which is rare, she generally calls me Karen.

Maybe I'm fooling myself, and I'm no more capable of mouthing the syllable "Mom" than she is of answering me with the syllable "Joan." Two puffs of sound. Too difficult for us. "Mom" requires lips to smack against each other twice, like a child smacking its lips over something good to eat. The vowel hums at the back of the throat. Ah-h. Mom.

And what about "Joan?" Lips have to purse, as if for a kiss. (Still, she gave me that name.) No wonder we're incapable of letting out either sound. And yet I suspect that we won't be able to let go of each other until we get what we want, if it's only the certainty that we'll never move any closer together than this.

Because this much I've learned from Martin: You have to give people permission to die, the people who're close to you, that is. They can't do it in a decent way without your consent.

There came a time when I had to stop fighting with Martin, had to stop holding him back and let him go his way, at his own pace toward death, as I let Peter go mountain climbing this summer, without reservation. Otherwise there might have come an instant when his foot groped along a ledge and his faith was unsteady, and the memory of my doubt, the doubt carried over from my doubt, might have been the pebble that came between him and his balance. I was able to let him go, as I was able to let his father go to death when his time came, because there was no guilt between us—but my mother and I are different. We may have grown so strong only to spite one another.

It's all right. She won't die soon. I spoke to Jack Nordlinger—the son, not the father—and he said that he expects a complete recovery.

"MOST arrogant sonafabitch you ever knew," my father, son of two Polish Jews, said about his father-in-law, Marion's father. "Tough as shoe leather, just like his daughter. A real German. Had no use for anyone who came from anyplace else. I suppose you know he was a certified paranoiac. Always sure everyone was out to take advantage of him." But of course they didn't need to take advantage of him after he was fifty. They already had it.

"Would you like to take a walk with me?" my grandfather asked one afternoon, when I was three years old. "Just the two of us?"

No one had ever made such an offer. Grown-ups had offered to walk me. My mother and grandmother, most often my governess, took me for my required daily airing. But this was to be nothing of the sort. I knew that right away. His tone made it clear that this was for his sake, not for mine. And this was my grandfather speaking.

He took my hand. Sometimes he brought me dresses or coats with velvet collars and velvet muffs when he returned from a business trip to Paris, this man who begrudged himself a new pair of eyeglasses, and I'm told that I recognized these as special garments and did my best to strut in them. I hope I was wearing one of his dresses that day, and that I poked out my rear end, as I liked to do, so that the starched skirt and the tips of the sash stuck out, and that I reached my hand up to his before he had to grope for it.

It was late spring or early summer, I know, because we were still in New York, spending the afternoon on West End Avenue where my grandparents lived, not in the summer home we rented on Long Island. The light swam in blue and purple streaks over his eyeglass lenses, the way I sometimes saw it swimming on oil puddles in the gutter.

"Not here," he said. "I want stronger light." We walked two or three blocks further down West End Avenue.

"Here," he said, coming to a corner where the sun shone full force from its height over the Hudson River. I decided he wanted to take my picture. "Stand against that wall, will you?" The light was so powerful that it struck sparks from the mica embedded in the sidewalk. He had chosen a building with a white foundation for a backdrop.

"I want to take a good look at you," he said.

I held out my skirt with both hands and smiled and waited, but couldn't see any camera. Instead, I felt his sight travel through the space between us, shrink me to the size of his pupils, draw me back along the same path, little speck that I was, and suck me in through his lenses, through the pupils I could scarcely see to some storage closet inside his head, where I'd be three years old forever, but also available forever after. For once in my life I was open to the grace that told me not to simper.

In the years after he became blind, whenever he wanted to find out how much I had grown, he would circle my wrist or upper arm with the thumb and middle finger of his right hand and measure the circumference. Oddly enough, although I didn't notice this at the time, he never ran his fingers over my face as I know now that other blind men do, or let his hands follow the outlines of my collarbones and elbow joint, down to the bumps of my wrist. For that matter, despite his great intelligence, he refused to attempt Braille. Blind and idle as he was, and gradually going mad as well, he was still in no sense a touching man.

Once, when I was a teenager, I took off my high-heeled platform shoe with its ankle strap and let him feel for himself that there was practically no leather there, only a sole an inch thick and a couple of skinny straps. But that was no longer me he was looking at with his fingers. That was America. Or profit margins. I didn't mind. He had seen me once.

Not long after he became blind, my grandfather sold his toy business. He sat in his bedroom for the next fifteen years, clicking his long fingernails against one another so loudly that the sound could be heard in the next room, and waiting for the six o'clock news. From time to time he went back to the sanitarium for another stay. "Nervous breakdown," my grandmother said on those occasions. Dementia praecox was the term I'd secretly read on the medical report I found lying on my grandmother's desk.

"His nerves cracked. But completely," my mother would explain more dramatically, as if he were the branch of a tree splitting off in a winter storm, a clear warning of what could happen to you if you were too smart for your own good. The bodies she knew were subject to drastic dislocations anyway. Nerves cracked or broke down. Eyes wore out. Minds snapped. She was forced to scream her guts out. Her daughter aggravated the guts out of her. Her insides dropped. Her daughter's insides would drop, too, if she hoisted those heavy sails. Life did these things to you.

"You're sure he tried to kill himself?" I asked my father, as the two of us walked along the beach at Pelican Key. "And my grandmother stopped him?"

"Twice."

"What?"

"Maybe more. Fan was having her own affairs, of course, but very discreetly. No one could blame her. Every friend they had was hers.

He'd have the biggest funeral in town, they said. Everyone would go to make sure the devil was really dead."

I picture him standing at the window, trying to open it and finding that it wouldn't go up more than a couple of inches, possibly because of paint caked along the edges, struggling to force it with arms that didn't have any muscle in them from lack of exercise. How far would he have to raise it? All the way, it seems to me. It would be possible to open it halfway, I suppose, and slither out headfirst like a belly whopper on a sled, but that's beyond imagining. Maybe it was the noise he made pounding at the window frame with the heel of his hand that alerted my grandmother. Maybe he wanted her to be alerted by the noise, or by a draft of cold air, while she was talking on the phone to her daughter in another room as usual, making heaven knows what complaints against him.

Still, there must have been a moment when Fanny walked into the room and understood what he had come to. Once during their marriage, my grandmother told me years later, she became so furious that she picked up a bronze bookend and threw it at his head, missing him by a few inches. "After that I swore I'd never lose my temper again," she said. "And I never did."

Does that mean that she hesitated for a moment when she came into the room and saw what she saw?

Of course not. Love and hate are nowhere near as pure or fierce as we suppose them to be. Other feelings, so common that they have no names, run much stronger.

Not that she would have lacked the nerve. She and her friends were the first generation of women in history to outlast their husbands, one way or another, by ten, twenty, forty years, thanks to birth control and improved obstetrical techniques working on their behalf, while the rigors of business life worked against their men. But even while the husbands were alive, it was clear they were no match for their wives. I remember a man with bulging thighs who sat with his knees wide apart and said he was a wholesale meat dealer. Not wholesale at all, my grandmother whispered. A butcher. Never mind. I wasn't to judge these women by the men they'd been forced to choose to support them, but by their charm in serving coffee from twelve different Royal Worcester cups, rather than all of a kind.

There weren't many German-Jewish women in New York when they were young. They stuck together as if they were a respectable small town all their own, a displaced Quincy or St. Louis or Des Moines; they dated one another's cousins, and married at more or less the same time, and wheeled their baby carriages together. When the wholesale meat dealer died without warning, it was my grandmother who got to the apartment first, found the empty bottle of sleeping pills in the trash basket and pocketed it, so that the insurance money was saved for the new widow, who would have had nothing to live on otherwise.

Oddly enough, my grandfather lasted longer than any of the other husbands, and when he died, it was from a heart attack. I got to my grandmother's apartment a half hour later, to find her searching in the drawers of the chifforobe, which was black walnut in those days, before Marion painted everything silver. "You see these pajamas?" she asked me. "They're still wrapped in tissue paper. You can put them right in the box and send them back to DePinna's for credit for me." After that she looked toward the bed, where a form lay hidden under a sheet. "Now nobody needs me," she said, which wasn't true, of course, and she knew it. Her daughter needed her as much as her husband ever had. But in her voice I heard a note that was regret, not relief, all the same.

Her daughter needs her still. Fanny saw to that. And who can blame her?

"YOU know what she say last night?" Sylvia demanded the following afternoon, as if Marion were deaf or unconscious or in another room, instead of right there in front of us. "She say I must look in her telephone book for the number and ring up her mother and find out what time she coming to dinner."

Marion was sitting in her crib, working a crossword puzzle and smoking. "Well?" Marion retorted, and the scorn of that initial "W" was enough to blow out a candle. "My mother didn't show up, did she?"

"You're writing with your right hand," I said.

The scorn turned itself ninety degrees and faced me. "And why wouldn't I write with my right hand? When have I ever used anything else?"

The apartment we were sitting in had been her mother's apartment. The chair I was sitting in had been used by her mother's nurse, who was heavy and wore out the springs, my mother and grandmother complained. The maintenance of the apartment, utilities and food were paid for with income from her mother's stocks, her father's municipal bonds. She never sold any security, but recorded the income in the same ledger that her father kept first, in his copperplate script, and her mother kept after her father went blind (with penciled notes after the names of certain stocks, reading "Don't tell C.H."), ledgers which she keeps faithfully up-to-date today. Her mother and father take care of their only child, their Tootsie, still. A good thing too, she'd say. Her alimony check—which doesn't amount to a tinker's dam, she'd add—was late again this month.

I expected Marion to ask how the hospital bed and tray table and commode got into her room, but she didn't seem to notice they were there.

"I have two nurses now," she said, relishing the words. Nothing was left except her body, but her body had turned out to be a source of unexpected drama. "Let me get us a drink and crackers." Sylvia had returned to the kitchen, where a friend of hers was about to relieve her for the evening. "Retinue!" She turned her head to speak directly into the intercom, but got no answer. "Retin-oo!" she bawled at the top of her lungs. "Retin-ooo! Sylvia! Mildred! Mildred! Sylvia! Left, right, left, right. Quick march."

If I'd told her I loved her at that minute, she would have thought I'd found her amusing. But even that much would have been a start between us.

"That girl doesn't get anything straight," she said.

"Who?"

"Sylvia. I didn't say my mother was coming for dinner. I said we were going out to dinner together."

"How nice. Where?"

"Luchow's. I think."

"The two of you?" A poke in the dark.

"No, with the girls. Aunt Florrie, Aunt Rose, Aunt Rosalind." Her courtesy aunts. Her mother's friends. Even in her dreams, I'm left out of the group.

But of course I'm left out. Only now, as I write this down, does it occur to me that I'm left out for good reason. All the women she named have been dead for twenty years or more.

PAY ATTENTION to entrances and exits, I reminded myself two days later at the airport, where I was waiting to greet Peter, who hiked up the ramp at the tail end of the passengers arriving from Albuquerque. See what you see. Every gesture is dated bread.

"It wasn't hard to spot him in a crowd," I told Karen later. "Middle of August, he was the one wearing a heavy wool cardigan down to his knees." A tone of light detachment in regard to my children was proper for her to hear.

LaGuardia airport had taken on its August air. A mustachioed young man, wearing sandals and a T-shirt from the North Carolina Swimming Team, napped on the terrazzo floor in his shorts. A group of girls went barefoot in calf-length dresses that made them look like dancers. Nobody was fully clothed except my son.

"I thought the pilot said temperature in New York in the forties," he volunteered. "It was a lot colder than that up in the mountains yesterday."

"I'll bet it was. How high were you?" His skin was rosy over his tan, but shadowed with gray where the pores were penetrated by dirt, which wasn't ordinary dirt but dirt that had come down from mountaintops.

"Thirteen thousand feet," he said. "But mostly starting from seven thousand," he added conscientiously.

"So high? But wasn't it hard to breathe at that altitude? Did you ever get above the tree line?"

Somewhat shamefaced, he pulled off the mud-colored sweater, whose sleeves dropped six inches below his fingertips when he lowered his arms. Maybe he was no taller, but he looked older all the same, his face leaner and less pretty. His braces jutted out more prominently, as if the past seven weeks had sharpened his teeth.

Peter caught sight of his backpack as it parted the leather streamers at the far end of the conveyor belt. Putting one foot in front of the other, he stood poised like a runner, but was afraid to shoulder aside the adults who stood in his way. Somehow, he made his snatch and shrugged himself into the metal frame that held the pack with the bedroll on top. Before the straps were fastened, he lunged again to retrieve his daypack.

"Can't I take something?" I asked, when he rejoined me.

"Nah. This is nothing. You think this is something? While we were hiking, we had to carry our food and stoves and tents on top of this. And a lot of the time, while we were in the desert, we had to carry our own water. A gallon and a half each. That's twelve pounds. On top of our gear."

"My son the schlepper. I mean Sherpa." He heard the admiration in my voice.

"I still can't carry my own weight," he added glumly. "Wait. I'll be back." He darted off to intercept a tall, skinny boy who was heading toward the exit with two people who were obviously his parents. When the boys leaned toward each other to exchange some final message, their bedrolls almost touched in an arch above their heads, the two of them loaded and clumsy but purposeful as astronauts, their hands locked in a secret grip. As he ran back, the bedroll bobbled.

"Where does that boy come from?"

Peter looked startled. "I don't know. New Jersey, I think."

"He looks nice."

"He is."

"He must be from around here, if both his parents came to meet him. You didn't get his address?" Peter shrugged, as if he'd known all along I was going to ruin his homecoming. "I don't mind getting you a plane or train ticket to visit a friend this winter. Or have someone visit us." Stop, I told myself fiercely. Not another word. When we left the terminal building I looked around, but the other family was out of sight. "What's in the paper bag?"

"An antler."

I already knew that. I'd seen the tip. "A real one? But that's sensational." That was no good either, the indulgent note in my voice, as if he were a kindergartener who'd caught a toad in the garden.

"Nah. They're common."

"Not at Bloomingdale's they're not. I'll have it mounted on a shelf in your room. How did you find it?"

"It was lying on the ground."

I saw antlers littering the forest floor like chandeliers. "Why don't the deer keep them and sharpen them and reuse them, I wonder, instead of growing a new crop every year?" Peter looked both ways for traffic as we made our way in between airport buses to the short-term parking lot before speaking.

"You know that fellow, the one from New Jersey I said goodbye to?" he asked, while we were on the way home. "He bought a bull whip. A real one. But I thought that was nuts. I mean, it cost ninety dollars for the six-foot size, because they're handmade, that's why, and what use would I have for it? Might look funny on the wall."

"You think so?"

"You know what I bought? I bought this sweater at a thrift shop for two dollars and a watch cap for fifty cents, and they're both pure wool. One hundred percent. Did you know wool can save your life? I didn't make that up. More climbers die from hypothermia than from falls or avalanches." He rolled the word "hypothermia" around in his mouth with terror and delight.

"Your parka wasn't warm enough?"

"Sure it was. But this is pure wool."

For a while it was difficult for me to talk, as I threaded my way in the dark through the access roads to the Whitestone Expressway.

"And something else. A doll. Not a doll, a wooden figure of an Indian woman weaving at a loom. Bought it for three dollars off a drunken Indian who needed money right away. You know how it is, you can get anything off them if they want money for another shot of booze."

"Pete!" Had I thought I could send him away for seven weeks where he'd hear nothing but the wind on the mountaintops?

"I'm not saying they're bad," he added judiciously. "Matter of fact, they make the best distance runners in the world." Now that he'd heard the outrage in my voice, he settled back happily in his seat.

"What about that blood blister on your heel you wrote about? Did it heal up?" Tell me something tough but virtuous, I meant.

"Sure. I can manage with nothing but a package of oatmeal, if I have to. Do you know I can live on eleven cents' worth a day? Plus water. Even without oatmeal, if there isn't any. Even in our own backyard. I know how to make tea from oak bark. I can make pancake flour from acorns." His voice dropped an octave in pitch. "There's one kind of acorn that's real bitter and one that's real sweet, and all you have to do is know which is which. I'll make it for you, if you want."

"That's terrific! You can sign up right away to go again next year."

"The best of the fellows in my group, the guys that like it most, can't come back. Their families can't pay for them twice."

"Don't feel guilty. I'm not doing anything for you that your father and I didn't do for your brother and sister. And don't worry, I'd never spend more money on vacations than we can afford."

Will I never learn not to drown those I intend to sprinkle with blessings? No. I'll never learn.

"Eight out of ten guys had to earn their air fare. Mowing lawns and stuff like that."

"Don't you see, I wouldn't want you to do that? You've got a job. Your job is school."

"They go to school too."

He knows what I mean. All he has to do is get himself through high school with a first-class record, get first-class scores on the SAT, first choice of college, first choice of graduate school, first choice on the fast track to wherever he wants, the weight of his entire life resting on his back at this moment, while the other boys have to mow their neighbors' lawns.

"You can earn a lot of money mowing lawns," he added fiercely. "And next year I'll be old enough to caddy. That's the way to make a mint. From tips, I mean. Tax free."

I know that I can earn my own living. What does the boy next to me know? He knows that he can live on eleven cents' worth of oatmeal a day, or failing that, on groundup acorns. "Want some Stimorol?" he asked.

It seems he also knows that the mature body, along with other frailties, is subject to bad breath.

Back at the house, Ralph hurled himself against the door, half out of his mind with delight, leaping and barking not at Peter but at me, so that I should have to continue to pay attention to him, my sixty-pound, mad-footed furry darling, and not to this interloper whose sneakers held wild, unsettling odors of the forest floor in their treads, whose sweater carried the scent of some unknown, possibly menacing male, and whose backpack and daypack, with their frame and straps and buckles, rattled disconcertingly from one side of the staircase to the other, as Peter made his way up to his room.

THE ROLLING STONES put us on notice full blast that "You cay-n't always get what you want," although he could as far as I was concerned, while Peter brushed his teeth with the faucet running full force. When he came into my room to say good-night, he was dressed in his running shorts—did he sleep in them, or were they being worn for my benefit? I followed him into his room.

"You found your pillow in the closet? Would you like me to turn on the air conditioner?" There were scars on his chest that might be permanent, from climbing over lava outcroppings in caves. There was a row of pale blisters like epaulet stars on top of each shoulder. I tried to imagine what sheets must feel like to someone who hadn't slept in a bed for seven weeks. When I bent down to kiss him goodnight, I could smell bacon smoke in his hair from the camp stoves he'd hung over.

At last he softened up a little, having done the job he'd undertaken and been relieved from duty. He'd carried his body around and tended it all summer long, no doubt fearfully at times, but now he'd brought it safely home, capable of surviving on oatmeal or acorns from here on.

"Guess I don't have to shake out my bedding tonight to check for scorpions," he said.

THE SILENCE was no longer hollow in its hum but stuffed up—temporarily, at least—by domesticity, like a bell muffled with two odd socks.

Two. That's what was wrong. Half a flight from his bedroom to mine. Twoness, twosome, duet but never couple, opposing poles, male and female, two at a time, but in no way a pair. Two, the power of two, rang its way down the stairwell from two bedrooms, two bathrooms, two televisions and two telephones between us, down to the kitchen, where there were two bowls for two kinds of cereal (I like corn flakes, he insists on bran), two kinds of juice (one fresh, one frozen), two spoons laid out for two tomorrows.

No number is so terrible as two, so terrible because so blasphemous, so perfect. The idea of it assaults the gods, claiming that they created two beings on earth equal and opposite. It demands the impossible, which is that nothing must change. Like every Eden, it heads straight for the Fall. With every breath, two exudes its threat of becoming one.

Three is a fine, safe number. Two is opposition, yes or no, either/or, but three is balance—what's more, an easy balance, where units needn't be equal to be stable. A three-legged stool is easier to build and yet steadier than a chair. A triangle, an A-frame, is the strongest straight-line form known to architecture. Three is steady, three is self-sufficient. (Karen and Kurt know that, which is why they've decided to have a child.) Three can progress to four, or it can regress to two; life will continue either way. Not an odd number but a round number, three is the trinity; the wheel; the basic building blocks of our world—proton, electron and neutron; the countdown of time—past, present and future; the moon in its phases; the number of atoms in a molecule of water, which is the beginning of life; the first number on which it is possible to rest.

Four is even better, or even and better; the square; the symbol of earth as three is the symbol of heaven; the measure of space as three is the measure of time, four-cornered, four points of the compass; four walls and a roof, a lovely symmetry, a pair of pairs and safe as houses; a junior couple and a senior couple, two females and two males. Karen and Ted, Martin and me.

Even one is safer than two, safer from risk and uncertainty, that is. One is the stroke, the digit, the beginning and end. One is barren. One is what is. One is the one that has nothing to lose but oneself.

One is the number that's waiting for me.

BY THE early part of October—three years earlier, I mean—the katydids sounded hoarser and slower at night, like a wind-up phonograph that has been allowed to run down, and two syllables were all they could muster most of the time instead of three—Ka-ty, Ka-ty, Ka-ty-did—while the field crickets, who'd finished laying their eggs and were dying off by this point, hushed their thrumming to a noise not much louder than the fluorescent light in the kitchen. Astonishing raps fell on the roofs of Shad Point, as an acorn or beechnut or tulip seed pod struck a slate. It was a particularly heavy year for mast. In response, I had to move the station wagon away from its usual parking place under a tree, for fear of having the windshield cracked. Amid this letting loose and falling off, this plopping and pelting like knuckles knocking on top of a desk for silence, once in a while I'd hear a muffled crash as an apple or squirrel dropped through the branches.

It was the time of year when small animals make themselves conspicuous. Our house cat, originally a stray, turned feral as he does every autumn, killed squirrels as big as he is, left the heads and legs of birds on the back steps, and nonetheless packed away his canned dinner, never confident of his own good luck but making himself fat in anticipation of hard times ahead. Ralph tangled with a skunk and had to be bathed in tomato juice. A fly the size of a bumblebee took refuge in the bathroom or clung to the bedroom windowpanes, quiet for a while and then banging furiously to be let out, as if it were a house pet. Spiders took over the corners.

September was the month of falling off. October was the month of scooping up. While the mail brought me oversized brochures from cosmetic companies, offering free samples if only I'd order eight dollars and fifty cents' worth of the company's products, the gardeners set to work in Shad Point in squads. One man in each group toted a leaf blower on his back that worked like a giant hair dryer, making more noise than ever as they blew leaves into paisley mounds to be scooped up later, just as the children were scooped off lawns and street corners every morning by car pools or school buses, just as the sailboats crowded two or three abreast at the boatyard docks, their halyards knocking against their metal spars like xylophones, as they waited to be hoisted out of the water in slings.

"Did Martin know the truth?" people asked me later about those months, as if life were some sort of detective novel, and it was all right to ask afterward what they wouldn't have had the bad taste to ask at the time. "Did he realize what he had?"

Which truth do they mean? And how many truths are there? More than enough to take care of both sides, Martin would have answered, out of his years of experience as a trial lawyer. The point isn't what truth or truths you may know, but whether you know any that are useful to your side. In the litigation department, there was a classic lesson he taught every associate during the first month of training: Never ask a witness a question unless you already know the answer. In private life, he would have added "Unless you know what you'll do with the answer once you have it," which is why this man who specialized in drawing up lists of questions for examinations before trial, or cross-examining hostile witnesses on the stand, never asked a single question on his own behalf. There was no need to lie to him this time, the way I had lied the first time round.

Or to anyone else. "How's Martin?" my father asked on the phone on Sunday nights, after each weekend bout of chemotherapy.

"Coming along. The doctors are trying a slightly different attack."

"But that's wonderful. Just wonderful. I'm awfully glad to hear that."

"He's more comfortable now that they've gotten rid of a lot of the fluid. For the time being."

"I can't tell you how happy you've made me. You know what you should do? Come down here, the two of you, and get some sun. Do you both a world of good. You can have the apartment to yourselves. Sally and I have been planning to go to Captiva for a few days anyway." In his voice I heard the satisfaction of a man who'd never had anything but a good report card from his beloved daughter, no matter how often she warned him that this year's crop of teachers were impossible.

"How's Martin?" my friends asked.

"Terribly busy. Trying to clean up his desk so we can go away in January. Did I tell you that we rented the same house as last year in Tortola?"

All truths were equally true, and all were equally fleeting, like weather changing overhead, clouds that obliterated the sun and silenced the birds, then blew away with a shift in the breeze. We lived under only one climate at a time. If I lied—if we lied—or didn't talk about all we knew, that was the reason, not because we were brave enough to put on a good act (for whom? what was to come would come) and not because we were cowardly, but because we couldn't help preferring to spend our time in scattered sunshine and mild air.

"We can go to Tortola before Christmas and bring the presents with us," I suggested, as we lay in bed together in October. "Limit ourselves to packable things. Diamonds and pearls."

"Why don't we wait and see?"

"Because I have to reserve plane tickets, that's why. Peter has almost three weeks' vacation. Ted and Kurt can come for ten days, around Christmas and New Year's. But American Airlines isn't going to sit around and hold seats for you."

"Why don't we wait and see?"

He was tired. A cough interrupted his sleep at night. I laid my head in his shoulder socket, where it fitted like a golf ball in its cup, and smelled his cheek, which smelled faintly, improbably, of suntan lotion. He was using a product called QT by then, to give his face an artificial tan, make himself look less sickly. By daylight, his coloring, too bronze and even, seemed to ride a quarter of an inch above his face, as if he'd become a museum replica of his own imperial bust, but QT was made by Coppertone, which is why I smelled coconut oil and thought of beaches when I kissed him.

A few hours later, the cough woke him. He stumbled into the bathroom and reached for the Robitussin, which he drank from the bottle. The cough meant that the fluid had reached his lungs. When he returned to bed, I saw that he'd left the bathroom door open and the light burning. I got up to turn it off.

"Don't," he groaned. "Don't. I'll be in the dark long enough."

Who tells me I have to love truth? What has truth ever done for me that I should love it?

Would I have abolished it altogether if I could? No, for all truths put together cancel one another out and sustain a life, but I would have said to this particular truth "Move gently. Don't close the door. Couldn't you have waited until a little later? Let my husband get his rest. In any case, don't flatter yourself that you're anywhere near as important as my hand in his hand while we sleep."

"How's Dad?" the older children asked.

"About the same."

"You never told me the truth," Peter accused me three years later. But which truth was it that he expected me to tell him, out of all the truths I knew?

SIXTEEN years earlier, the surgeon who'd operated on the first cancer had given Martin a fifty-fifty chance to live five years, or rather, to be accurate, had given me a fifty-fifty chance that Martin would live. Before the time was up, the surgeon himself, a tall young redhead who'd obviously been top of his class ever since grade school, was dead of a heart attack. I've seen the record of that first hospitalization now. Truths have a way of coming out of the ground at last.

Tumors of the colon are graded like my grandfather's municipal bonds, it seems, not by Moody's or Standard & Poor's but on a scale devised by a researcher named Duke. "A" is suitable for long-term planners; "A" restricts itself within the lumen of the bowel, assumes risk, but still can be considered investment grade. "B-1" and "B-2" are more speculative, but could be turnaround situations all the same. "C" carries a strong likelihood of default. "D" is not to be discussed. Martin's original tumor was Duke's "C." His chance of survival, given such a tumor and radical surgery at that stage of medical knowledge, was actually no better than one out of three. The only truth I'd caught on to was that the surgeon was distorting what he knew when he tucked in his chin and talked in such measured tones.

At the time of the first operation, Martin asked for a postponement of trial from another lawyer who was unwilling to grant it. "I'm informed that the human body contains about thirty feet of intestine," Martin wrote to him, "and I have had about two feet removed. Rest assured that leaves me occasion for only fourteen additional requests for postponement." So what did he know, then or later, and does it matter what he knew? Silence on any subject includes all possibilities.

September, sixteen years later. The early part of October. Martin went to work wearing Mr. Pellitteri's insets of cloth from the cuffs in the back seams of his trousers, and into the hospital for chemotherapy every other weekend or so, but it wasn't the same hospital where he'd had his operation. He'd been lucky enough to be accepted as a patient by a leading research oncologist at Mount Sinai, a man so kind that he remembered why he was doing what he did every day. Getting on this man's list was tougher than being accepted by Harvard or Yale; no one could afford to stay on this particular waiting list very long.

"Poached salmon," I said during our hospital weekends. "Canned asparagus tips. Blueberry muffins." I brought them from home. I brought a toaster and hid it behind the curtains of Martin's private room, because he complained that the toast on his breakfast tray was cold by the time it reached him. I brought Yardley soap and Lipton's iced-tea mix, I brought his own pillow and toilet paper, so that he would be touched as little as possible—contaminated as little as possible—by the products of the Underworld that he was visiting.

"Are you nauseated?" the youngest medical students on the floor asked him, popping their heads in the door and proving that they'd learned the difference between nauseous and nauseated, if nothing else. An IV tube dripped the secret recipe that had replaced 5FU into his vein, while he dangled an asparagus tip at the level of his nose with his unemployed arm. "My, doesn't that look good."

"Don't worry if he throws up and loses his hair," my friends advised me. "That's the way it's supposed to be. That shows the chemicals are working." But his hair was as thick as ever, even if the texture had changed, and it still fell over the bronzed face in the mornings before he took the time to comb it.

"No correlation," the doctor assured me privately, as Martin went on eating his cold jellied soup, his shrimp salad and biscuits and miniature Danish.

On every hospital visit, even if Martin had left only two weeks before, a new medical student, with a stethoscope riding his hip pocket like a Colt .38, came into the room clutching a clipboard to do a medical history. The female residents, who numbered one out of three or four at that time, were subtler than the men in their interviews and unafraid to be charming, as they were unafraid to wear gold earrings or to pin their identification badges askew, to make sure you looked at their faces.

But it seemed that it was always a man—not a man but a boy, younger than Ted and still in the midst of his professional training, while Ted was a full-fledged lawyer already—a boy subtle as a plow horse, who went through the sheaf of questions. Childhood illnesses, allergies, dizziness, spots before the eyes, coughing, palpitations of the heart, chest pain, indigestion, headaches. Father's age at death. Cause. Mother's age at death. Cause. Hm-m. How many other cancers in the family? Onset of symptoms. How long ago? Show me the spot. Ah. Results of the last operation? And all this time, attached to his clipboard, he had (or could have had, or should have had) the surgeon's and pathologist's reports on the operation.

Martin wasn't a tolerant man. Any waste of time or energy irked him. Repetition irked him. But above all else, he believed in the necessity of training the young, his own young or anybody else's, in his own profession or any other, and so he played his role as if he were taking part in one final moot court trial. Hobbies? None. Exercise? None. Except going downstairs to empty trash baskets. Tension, overwork, fatigue, insomnia? Need you ask? Any trip shortly before the onset of symptoms? Yes. Business? Vacation. When? In March. Ah. Really? Where? To the Virgin Islands.

The student's eyes gleamed. What foods had Martin eaten in those treacherous tropics? Unwashed fruit? Gastrointestinal symptoms: diarrhea, vomiting? No. Never mind. Did he like to swim in the ocean?

But the patient had had enough. "Only when the boat is going down," Martin answered.

This much I'm prepared to swear to: Laughter is real. Courage is not real. Everyone I've known is a coward at one time of day, a lion at another. The question to ask, when you take the measure of a man, is whether in the face of death this person will brandish his sense of humor, because death is, among other things, the archetypal joke against which all others are measured. It's the kicker that intrudes into the same old hackneyed situation an unexpected and yet instantly recognizable level of truth.

So. Find me another man who can make me laugh in the same way, and I may wake up from my spell.

The question confronting the interviewer, as he eyed the fruit salad and said "My, doesn't that look good," and helped himself to Martin's miniature Danish, was the distinction between right hope and wrong hope, even if he never suspected that was the nature of his problem. It was a distinction that was causing me a good deal of trouble that summer and autumn. The answer turned out to be more obvious than I expected, a matter of grammar, really.

Wrong hope—treacherous hope, debilitating hope—always requires a preposition. It's not hope, it's hope for a specific result. Wrong diagnosis. Cure. Remission. Time. Above all, time. Twenty-eight years we'd spent together, and suddenly I discovered that I'd wasted all but a few hours of them, and there was nothing else I wanted but a credit to my account of months, or better yet years, I hadn't earned. The feeling was the same as the one that came over me in college, when an exam ended and the proctor told us to hand in our papers, and not until that moment did the adrenaline pump through me full strength, so that the essential paragraphs flashed into my mind, the paragraphs that would synthesize what I'd been trying to say all along, if only I could scribble them down while my classmates were screwing the caps on their pens and standing up and moving to the front of the room with bluebooks in hand. The anguish I felt when I dropped my own bluebooks on the proctor's desk wasn't that the time wasn't longer, but that I hadn't used what was given me to become something closer to what I knew now I could have been.

Right hope, another matter syntactically, has nothing to do with prepositions. It's hope pure and simple, a condition not unlike being drunk, or falling in love, or glowing after exercise. Wrong hope whispered that a new cure might be discovered next week, or that, given his fighting spirit, Martin might beat the rap and prove to be the exception that proves the rule. Right hope was wordless as Cordelia, too proud to stoop to promises. It was hope that existed not because of anything in the outside world, but in spite of everything.

BY THE end of October, Martin swelled up with fluid like a pregnant cow. There was no way he could get into his trousers any longer. From that time on, he had to wear slacks and leave them unbuttoned with a baggy sweater pulled over the waist, or else wear a bathrobe at home, as if he were prowling around with a perpetual hangover. He went into the hospital now not only for chemotherapy, but to have the doctor make an incision and drain his belly of pinkish fluid, great jugs full of it, half-gallon size, that collected in a corner of the room like strawberry milk shakes for the doctors to count. It was his private vintage, Martin said. He was going to have it estate bottled and send it to his friends for Christmas.

There was something appropriate about all this. My grandmother had never nursed a baby, my mother had never nursed a baby and neither had I; we took food in but never gave food out, but here was Martin producing gallon after gallon of a liquid that looked exactly like Nestlé's strawberry Quik. Excess had always been his style. Cancer was only one more sign of his extravagance, of which he knew I was bound to disapprove, like the wad of Kleenex stuffed into his trouser pocket when a couple of them would do the job just as well.

By this time he could no longer afford a private room, not in terms of money but in terms of the slightest chance of survival. He didn't need his own toaster any more. He needed high-powered technicians and nurses with state-of-the-art training and lights burning all night and carts rumbling and all-out war in the final bunker, which meant the research cancer ward, where the nurses and technicians were specially trained. The best people were reserved for the worst people, we'd learned by that time. Being crowded into a hutch of a room that had to be shared with a stranger, that was the signal that Martin was losing control over the shape of his life.

Neither of us could have stood it if he had withered away like his roommate, who was nothing but a belly and a yellow skull—the disease must have struck his liver—that lay on top of the sheets and stared in silence at the ceiling, plus a few bones that lifted in polite dissent when we asked whether our conversation or Martin's phone calls were disturbing him. There was never any visitor or phone call for that man. His lunch and dinner trays went untouched, although nurses came in afterward and tried to coax him to eat. Martin would share the room with him for a weekend, go back home and back to the office and return to the same room a week or two later, and the man would be lying there, in the senior bed next to the window, still studying the ceiling, a Halloween goblin made out of two yellow globes and a few dry sticks.

I never remembered his name, even though it was written on the file card attached to the door. I saw him move only once, on a weekend at the end of October. Martin was feeling low that Saturday night, when he was scheduled to get a drug even newer than the new one that replaced 5FU, and so I stowed away in his hospital room when visiting hours ended and winked at the nurses who pretended not to see me curled in the chair at the foot of his bed. Eventually he slept the stolid sleep of the drugged, one tube leading into his arm and another tube leading out of the incision in his belly and under the sheets, as if he were suspended on wires between heaven and earth.

After a while I slept too, but I was awakened by a puff of air, and opening my eyes I saw the roommate, bare knees sticking out beneath the hospital gown, bare feet stuck into paper slippers, sitting rigid on a stiff-backed chair, his hands gripping the arms, staring straight at me like a hobgoblin king on a throne, only the throne wasn't a throne or even a chair but a commode, and the sounds I heard, like sighs coming out of his body, were his bowels expressing themselves sadly in the night. He got up and stalked the length of the room, turned around and stalked back. I hadn't known he could walk.

I glanced at Martin. It seemed to me that his face looked softer, maybe even that his color was better, although it was hard to tell in the dim light. I could feel the drug spread from the needle in the crook of his elbow up to his shoulder, across his shoulder blades, down the other side and into his belly. My own arms and legs tingled. After all, here was a drug so untested that no one could swear it wouldn't work.

A little while later, Martin woke up. I produced a box of gingersnaps and made iced tea from powdered mix and the water in his bedside thermos. We invited the roommate to join us, but he only waved his arm bones in the air, in the polite waggle that we had learned to construe as "No, thank you," so we drew the curtain around the bed and ate our midnight snack in private. I have no idea which of the two roommates lasted longer.

When Martin went back to work that Monday, the leading partner of his firm told him that a new client had come into the office, a Fortune 500 corporation with a staggering product liability problem, the kind of problem that would go on for years and involve dozens—no, hundreds—of plaintiffs and dozens of trials or settlements. The partner wanted him to take charge at once, set up his own task force; lawsuits had been filed already. No one in his right mind would ask a dying man to take on such a representation. Martin was reborn. After five or six days, his belly was noticeably less swollen.

But that was the end of October, and November was November, and truths changed, as I said, like autumn weather over our heads, while wrong hope was soothing and fruitless as Indian summer. A man might put on his bathrobe and sit in the den and work at noon, but at night he was a different creature, and his wife was a different creature too. Between us there was the fundamental enmity of the sick and the well, when the sick one wants to talk and the well one needs to sleep, when the sick one knows this is it, this is all there is, and the well one knows this is not it, there are years ahead and someone has to get up in the morning and cope with the refrigerator repair man. What I wanted most was ten hours of sleep.

On this particular night, when we were into December, I woke up at the sound of sleeping pills rattling on Martin's side of the bed.

The incision that had been left open in his belly to drain out the strawberry milk shake had leaked through his bandage, through his pajamas, through the towels that we had wrapped around his middle in the hope that they would keep his bedding dry long enough for both of us to get a night's sleep. I took off the bandage but didn't have another in the house, so I used a sanitary napkin, the only thing I could find that was thick enough and anywhere near sterile. I changed his pajamas. I changed his sheet. I gave him the urinal and cough medicine, and I arranged his pillows as best I could, hoisting him up with one arm behind his shoulders, since we had passed the time when he could do that for himself.

"Is there anything else I can bring you?" I asked.

Asleep or nearly so, from the depth of his self, Martin answered me, "Only my dancing shoes."

It isn't a good idea to fall in love with your husband all over again on his deathbed, I thought in the months that followed, but I was wrong. If you don't fall in love with him all over again on such an occasion, and if you don't get engaged to him for some unspecified future in which you'll have a great deal to say to each other, because he has proved himself worthy of the only death he's going to get, the single perfect test we face—why, then he doesn't deserve your love, and probably hasn't deserved it for years. Your marriage lost its luster long ago. You might as well admit it, and get done with the condolence letters and get on to something else.

I speak, of course, as a woman in love.

Chapter 7

I'VE BEEN to the doctor," Karen said on October fifth. "The cervix is effacing. I'm dilated two centimeters."

"The cervix," she said, not "my cervix," as if it belonged to someone else.

"You can't be early. You promised." When she was twelve, she worried for a week about visiting the orthodontist to have a mold made of her teeth before she got braces. Would it hurt terribly? she wanted to know. Terribly, Ted assured her. She'd probably vomit. Lots of kids did. But she wouldn't vomit if she thought of it as a big fat mouthful of pink bubble gum.

"I promised?" Karen said. "Well, all I know is that the head's engaging."

"She won't be early. I'll bet on that," Ted volunteered.

"And how do you know?"

"She's too much of a camel. Remember the car trips we took when we were little? She wouldn't go to the toilet for days and days, I think it was two weeks once when we drove through France, because she couldn't find a place that was clean enough to suit her. Without footrests and a hole in the floor."

Felicia turned toward me. "First children are always late, aren't they? Wasn't Ted?"

"I'm not sure."

"She's not sure because she's always late herself. If I'd showed up on time she wouldn't have been home yet."

"Twilight sleep was the big thing in those days. The doctor knocked you for a loop as soon as you came through the door of the hospital. You were supposed to go home and tell your friends 'I don't remember a thing after I took my clothes off.'"

"Twilight sleep as distinguished from midnight sleep or noontime naps?" Ted wanted to know.

I went to sleep and had a dream, and when I woke up a child was handed to me. The story of the stork had to be the true one. This couldn't be anything I had done myself. But forever after, between that child and me, a gap existed, a gap of wonder and undeserving that was central to our lives. It was my child who was the older of us two, the proficient one, the creator who stayed awake, and did his job, and created me a mother while I slept.

"Doesn't sound like a bad idea," Felicia murmured. "Twilight sleep."

"Personally, I'd rather let a junior associate do it," Kurt broke in.

"You going to have the lithotomy position?" Ted asked his sister. "It's only for your doctor's convenience, you know. Shows he's boss."

"Even if my doctor's a woman?"

"She's going to have a baby, that's what she's going to have," Felicia snapped.

"Your doctor says it's all right to go to your office when you're already dilated?" I asked Karen.

"Of course. Don't fuss. I could go on like this for another two, three weeks. Besides, my doctor's still in Switzerland on vacation and won't be back until the fourteenth. She was supposed to go last month, but an emergency came up and she had to postpone her trip, so I've been seeing the woman who covers for her." A trace of the old uncertainty raised the pitch of her voice. "I told her I wouldn't dream of having the baby until she gets back."

"See? What did I tell you?" Ted demanded. "The baby's head will be popping out, and she'll be stuffing it back in and taking a plane and a train and a trolley, because a trolley is cheaper than a taxi, and then a cable car, because her doctor's up on top of the Jungfrau, but that's the doctor she's going to have, because that's the way she planned it. The way I figure it, she's not going to give birth until the baby's toilet trained anyway."

"Will you promise that you won't pick this weekend to go into labor?" I asked. "I'm supposed to be up in Connecticut on Saturday and Sunday, sailing in our team races." The quirkier races are scheduled after the end of the regular season.

"What's the difference?" Kurt interjected. "You weren't planning to come to the hospital, were you?"

"I'm not coming?"

"What good could you do?" Karen asked.

"Of course I'm coming. But not for your sake," I said to Karen. "I'm coming to keep Kurt company."

"But he won't be in the waiting room. He's Coach. He has to be in the labor room with me. And the delivery room. Even if it's a C-section."

"Oh." Had her doctor said anything about the possibility of a Cesarean? If not, why had the subject even been mentioned? C-section. She made herself sound like a melon about to be sliced.

"The Lamaze book specifically says grandparents should be kept away, because otherwise the husband is distracted. He thinks he has to run outside and keep you posted."

"I see."

"So you can sail. No reason why not."

No reason at all.

How ponderous and dull-hearted, like the work of leveling a pyramid, was this labor I'd undertaken for love of my daughter, the labor of perceiving myself as unnecessary.

"You see what happens when she finally reads a book?" Kurt asked Ted.

"Anyway, I refuse to go into the hospital until after the trustees' meeting a week from Monday—that was the earliest date I could get for it. And then I have to clean up the jobs that've piled up while I've been doing the annual reports for the meeting." I heard her promise, no matter what she said, that she'd wait until October twenty-sixth to give birth to her child, or at least until the twenty-fourth, when the child would be born a Scorpio, like his grandfather, like his two uncles, like all my fiery and intractable males.

"ANY day now," Karen said on October twentieth. Her Lamaze bag had been packed for three weeks, with lip pomade and cornstarch (for massaging the abdomen) and a tennis ball (a brand-new, clean one) in case of something called back labor, along with sour lollipops, while in the freezer a Jiffy icepack was kept at the ready. "Dilated five centimeters and well effaced. I saw Deedee Hopkins, you remember her from high school? She has a girl nine months old who walks already."

"Karen. I beg you. Don't upset yourself with children who walk or talk or program their computers . . ."

Her voice rose to its familiar whine. "Do you think I'm so dumb? All I said was the baby walks. So they've just adjusted to having three people in a one-bedroom apartment, and now they have to rearrange everything so it's over three feet high. And that's all I said."

But Ted was right, as always. After midnight, between the twenty-fourth and twenty-fifth of the month, during the dark of the moon, the sun on one side of the earth moved into the house of Scorpio, while on our side the clocks were turned back an hour, the thermostats were reset, and the United States left daylight saving and the last of the dawdling drive-home-before-dark twilights behind.

On the twenty-eighth, I drove into the city to meet Karen at her office for lunch, which was something I'd never done before. The wind came out of the northwest that day, hard dry air, straight from the Arctic, that lifted me to a quick high like the barometer, every racing sailor's favorite wind but a land wind all the same, shifting every three minutes, regular as clockwork, from three-thirty on the compass to three hundred and back again, from gust to lull, from cold hard upper air to warm soft lower air, with no deviation. By afternoon, clouds marking those lulls would form lines of white dots in the sky, with blank blue stretches in between, as if someone were tapping out messages that have to do with switching over from sea to land, from country to city, from summer to winter. From myself to the rest of the world. From present to future.

Getting dressed up at eleven in the morning was a celebration all its own that reminded me of the excitement of putting on my city clothes when I was a child, the morning when I was let out of camp. Even through pantyhose, the heavy wool skirt itched. The high-heeled boots and velvet blazer made me feel young and competent.

By the time I reached the highway, the morning rush hour was over. At 103rd Street, the purple-and-orange pedestrian bridge over to Wards Island, where no one ever seems to set foot, was fantastic and dangerous as a gypsy wagon. A sloop with a mast-high genoa moved toward the harbor, probably heading for Sandy Hook and the Jersey shore and then south on the Intracoastal Waterway.

The Detwirth-Manning Institute, where Karen works, is in the East Sixties, between Lexington and Park. It owns one of the last of the private mansions squeezed in among the high-rises, with a bare flagpole over the great wooden double doors that are never used, and only a small plaque to identify the side door, which was once the servants' entrance. Visitors who don't know where and what the Institute is have no business finding it, that plaque announces.

Two granite steps led from the street up to the entrance hall. Two wooden steps led down from the entrance hall into the former front parlor, now converted into a waiting room with an Oriental carpet. "Her mother," I said to the receptionist, who sat in a cubicle that must once have been a closet. I was ashamed to admit that I had no professional reason to be there.

As I climbed the flight of stairs that rose over the sixteen-foot ceiling of the main salon to the offices on the second floor, I thought of the generations of housemaids who had passed up and down them carrying scrub pails and and carpet sweepers. Karen's office was junior administrative, in the back of the building, which meant that it still had a working fireplace, a window overlooking the garden and a parquetry floor that had been patched with plain strips of wood near the door.

"But that's fan-tastic," she was saying on the telephone as I came in, gripping the receiver with her shoulder while she sorted papers on her desk and packed up her briefcase. "You made exactly the same choice of which one to hire for the job that I did. And you got through that stack of CV's so fast."

Thank heavens she'd had her hair cut (by La Coupe, for an outrageous price, she complained to me on the phone one evening, and what kind of tip were you supposed to leave on top of a bill like that?). She was getting herself ready. I was willing to bet that her eyebrows had been freshly waxed.

"I'll notify the other candidates that they're out. But I'll keep the name of the fellow from New Jersey in my file, just in case we need him some other time."

I try to imagine what she does at her job all day, what they pay her for in this elegant building where she looks like the daughter of the house, dressed in pale pongee in one era, wearing a maternity dress and five centimeters dilated behind her desk right now.

My children's work lives are hidden from me. They fascinate me but intimidate me, they go on behind closed doors, they seem more adult than anything I could achieve. I'm supposed to know that they exist, but not to think about them, any more than I was supposed to think about my parents' sex lives. I believe firmly in the extraordinary value of my children's careers.

My mother, on the other hand, believes that careers for women whose husbands can support them fall in the same category as extramarital affairs. What nice woman would want to leave her comfortable apartment and go to seek out either one? In her world, women play a more subtle role: Men are supposed to impregnate their wives and take care of them forever after, chiefly so that there should be daughters in the next generation who will sit motionless at the center of the day, listening to their mothers' voices.

"What do you mean, you have to work?" Marion has accused me for thirty years. "You don't work. You write at home. But if you need money that badly, I'll have to give it to you." By that she means there's no need for me to work and she knows it, so that if I insist on doing it, it's only another crazy waste of energy, like sailing. No, it's not. It's done to avoid her, it's a deliberate renunciation of the afternoons we might have spent together in her bedroom, or more wicked yet, the afternoons she spent with her mother. Every time I say the word "work," she supposes I spit on her; I shrivel her domestic life to nothing.

But for Karen, whether she needs money or not, work is a necessity—if she wants to be a respectable young woman, that is. She can share a man's bed if she chooses, whether married to him or not, and still be a pillar of virtue in the community, but she can't share his American Express card, not even if he's her husband, at least not at her present age, while she's childless.

At that moment, her caller must have said something unexpected.

"How does everyone seem to know?" she asked in astonishment, rolling her foot outward until the anklebone almost touched the floor. She'd crack her shoe leather if she didn't stop that. "Was it published in the paper? But don't worry. I'll mail you my memo first." To counterbalance her new proportions, La Coupe had cut her hair into what used to be called the gamin style, which gave her, more than ever, the look of innocence combined with burden that young women carry while they're pregnant, never so chaste in their expressions, like pearls worn above black velvet.

"Sorry to keep you. I've already washed up." She opened the closet in her office and pulled out an old unfitted raincoat of mine, borrowed for the duration. "Well, you picked the right day to come for lunch. Your lunch, I mean, because I'm not having any. We're inducing labor this evening. Too much risk of infection if I go on this way. I'm dilated six centimeters already." Six, not five. Her desk, I noticed, had been swept as clean as if she'd been fired.

"Back in an hour," she said to the receptionist as we left the building. "I have an appointment Doctor Hollander set up with the young man from the University of Pennsylvania. You can count on my being here until four, anyway. Does Peppermint Park suit you?" she asked me.

"You be sure you get home early enough to shave your legs, you hear now?" a young secretary called after her, brimming with the event that she was privy to.

Peppermint Park is a restaurant that likes to think of itself as a garden, with green acrylic partitions and white tables, with frilled green-glass shades around the light fixtures and hanging plants with green-and-white leaves, where waiters serve chicken salad with celery and walnuts, cucumbers in sour-cream sauce with flecks of dill, spiced chicken crepes with cream sauce, and peppermint ice-cream sodas, as if the food has been selected solely to carry out the green-and-white color scheme.

"A glass of Perrier. Nothing else. Will you look at these spiders?"

She laid her hands on the table and pointed to small eruptions on her hands and face. "That's because I have so much blood in me right now. It's all right for you to come to the hospital any time after six. That's when Kurt and I will get there. The doctor's breaking the water at seven."

"Would you like me to go with you?" is what I stopped myself from saying. "You're going back to your office after lunch?"

"Of course. I have to clean up."

For an instant, I loved her not as my child but as my superior, my boss, a woman of six years' work seniority over me, who was good at her job and needed at her job and knew it, a woman who went on working no matter what happened, aware that husbands die or desert their wives, and children leave home (as mothers become a burden), but her career is her career until she quits or grows old. How many candidates for whatever job she was filling had she thrown in her trash basket during that phone call before lunch? A number of families were going to be knocked for a loop at supper tonight by what she'd decided.

Outside the restaurant, we kissed good-bye. "Just think. By tomorrow at this time, I'll be two people," Karen said.

IT MIGHT have been midnight, that's how dark it was at a quarter to six when I walked from the subway to my mother's apartment house.

Only the biggest handball players were left in the Ninety-sixth Street playground on the edge of Harlem, where a police car had taken up its nightly vigil. The owner of a newspaper delivery store rolled down his iron shutter and padlocked it.

Looking downhill toward the river, I could see the apartment house where Ted was born and Karen was conceived, where Karen and Kurt now live. I could imagine that I saw a radio cab turn the corner and draw up at the door to take them to the hospital. Was a cab really there? This was the hour, after all. Wasn't that Karen coming out of the house now? I wanted to say good-bye. I wanted to kiss her again.

When I was little, my grandmother was convinced, or pretended to be convinced, that it brought good luck to touch a nun's garments, and so she would walk down the street, a Jewish matron from the banks of the Mississippi River, with blue-gray hair and burgundy fingernails and a baum marten skin draped over the shoulders of her tailormade suit, its toothy little jaw fitted with a clip to grip its rear paw, while three other paws dangled over her shoulders, and if by chance a pair of nuns passed (pairs of nuns on foot were common on the streets of Manhattan in those days, especially on the Upper East Side), she'd tweak the habit of the one closer to her, tickled by her own naughtiness, while my mother snorted with laughter at her side. That's what I wanted. I wanted a nun to walk up the block at the exact minute, so that the black wool of her habit would brush against my daughter's leg and touch her skin, just when she bent double to get into the cab, squeezing my grandchild's head as she did so.

Block by block, I walked past my past. The fruit and vegetable store was the same, even if the owners were Korean now. The barbershop was the same, with an electric barber pole in the window and a sign offering "razor hair styles," as if these were the latest thing. Kurt looked terrible when I saw him the week before, ashy-gray, as if he'd forgotten how to sleep; Karen was blooming. I wanted to stop in every store still open and buy her a pint of raspberries, a bottle of bath splash. All the daisies in the florist's pail.

So the doctor was going to prick her bag of waters. Make a hole and let the fluid out. She sounded like a balloon. She sounded like someone else I'd known well. As I turned west on Eighty-ninth Street, one more middle-aged woman with a shopping bag over her arm who bustled from Lexington to Park shortly before dinnertime, I felt with astonishment a feeling I'd never expected to feel again. I felt myself wetting my pants. No doubt about it. I was wet between the legs, not with the clotted, pulling sensation of a period, and not with the helpless gush of amniotic fluid or the fishy slipperiness of sex, but with a meager and decent wetness like that of a child, just one more time, but this time out of love for my daughter. All the same, I couldn't be sure whether it was sympathy or envy that was commingled with my love.

"IT SHOULDN'T happen to her what happened to me," Marion said. "That's all I ask. Losing her water."

Sylvia had washed Marion's hair that afternoon and rolled it on curlers while sopping wet, held by a pale-blue hairnet tied up like a turban. (Where would anyone find a hairnet like that these days, I wondered—is such a thing even made any longer?) With her red-rimmed eyes, redder and sorer than ever, it seemed, Marion looked like a crested blue jay. "Next time I come—remind me—I'll bring you a hair dryer."

"Don't you dare do anything of the sort. I have no room for one more thing in this house."

"I have an extra that's made for travel. It's all of eight or ten inches long."

"Not another thing. I'm telling you." She's full to bursting; she's dying of undernourishment. Anorexia of the spirit is what's killing her.

"Otherwise you're going to catch pneumonia this winter for sure. In six big rooms, it ought to be possible to find ten inches of space somewhere. Stick it under the sink." Or just plain stick it. Who was trying to force-feed whom now?

Reminded by the word "pneumonia," she coughed so that I could hear the rales. The single lamp next to her elbow showed the cords in her throat as she thrust her neck out and retracted it. "Those damn cigarettes," she said, hunching her back as she coughed until she retched. Her lower lip stuck out an inch further than the upper to spew out air. When she was done with the cough, she remained bowed over, a look on her face as if she were about to be tortured by having a hair dryer thrust into her room.

She couldn't do this to me. I wouldn't let her slip away like this and leave a dying old woman in her chair.

"Don't worry about her," Jack Nordlinger had said, when I phoned him earlier in the week to find out if the cough that wouldn't go away could possibly be lung cancer. "Cancer of the colon would be more likely. But the sigmoidoscopy was negative."

"I don't understand why she's so weak, then. Last night I called at half-past seven, and she was in bed already."

"Emphysema. Aside from that, all her tests have been normal, not only for her age but for a twenty-five-year-old woman." There was admiration in his tone.

"Little things have happened. *Not* happened, I mean. Nothing important. I mean, this year, for the first time, she didn't send me a thing for my birthday. Not even a card. Not even a phone call. She ignored the day." Why was I burdening him with a petty story that I hadn't told my children?

I could have told him that only a few weeks ago, when the question of sending Gitte a birthday card came up and she said it was impossible for her to get out to buy one, I'd answered with a sigh that that had to be the truth. After all, she'd let her daughter's birthday pass altogether. She'd been appalled, as I'd hoped she'd be, and announced that she was going to send me a check—a big check—but immediately.

And I cried out like a child that I didn't *want* a check, I had enough money and she knew it. What I wanted was a gift I could touch from my mother. I never remember getting a gift I could touch from her.

But that was the point, how could she manage it? she'd protested, shocked by my violence. She couldn't get out of the house to go around the block. But it wasn't too late. I must pick out something she owned, the repoussé silver water pitcher I'd always admired, or the little white Nymphenburg pigeon that sat on her coffee table. Anything I wanted. She insisted.

No. No thanks to you, I meant, not no, thank you. Because I knew what I wanted. I wanted my mother to comb through the catalogues arriving in the mail these days—the thick, expensive sort with one picture to a page—and read the captions while she thought about me. Lavished with lace, she'd read and think about me. Color-soaked separates. The most poetic collar, get the jumpsuit on fashion, cashmere with cream, the most delicate blouse, fab fur, faux tortoise, faux pearl, butter-soft, for the long-stemmed rose in your life. I wanted her to study the pictures and turn down the corners of certain pages, which she'd refer back to later while she said to herself, no, not that one, it's not really her type, but maybe this one, if only because she never had anything like it, it's a new look, or maybe this, but which color? and am I absolutely sure of her size? And I'd want her to turn it over in her mind, maybe have two things sent home so that she could choose between them, and even then console herself with the thought that, whatever it is, it can be returned if it's not right, because it comes from a regular store. (How long is it—twenty years, thirty years?—since she bought anything from a regular store?) And then I'd wear it or hold it up, whatever it might be, and show it to my friends some day and say see, how do you like this on me? This is what my mother picked out for me. She saw it in a catalogue and got carried away and called up and ordered it sent C.O.D. Just like that. She knew what I looked like, after all.

"It seems to me she's losing her grip on life," I said to the doctor on the phone. So far, she has sent me neither the gift nor the check. "You think her weakness is psychological? Depression, perhaps?"

"Emphysema is plenty good reason to be exhausted," he said angrily. "Just breathing uses up her strength." He stopped for breath himself. "Of course it would help if she gave up smoking."

"I think she wants to die," I said.

"Don't let her fool you." He spoke more gently. "She uses that threat to keep us in line." Us, he said, as if we were brother and sister. "Anyway, the baby's going to give her a new lease on life. That's all she talks about."

"Unless it's the other way round," I said. "Unless she's only waiting for the baby to be born so she can see it, and then that's it, she has no more reason to go on breathing."

"WHAT do you hear from Karen?" Marion asked, as she took her daily Scotch. When she reached for a cracker and brought it up to her mouth, I saw that her fingers were thin, the knuckles straight, not arthritic like mine. Sylvia manicured and polished her beautiful long nails every week. "Did you speak to her today?"

"Yes. I wouldn't be surprised if she has her baby soon."

"Why? What do you know? Do you know something you're not saying?" Suspicion spurted up between us like pond water struck by a stone.

I could never be simple. But then, she could never be tender. If I told her the truth, that Karen was on her way to the hospital at this minute, she'd take over the scene and create hysteria the way she did on the night that Ted was born. I needed quiet tonight. My tenderness belonged to my daughter. And to myself. Something was being born in me, too.

"What is there you're not saying?" Marion demanded.

"You know as well as I do. She's more than a week overdue."

"I don't know a thing. Except what you tell me."

"I can tell you this much. She was working in her office this afternoon."

"What? Suppose something happened?"

"What could happen?"

"Suppose she had happen to her what happened to me? Suppose her waters broke?"

"Well? Suppose they did?" Waters, she said. Cataracts of the Nile. "It has to happen, after all. What's the difference where?"

"A dry labor. That's what I went through."

"Look, you don't know the first thing about having babies. The sac of fluid has to break sooner or later during labor. If you're not in the hospital, you get there."

"A dry labor for twenty-four hours. Karen should never know what that's like, that's what I pray."

For an instant I saw it, how many reasons my mother had to hate me, this twenty-year-old girl who'd been drained of her body fluids one after the other by her untimely daughter, her menstruation corked up while she was still on her honeymoon, as she must have seen in a string of anxious visits to bathrooms in Banff and Jasper and all the way home on the Canadian Pacific, while other young girls made a play for her husband, with his mustache and his plus fours and his pastel-colored golf sweaters. "What did I know when I got married?" she said to me years ago. "My mother put a douche bag in my suitcase. With printed instructions. That was all."

But that wasn't all. In less than nine months, there was a puddle on the floor between her legs. No one had told her a thing. "A dry labor. I remember the doctor standing over me and saying to somebody, I don't know who, 'This woman is exhausted.'"

Afterward, while she was lying in the hospital bed with an infant in her arms, it's possible that her mother—who was forty years old at that point, the same age that I was when I gave birth to Peter—may have smiled at the baby, may have promised to give the baby a taste of chocolate one day very soon, a tiny taste from the tip of her fingernail, no bigger than *that,* a promise she would have kept. My grandmother loved chocolate. I love chocolate. My mother doesn't care for it and never kept any in the house. It's possible that I still don't know whose child I am.

"You were so young, you might have been my sister," I cried. Is this why she remembers the casual remark the doctor made when he stood next to her bed, because no one had spoken of her as a woman before? "There's only four more years between you and me than between Ted and Peter." In which case, your mother would have been my mother too.

She looked up as if I were accusing her of not being grown-up enough to do her job. But why do I assume that she had a duty to love me (*has* a duty to love me) just because I was born to her, and not only that, but love me with the full-blown love of a parent for a child? And yet I make that assumption, and so does she. It may be the primary thing we share.

"Honor thy father and thy mother," the commandment says—not love, not like, not be good to, but honor, as if our parents are not only grown-up but godlike, but here's this one looking at me as uneasily as if she's the defenseless child and I'm the unpredictable old witch, likely to explode at any instant. "Honor thy father and thy mother." But no commandment says "Love thy children," as if that directive is unnecessary, because there's no way we can help ourselves, and therefore we get no credit for obedience, or as if mother love is a talent that some women have in greater abundance than others, like intelligence or musical pitch or a plentiful flow of breast milk.

"And you came four weeks early. You were premature. Whether you think so or not."

Weighing six pounds? "Maybe that's why I've been late ever since. Anyway, what difference does it make what I think? Now." She opened her mouth. I overrode her. "You were too young. You never had a chance to get your marriage started."

"And how much older is Karen?"

"Eight years."

"So? What does she know about babies? You want to know the right way to feed one? Well, I'll show you." Sitting in her chair, Marion lifted her left leg, still so startling in its shapeliness, and put her ankle on top of her knee to make a V-shaped hole, where she laid an imaginary infant. She pushed an imaginary nipple into its mouth with her right hand.

"Whoever taught you that?" That rape, I meant. Was that the way I was fed?

"Never mind. I know."

"I see."

When I gave Peter his bottle during his first weeks, as I sat in the rocking chair, I felt my uterus shrink to its proper size under the weight and warmth of his body. He snorted, he sucked, four, five times in rapid succession, then relaxed and let the air bubble back into the milk. His head rested on my breast. My nipple perked up and pointed at him. I could feel its tug right down to my genitals, exactly as if the milk wasn't made from a powder that came in a can, but was my own. Rocking chairs had been reinvented sometime between Karen's birth and Peter's, along with Snuglis and pacifiers and all things close to the body and easy to hold.

"Dinner." Sylvia came into the room to make the announcement. "You coming into the dining room to get it?" From her tone, I gathered that a week might have passed since her employer visited any of the other rooms in the apartment. "Your daughter going to have her baby any day now?" she asked me.

My mother looked up in astonishment. To a woman who never went outdoors any more, who lived in a world without weather, much less seasons, without the change of hour implied by bedspreads put on in the morning and taken off again at night, whose weeks were marked only by the alternation of weekday nurse and weekend nurse, whose months consisted of the gaps between holiday dinners, or the rotation of quarterly tax payments, it was inconceivable that an outsider could keep track of the date her great-grandchild was due to be born.

But Marion had started a fresh cigarette a few minutes earlier. From the lamp table next to her chair she produced a pair of sewing scissors, which must have been placed there for the purpose, and snipped off the lighted end. With religious care, she ground it with the end of a pencil to make sure that it was extinguished before she put the butt back into its pack.

"BORN with a caul," I heard about my second child, before I knew whether it was a boy or a girl. I suppose that the doctor saw the head slip out, draw back into the birth canal and slip out again, still wearing its veil, and knew that the infant was a myth-bringer before he knew its sex. I never saw the caul. Mothers weren't supposed to have eyes on the delivery table in those days, so I never found out if she showed up with a membrane covering only her head, like a child taking First Communion, or with a sac covering her entire body and sealed at the edges (the child born under a caul is forever safe from drowning), as if she were a package of frozen food.

"I hope to goodness you didn't let the delivery-room attendants steal it," Marion said as soon as she heard the news. "Sailors pay big money to get their hands on one of those things, I hope you know."

No, I didn't know, but I'm glad I do now. I hope some sailor got hold of it and hung it in a chamois bag around his neck and touched it whenever a gale warning was broadcast at sea, even if he made believe that he was scratching his chest. I hope the caul carried him around both Capes with easy quartering winds. I hope it serves him still as a life preserver whenever the waves turn green, or fog closes down, or ice floes wander in the night.

Some people, no matter where they may go, are forever safe from drowning.

NO, nothing had happened yet, and no, I couldn't go in to see my daughter.

Central Casting had been at work in the waiting room on the obstetrical floor. Well, what else would I expect in a great teaching hospital in the capital of the land of Blue Cross? In the corner, facing a blank wall, a young bearded Hasid, an Orthodox Jew, was praying, dressed in a black overcoat that reached to his ankles and a black fedora that was a size too small for him. He bowed from the hips, hunched his shoulders as he recited a prayer, straightened his back and bowed again.

An Oriental boy, about four years old, poked his face under the nose of the *davening* Jew and peered up at him. The child's father came into the room, said a few words and vanished into the area behind the leather door in the corridor that was forbidden territory to anyone but fathers.

The rest of us looked at one another, sympathy mingled with vague competition in the push for salvation, like passengers in an elevator that's stuck between floors. At the far end of the room, a blonde woman was speaking Spanish to her daughter with the high clear syllables and exaggerated stresses of the upper classes in every country, wearing five jeweled rings on each hand. The daughter's broad nose and high cheekbones showed there was Indian blood in her. Through a single braid of black hair that reached to her hips, she had wound yellow ribbons to match her silk blouse, a bit of throwaway chic that may have been for the benefit of the expectant father and the paternal grandparents, who were getting off the elevator at that minute, carrying their travel cases.

But here came the figure who was the center of their attention, a young woman in labor, scuffing along in flat slippers and an old wool bathrobe, her hair lanky with sweat. "Ai-ee," cried the girl in labor. Her mother opened a Gucci suitcase. Out tumbled a standard size pillow in a linen case piped in pink, a miniature pillow to match, a peignoir embroidered with butterflies. The girl reached for a toilet kit and found a bottle of Afrin, which she inhaled, sending out a series of small whistles.

Each language has its syllables reserved for groans, all of them based on open-mouthed vowels. "Ai-ee," the South American girl said during her next contraction, which rippled through her relatives like wind.

"Oy," the Hasid's wife must be crying out, as she brought forth a child under Old Testament strictures about suffering and woe. "Oy." Not to call out would be impious, a denial that something significant was happening in her life. After she left the hospital, she would refuse to have sex with her husband again for forty days, and even then not until she had been cleansed in a ritual bath. Scholars may say what they like about the meaning of this custom. New mothers know that it's meant to release them from the vows they take during labor: Never, no never again, will they make the mistake of sleeping with a man.

"Ah," my daughter Karen would exclaim, her mouth open in slight shock as if a dance partner had stepped on her foot, but then she'd turn the gasp into a laugh at the wonder of the occasion, so that her partner would realize that he wasn't responsible, and anyway there was nothing she wanted so much as to go on with the dance.

I'd no idea what sound the Oriental woman would make, or had already made; maybe a helpless tinkle, like wind chimes in a gust.

The South American husband marched his wife and her Afrin to the nursery at the end of the corridor, where the newborns were on display during visiting hours, each in a clear plastic case like a potato bin, with pink index cards at the head of some bins and blue at the head of others. I followed.

Tell me, I demanded—a question central to me, as well as to them—why I ought to assume that one particular woman is bound to love each of you, instantly and without question, long before you've proved yourselves beautiful or lovable or anything else? A million pages of literature tell me why Jack loves Jill and why Jill can't stand the sight of Jack, but no one writes books about mothers who fail to love their children, at least not since the fairy tales let slip the word about women who peddled poisoned apples at a pretty girl's cottage door, or women who ordered their husbands to lose their children in the woods, or who locked them in towers, or who shoved the little ones into ovens.

Child abuse is epidemic in our land, I said to the rows of plastic bins. One of you in this nursery, who's pretending to sleep on the other side of the glass, one out of thirty-three, will be brought back to a doctor's office within a few years with bruises or scalds or broken bones. How fortunate that you're swaddled so tight that no air touches your skin. We wouldn't want you to suspect that you're out of the womb now and exposed to our moods.

The babies lay on their right sides, wrapped from toe to neck like papooses, mocking the masculine idea that it's freedom that human beings are born for. Two new mothers in bathrobes that still puffed out below their belts stared through the glass at an infant born a few minutes ago, the only naked one, laid out under a heat lamp with his umbilical cord sticking up in the air. "Cold as hell in that delivery room," a young man said authoritatively. "You should've seen him, he was purple when they brought him in here. They never get the heat right in these old places."

Could that be my grandson I was looking at?

We're animals, we're more than animals, we're less than animals. Word sifts back from laboratories at Rutgers and other universities about mother love among our mammal cousins. Pregnant rats, for instance, change their behavior even before they give birth, build nests for their young or retrieve lost pups. But if scientists give a virgin rat a blood transfusion from one who has just given birth, or inject her with the same hormones, what they soon see is a new mother in action, full of motherly cares, even though she's still a virgin.

("Be quiet," I said to Peter a few hours before he was born. "Stop pushing, will you? I'll be with you in a few minutes. I haven't finished lining your bureau drawers with Con-Tact yet, although I can't imagine why I didn't get to them weeks ago.")

So mother love is as simple as that, the result of an altered chemical balance in the blood? Of course. How could nature afford anything else to offset that first shock of dismay none of us talk about, at the instant when we confront the ugliness of a newborn child, a face that only a mother could love? In rats, it's not the sight but the smell—the stink—that disgusts adult rats other than the mothers and keeps them away, which is the way it has to be, or else the litters would be eaten in their nests.

Shortly before the pups are born, however, hormones in the mother rat's body change her reception of odors. This may even be accomplished by the same hormones that work on her uterus and bring about the birth contractions. In any case, at the time of birth, the rat is no longer the rat that she used to be. She can still smell; there's nothing wrong with her nose's ability to catch odors, but her pattern of likes and dislikes has turned topsy-turvy. The smell that used to disgust her now entices her—entices her just enough to make her eat the placenta, thus cutting the umbilical cord and initiating breathing, without also tempting her to gulp down her brand-new pup.

There's a delicate balance here, a crucial balance between the perils of not enough love and too much love. Make the offspring too foul-smelling, too ugly, and it will die of neglect or mistreatment. Make it too attractive—even to its mother—and it will be devoured. The witch in the woods who likes to eat little children is not, as the scientists would say, species-specific.

("Don't cry," I said to my babies when I lived on 94th Street. "Of course I know what I put in the garbage bag that I threw down the incinerator chute into the furnace. And it wasn't you. How could it be you? And I know it was only a roasting chicken whose legs I tied together and whose arms I fastened behind its back before I popped it into the oven. What right do you have to suggest anything else?")

But at birth another drama begins—gesture and response, creatures making love before they can see each other, even before the younger one breathes—an instinct as irresistible as the mother's urge to bear down when the head appears. Pups nuzzle, even during delivery. Prompted by hormones, the mother rat sniffs them, licks them, warms them, feels warmed by their bodies against her belly. She tastes them. She smells them. She licks the anus and genitals. These are delicious to her.

If a virgin rat, with no artificial hormones to help her, is placed in a cage with newborn pups, she will cower in a corner at first, but within a few days she will let them touch her. Once she does that, once she dares to touch them in return—and the smaller the cage, the faster she succumbs—she's done for. She's touched to the quick. The feel of their bodies overcomes her aversion. By the end of a week of this intercourse of flesh with flesh, more consistently satisfying though less varied than sex, she's a mother as tender as any other.

("You're there," I said to my babies, each in turn. "You're hideous. I can't bear you. I can't bear myself for not bearing you. I love you into beauty. See? What did I tell you? Look at you now." I drew their arms and legs away from their bodies to see the miracle, which was that they looked like every other body, they were in perfect disguise as human beings, down to the hairs of each eyebrow. But this meant nothing until the next minute, when I said "Open your eyes and look at me, because I am here. I exist. I am real, if you will only look at me, because I am necessary to your life. As long as I am necessary, I shall go on being real.")

There are incidents we know are true long before they are reported in scientific journals, because they correspond so closely to dreams.

A few years ago, in an Israeli maternity ward, two mothers were given the wrong babies by mistake, babies they took home and cared for. When they returned with the infants for their two-week check-ups, the mistake was discovered, and the hospital prepared to arrange the exchange—what else could be done?—but by that time, each mother had fallen in love with the baby in her own home and refused to give it up. How could she? Promises had been given. Divorce wasn't possible. It was because of her that the child was clean, content and gaining weight. What she loved wasn't simply the new baby himself but the new mother awakened in her, the comfort she had brought him.

The fathers felt otherwise. What did each of them know about the intelligence, health, energy, ambition, humor, holy zeal of the other family's genes? He had swapped his semen for what sort of soup? The fathers' bond was rational, vertical and abstract, drawn to the line of family, the chains of chromosomes, looking backward to the past and forward to the future. The mothers' bond was passionate, horizontal and immediate, flesh to flesh.

I have no idea which sex won.

IN THE bins, the babies swatted their faces as they grew hungry in their sleep. Visiting hours were over except for fathers, who could stay as long as they wanted. A hospital cart arrived loaded with flower arrangements, many of them bearing Mylar balloons tasseled with streamers and painted with butterflies or unicorns—unicorns with curly manes were very big this year, especially for boys. The pair of mothers in their terry robes flapped around the cart and checked address tags, as if they were college roommates dogging the mailman's footsteps.

When we got back to our seats in the waiting room, the white-socked Hasid took out a plastic bag and produced an orange, which he peeled, while the Oriental child at his elbow looked on expectantly but wasn't given any. No one was alone except this child and me. His father walked in, wearing a surgical mask and gown, and squatted down and talked to him, while the rest of us looked on with meaningful glances that put us on record as saying how adorable we found him, and it wasn't our fault that he hadn't been given a piece of orange.

I went to a phone booth in the corridor and called Ted and Felicia, but no one was home. The receptionist at Ted's office told me that he'd signed out for the night. At this hour, the only other person I could call—it was a shock to me that I thought about calling her—was my mother, but I'd boxed myself in. There was no way I could explain that I hadn't gone home to Westchester, as she thought, but had come to the hospital instead.

"If there's one thing I can't stand, it's a liar," she often said.

The Hasid left the room, beckoned by a nurse. The Oriental father returned to his wife. I had no candy in my pocketbook for the boy, but found an old marketing list from which I made a paper airplane that refused to fly, but delighted him nonetheless. He ran around the room with it and banked and swooped and buzzed.

Deception was my means of distancing, I saw that at last. Deception or silence. And yet I considered myself honorable, if not honest. I had held back on Martin. I had kept silent on the one subject on which we had nothing that we chose to say to each other (never ask a question if you're powerless to change the answer), for my sake more than for his. I'd held back the truth about Martin from Peter as long as I could, because a truth unspoken isn't the whole truth yet. With a different intent but the same result, I'd held back the truth from Marion about Martin's illnesses, and now about Karen's labor.

I felt further than ever from the events going on behind the leather doors.

There must have been a language that my mother and I never mastered, sometime after the water gushed out and the doctor declared "This woman is exhausted,"—not conversation, but a slippery babble full of vowels: private babble on her part, mews or cries on mine, some mouth work we missed, while she spent two weeks in the hospital accepting visitors and phone calls, with the baby in the nursery (which was standard in those days), before she came home to an apartment where a cook and nurse waited for her. Each of them was old enough to be her mother. What could she do for her daughter that someone else couldn't do better—hadn't already done, in fact? What need could she fill?

Whenever we were closest, it occurs to me now, no words were used. When I was young, when she threw me on her big double bed, where we tussled and laughed and kissed and rolled over and over, the ecstasy took place without words. Passion we were able to manage; it's tenderness that we've never been able to handle. The cage we were originally locked in together must have been too big.

What a terrible airplane I'd made. I beckoned to the boy, and when he came over to me I took my marketing list and smoothed it out and started over again, more carefully this time, trying to remember what would make it fly. It had to form an M, that was it. I shaped the nose with my thumbnail and launched the new model, which flew by itself across the room. "See what a fine grandmother I am," I said to myself, as he chased the plane to its landing place.

"Y O U didn't finish your dessert," Marion had said to me a few hours earlier at dinner, even though she'd been served only half a Pepperidge Farm apple turnover herself and hadn't finished that much. Hunger seemed to be falling away, along with everything else. "Look how I've lost my appetite." She raised her arms in the sleeveless gray sweater she'd knitted forty years ago, when knitting argyles with several needles at the same time was in fashion, to show that the armholes drooped halfway to her waist. "Tastes change with age." She has to be right. Pete told me that since his wilderness trip this summer he doesn't like Yodels or Hostess cupcakes any more. I'm not to buy them from now on.

Using her walker, Marion thumped foot by foot from the dining room back to the bedroom, but stopped a minute to look at the double line of photographs hung in the hallway outside her door, her mother and Karen and me in the top row, with Martin and Ted and Peter below us. "How I loved that man," she said, shaking her head as she stared at Martin.

Back in her chair, she squinted toward the hall, scrutinizing the contents of her apartment. "Switch those two pictures, will you?" she demanded, pointing to the wall.

"Which pictures?" I knew perfectly well.

"Yours and Martin's."

"You mean these two?"

"I can't see Martin from where I sit."

"Well, of course."

Did she think it would be that easy to trap me? All I had to do was keep my eyes on the wall six inches above his head, while I unhooked the frames and switched them. "There. Are they hanging straight? I can't see from this close up."

She studied the arrangement as if she were a museum curator. "That's much better," she said with satisfaction.

"Any others you want moved?"

Is it conceivable that she loved Martin and still never came to visit him in the hospital, all of ten blocks away from her apartment? My father didn't come to the hospital either. I don't fool myself; he wouldn't have come even if he'd lived in New York. I can understand that in my father, I admire his genius for self-protection, his determination to think only blood-building thoughts. I find it courtly, in a way. Old people don't like to see a younger person shove ahead of them through the revolving door that leads to death.

Then why don't I feel the same way about Marion's failure to visit? And why do I mistrust her passion for Martin tonight, now that he's no longer here to defend himself? Is she trying to take him away from me?

Or is it possible that she has learned to love him at last, now that he's gone, along with her mother and father (she could never tolerate that man either, while he was alive), because she's growing old, and old people are partial to the dead? The dead are what has happened. The dead are authentic. They are the only people left who need her, in their wordless way, to remember them. They belong to the small group to whom she feels superior, even responsible, like her elevator men and doormen, who also have no clothes of their own, no existence until she calls on them. These people surround her and watch her and know her apartment number even if she never goes out of the door; they are on hand when she calls them, they are always tactful, they never show up late or threaten to leave early or interrupt a visit to go downstairs and feed the parking meter.

In any case, she no longer has to look at my face hanging on the wall opposite her chair all day.

THE SOUTH AMERICAN woman who'd arrived last, bringing her traveling case with her, got up, as if she couldn't stand this any longer, and walked along the corridor to the leather doors that sealed off the delivery and recovery rooms. I followed. The infants had long since been fed and wheeled back to the nursery, where they lay on their left sides this time. The visiting fathers had gone home an hour ago.

"Venezuela," the woman said. "My daughter-in-law. My husband and I arrived by plane this evening." The two of us leaned against the padded surface. I pointed out the seat in the telephone booth I'd used, but she refused the offer, if only because she hadn't enough energy left to bend her joints and sit down.

"Your first grandchild?" I asked, to break our silence. She nodded. "Like me." We waited. "And what do you want, a girl or a boy?"

"I want her to be safe," she said. "I want she should pass the baby safe."

I stood shamed. This woman who wasn't even the girl's mother hadn't thought about her first grandchild but about her daughter-in-law's safety, having come all this distance to guard it.

"How do we know it when she passes?" We walked back to the waiting room side by side. At least her husband, her son, her daughter-in-law's mother were with her.

Kurt was beside me. "A girl," he said. "The baby's wonderful. Karen's wonderful. She's so heavy. The baby, I mean." We kissed. He leaned against me.

"And what's her name?"

"We don't have a name for a girl yet." It didn't matter. All names would sound unfamiliar to me except one, a man's name that wasn't going to be used.

"I'm so happy it's a girl," I said, realizing the truth of what I was saying. We don't start over, we start afresh.

"But when the baby was put into her arms, Karen cried and cried. She couldn't stop crying." He leaned back far enough to look into my face and find out if something was wrong.

"Of course she did."

So another breaking of the water had taken place. It marked another birth, but one that took place where no one could see it, not out there under the delivery-room lights. "Don't worry about it. Bless her." Kurt disappeared behind the leather doors to rejoin Karen. I waited another two hours for a glimpse of her being wheeled from the recovery area back to her own room.

GRANDMOTHER, stepmother, mother-in-law. These aren't beautiful words. Only one term has dignity, and Karen had earned it.

I stood in front of the window and looked at the bin that carried a new index card. By this time, Martin would have been monopolizing the pay phone, calling family members at eleven at night, sending telegrams, ordering sandwiches to be sent in for Kurt and us, calling his office to announce he'd come in late in the morning. He'd have thrown open those doors that say "Operating room personnel only" and barged into the recovery room, with a surgical gown or without one, demanding to see his daughter.

I called my mother and woke her. She didn't ask where I was or how I'd known so soon about the birth. Had something ended for her tonight too, or something opened up, now that her daughter had moved along to another level, which seemed to be approaching so much closer to her own? Before I hung up, I promised to call her in the morning.

So this too was part of birth, I thought to myself, the last part, the afterbirth long after the afterbirth, when it's over at last, the cycle has come round, the mother isn't known as a mother any more but by another title which I couldn't bring myself to pronounce yet, when she becomes useless as a placenta after a new life has begun.

Tonight I had finished giving birth to my daughter. My part was done. There was nothing else anyone wanted from me except silence. Karen's turn would come round too, with her daughter, which she must know tonight, as she knew everything tonight, in the place where parallel lines meet. If only by five minutes, the whole road of motherhood no longer lay ahead of her. She'd already used up part of her time—that must account for a few of her tears—but it didn't matter. By tomorrow she'd forget that fact in the busyness of the present moment.

Did my grandchild, baby nameless in her bin, look any different from the others? She was bigger than most, which made her face fuller and more babylike. And she was strong-willed. Look at the way those fists were clenched, a person to be taken into account, pure Scorpio for sure, a woman I didn't seem to meet so much as recognize—my companion, my equal. The future was laid out in front of me on display. It was all there. Nothing could be changed or added.

Well then, what did I feel toward my granddaughter?

Nothing. How could I have feelings for someone I hadn't felt—with my hands, that is, through my skin? We hadn't been put in touch with each other yet.

Now I know why people shake hands when they meet. Meeting is touch. Sex is touch and nothing but touch, but way down deep where it counts. Licking is touch through our most delicate finger. Smell is touch. Mathematics and music and sculpture are touch. Writing is not touch but memory of touch, which is why it is more dubious and susceptible to excess. Marriage is touch, in the few minutes when it's marriage. Children, above all, are touch.

I wanted to break through the glass, hold her in my arms, with none of that swaddling coming between us, and kiss her. No, that's a subterfuge for what I really wanted to do. I wanted to lick her.

Mother goats, prevented from licking their kids within the first five minutes after birth, will reject them, even butt them if given the chance, forever after. Expectant rats lick themselves further and further down their bodies as pregnancy advances. If kept from doing so, their mammary glands grow to only half their normal size. In a study in Guatemala, doctors found that there was a high rate of skin infections among Indian infants born in hospitals, while among infants born at home in the villages to the same sort of families, the rate of infection was extremely low. The doctors theorized that the mothers who kissed their newborn children gave them their own organisms, such as staphylococci, in prophylactic doses.

Or maybe it worked the other way round, and the mothers transmitted antibiotics from their mouths. My dinner-table chatter with Stanley Berkman may not have been as ridiculous as I thought. What I have, I share. What I am, my baby is also. When I kiss, I lick. When I lick, I taste. I am the witch who devours, but I am also the mother tongue that licks the hazards of the world into my child's system.

My grandmother may have been right, too—in fact, all of us women may be rightest whenever we're silliest: Twitch the nun's skirt. Before history began, for all we know, there may have been a time when holy men and women passed their holiness through their clothes like body odor, and those who touched them yanked loose a bit of luck. Maybe a king's touch really had the power to heal. Maybe there was an authentic laying on of hands. Maybe the purpose of biology is nothing but this, to draw living organisms closer and closer together, so that they may become more and more complex, as the normal cells in my body, if isolated on a glass plate in a laboratory, will draw toward one another, riffling their borders in anxiety and reproducing as they go, until each encounters another cell, at which point they no longer move or reproduce but settle down, having fulfilled their purpose, content to rest in a single incestuous kiss.

Cancer cells lack this sense. They have no contact inhibitions; they go on reproducing even while they pile up on top of one another, which means they have lost touch with their world.

"LOOKS like something Frank Perdue dreamed up," Ted said the next evening, standing in front of the nursery window and studying the bins, with a measure of awe in his voice. He'd come straight from the office, carrying his battered attaché case, five inches deep with a combination lock. I couldn't be sure whether this was still his father's old case that I'd given him, or whether in the past three years he'd had to replace it and worn the new one down already. Felicia had a cold and hadn't come with him.

"You're losing weight," I said in surprise. Something had come over him. Where he used to be puffy and flyaway, his eyes popping slightly as if straining to catch the light a thousandth of a second faster than anyone else, there was a controlled strength now, but there was also a shadow. When I kissed him, I could smell the after-shave lotion on his cheek. His shirt was one hundred percent cotton with stays in the collar. It affects a young man to have his time sold to clients in fifteen-minute packages over a period of five years, I reminded myself. It wears him down to think that any minute he spends looking out of the window comes out of somebody else's pocket. It glorifies, but at the same time depresses him, to know that he's so close to his goal, there's not much farther he can go. He's a sure bet to become a partner, I hear.

"I run three times a week," he said. "Twice around Central Park on Sunday, that's ten miles. I have to have my suits taken in." The hand that he raised to pull the front of his jacket forward in order to show me the excessive space was carefully manicured.

"Alterations are expensive," Kurt said sympathetically. "Maybe you should give up running."

"Never mind. You look wonderful," I said. "It's very becoming."

But for once in our lives my crown prince, my *stupor mundi*, the baby who had invented me as a mother, wasn't the first in the family to do something. He, who had always been the bountiful one, the giver and teacher, had nothing to give or teach his younger sister today.

RUSHING the carriage up Lexington in the blackness that first winter, late as usual, I could almost feel the lump of cold wet cloth diaper, not changed recently enough, between the baby's thighs, which were dirty too, two different kinds of acid making his privates sore. He screamed. The sound, closer to the screech of faulty brakes than to human speech—any animal that purrs or whines sounds more nearly human than a squalling baby—came from behind his palate with no inflection or rhythm of its own, except the rhythm of breathing. He could keep it up forever.

Men hurrying from the subway, on their way home from their downtown world to the city of women and children, stared at the delinquent mother, the child whose eyes were squeezed shut with exhaustion. The kind of women who lived around here belonged indoors by this hour. I was the only one left outside, exposing my baby in his carriage to the blackness that would somehow leave its mark on him. I prayed that the elevator would be in the lobby for once, waiting for us.

Even after we reached the apartment, there was a delay. I had to strip off his pram suit, his overalls, his filthy underclothes, and fill his bathinette from the tub while the bottle of milk jiggled in a saucepan of water. If I lingered a minute too long with his bath, the milk would be too hot and I'd have to take time to run it under cold water at the sink. At last the moment came when I could thrust the nipple into the mouth too angry to receive it. The baby felt a squirt against the back of his throat, choked, coughed, cried in shock or in declaration that he wasn't to be bought off so easily, then cried because he wanted milk and couldn't have it unless he sacrificed his crying, swallowed again and shuddered through the length of his body but went on sucking and sucking, stopping only for another few gasps of memory, and quickly lapsed into another state, as did I, two orgasms perfectly timed.

When the baby's father came home a short time later, he saw a child fresh from his bath, wrapped in a receiving blanket in his mother's arms, sleepily emptying his bottle of milk.

"I'M THINKING of getting a home gym," Ted said to Kurt rather than to me. "The Marcy M-1, maybe. Carries two hundred-pound weights."

It was the sight of the manicured nails that made me want to cry. None of the marvels I'd been given could make up for what I'd lost.

"What are you going to name the baby?" he asked.

"Carrie," Kurt said.

"I didn't know you'd picked a name," I said, because I had to say something.

"Short for Karen. Sort of."

"Oh," Ted said, humbly accepting the fact that was given him. "I thought it was short for Cash And."

I'd been so caught up in my own life that I'd overlooked the most obvious possibility of all—the possibility that a child may be named for its mother.

Chapter 8

EVERY death is followed in its own way by a sort of liberation, whether we want to be liberated or not.

All during Martin's life, if he was sleepless, the point of no return was the hour between three and four, when it was too late to go to the bathroom and take another sleeping pill but too long to wait until morning, when the furnace would start up in winter or the underground sprinklers turn on with a clang in summer, after which the newspaper hit the driveway with a thud that startled the crows.

No one told me to stay at the hospital with Martin that night in December, three years past. No one called me to put down the book I was reading in bed at home and drive back to New York. Martin had no roommate any more, which was a signal of its own that this is what you get in the way of luxury if you're a terminal case and rich enough to die in style: a room to yourself in New York, with the door shut and a wife who reads her book in bed in Westchester.

If he was still awake at half-past three, which is the hour I read on the death certificate later, or if he woke up for the event and coughed, or cried out, or said he was in pain, or left a message, or didn't leave a message because he was choking on the fluid that filled up his lungs, nobody told me about it. He must have been choking on his own fluid, because he didn't leave any message. So Martin was the one who died by drowning after all, the man who would never set foot in a boat.

For the first time, there was no one to attend to his words or the lack of them.

Just as well. If I'd been there, I might not have been able to stop myself. I might have tried to hold him back.

If there was one thing about me that Martin couldn't stand, it was my habit of dawdling in the doorway at a party after I'd said goodbye, for one more snatch of conversation with someone I'd neglected until that part of the evening, one more point to make, as if I hadn't had plenty of time already to make it. In the back of my head was the vague idea that this was some sort of compliment to my hosts, showing that I'd had such a good time I didn't want to leave. It showed I was neither here nor there, said Martin, who didn't care for things that were neither here nor there.

Now that I look back at my habit and his response, I realize that I've never been good at putting anything behind me. I stay in bed too late in the morning; I run behind schedule all day and then putter in the kitchen long after midnight; I put off writing a letter but once started I can't put an end to it. I constantly fall off the margins of my day, which has to be the reason—how could it have taken me so long to see this?—that I was determined to have another baby when I was almost forty. It wasn't because I was such a success as a mother that I wanted to succeed again, but because I'd missed so many opportunities. I'd never given a single day, not even a single hour, the attention it deserved and that I meant to bring it, but never mind the past, I was just getting warmed up for the task around the time that Ted and Karen began to think about college. By then I was charged with energy, the way I was charged with a sure sense of what ought to be done the next day while I rambled around the kitchen after midnight.

Martin was nothing like me. When it was time to leave a party, he stood up and said good-bye and walked out the door, taking me by the arm. "Of course you have a choice," he'd tell me. "You can come with me, or you can run behind the car."

No, he wasn't the sort to linger at half-past three in the morning because he'd thought of something that hadn't been said in twenty-eight years. Or if he thought of something, I didn't know about it. I only knew that he disappeared between night and breakfast. There was no dying, much less death; there was only disappearance. I never saw him again. I never went back to the hospital room—why should I? The coffin would have been closed in any case, even if the doctor hadn't asked of me what he did. That way I could tell myself that Martin wasn't with me because he was away on a long business trip. Captains of sailing ships had often been gone for two, three years at a time, hadn't they?—and nobody thought to feel sorry for their wives.

Permission to do an autopsy was what the doctor asked of me. (I was never sure if it was the same call with a break in the middle, or if we'd hung up and he had called back later on that morning.) Clearer diagnosis. Possible benefit to my children in future years. "I understand," I said. "But wait three or four hours. At least." Lingering, I knew, was my habit, not Martin's, but still I couldn't be sure but that those who have been loved so ferociously and with so many of the accoutrements of love can only little by little pack up and remove themselves from the places that have served them. The incisions would be stitched up, of course, as in any other operation; the body would look quite normal. But Martin might need to use his body, for all I knew, a few hours longer, while he grew accustomed to new conditions, the way he used to need his lounge chair in the backyard—who was I to take it away from him?—so long as there was a patch of sunshine, however slanted, anyplace in the garden where he could park it.

In any case, the coffin would have been closed for the funeral, because German Jews value restraint above all other virtues, if only to prove how non-Russian we are, particularly if restraint is combined with breeding, education, achievements and family, so that there's something worth being restrained about. During visiting hours at the funeral chapel, the coffin, which was mahogany, not rosewood (nothing flamboyant in the ground), would lie at the back of the room with its lid shut, like a dining-room sideboard with drawer partitions lined in velvet to hold the family silver, while the callers chatted about any subject under the sun except the obvious one. (Martin was always particularly amusing when he paid condolence calls.)

At the funeral, no one would be expected to cry, especially not me, most especially not as I walked back up the aisle after the coffin, when everyone could see me. Let the Russian Jews wail, fall on one another's shoulders, tear their clothes, or, in a more practical vein, pin squares of fabric to their lapels and tear those, shroud their mirrors, bury the dead in pine coffins, and listen for the thumps as they threw the first shovelfuls of dirt on the coffin themselves, instead of leaving the job for the cemetery workers to do in decent obscurity. Let them sit on wooden boxes instead of chairs for a week of mourning. For us Germans, the less that showed, whether it was silverware or tears, the more was assumed to exist underneath. A weeping widow meant that a lover must be waiting in the wings. Of course, only our mothers were of German ancestry, Martin's and mine—our fathers were Russian—which was an extra incentive to show restraint.

True to the traditions of the tribe, on the day after the funeral,

Peter went back to school with a note excusing his absence for the past three days on the ground that he'd had a cold. That was the way he insisted it be done.

Later, a brown-paper bag was left for me at the hospital office, containing Martin's watch—the cheap one, not the good one—his eyeglasses and office telephone directory, plus a pajama top with the collar seam bleached white, still holding the damp, minty smell of sweat and Noxzema. Also his gold wedding ring, which disturbed me. I hadn't supposed it was big enough to slip over his knuckle.

so I wasn't there. I'm never there. I'm never even aware of the instant of change until afterward. Three times I've lain in bed and faced the ceiling and told myself this is it, I feel a feeling of fullness, I've conceived, I'm pregnant, but each time I doubted my feeling an hour later and didn't think about it again for another six or eight weeks, after which I discovered that I must have been right in the first place. I was sound asleep for Ted's birth. I missed seeing Karen's head sticking out in her caul. I came closest to catching a glimpse of Peter. I wasn't with my mother the day my father walked out on her or the day my grandmother died, either. I finally told Peter what was going to happen to his father, but by the time that I sat down with him and told him that we had a couple of days left to us, I was wrong. We had only a few hours, and Peter and I slept through them.

I can't even say that I'm not there at the instant when I'm needed, because that's the worst of it: I'm never needed for these events, they simply happen without me.

When the phone rang at a few minutes after seven in the morning, I knew what I was going to hear before I lifted the receiver. (If the call had come earlier, the message would have been that Martin was still alive.) I could imagine the doctor—someone—saying, Why not let her get her rest? What can she do about it anyway? Seven o'clock gives her a night's sleep, but it's still early enough to catch her at home before the day begins. Besides, at this hour it'll be all right for her to call her children. I knew the voice could only tell me I'd missed the moment I'd been waiting for once again. For several hours now, I hadn't been what I thought I was when I went to sleep.

Continuity, the scientists tell us, is an illusion imposed by the limits of our perception, like seeing motion on a screen from a series of still frames on film. The truth is that each second annihilates the cosmos. Each second creates the cosmos all over again. The universe leaps like a mountain goat across a series of gaps. From the void to the creation of matter, the universe leaps a gap. From inorganic matter on innumerable bodies to organic matter on one that we know about, another gap is leaped. From nonnucleated cells to nucleated cells, perhaps the greatest transit of all occurs; from algae to plants, from water creatures to land creatures, from animal to human, more gaps, more leaps, with precious little left in between to show us that there has to be a track.

We never can rest so long as we're half of something else. An atom is carbon, or perhaps it's gold. We never catch carbon while it's in the act of turning into gold. Not even the alchemists were able to do that, catch what they were after, which wasn't anything as ordinary as gold, but the energy that was needed to make gold—not change, but transformation, which lifts a substance out of its ordinary state and carries it to a higher level.

So I tell myself, for whatever it's worth, that it wouldn't have made any difference if a night nurse had phoned me that night and told me to come down to the hospital at once, and I'd driven to New York as fast as I could. (But it would have made a difference. It would.) I still wouldn't have seen Martin dying. I would have seen Martin alive, and I would have seen him dead, but I wouldn't have caught the instant in between. I can't help it, I always blink, so that my eyes are shut whenever something real is coming at me.

WINTER solstice. Cloudy and cold, with a chance of snow, and that particular year, the Shah falling. Christmas. Chanukah. Light shrunk to a single point. Darkness about to engulf us. Starting from that point, the Virgin Birth, attended only by angels and animals, higher powers and lower powers, or the flame that goes on burning for eight days without fuel, straight through the octave of time. Something out of nothing, that's what's demanded of us, something impossible with what we've got, demanded at the moment when we can muster the least strength to manage it, something beyond our capacity, not to be salvaged or extrapolated from what we already know we possess: a child or a flame born without a source, a child kept going without a father, a flame that burns without oil.

Something out of something alien, that's what's required. A cathedral spire in the snow. Love of God in a rigorous climate. Tomorrow after today.

At the end, during those last days in the hospital, a time came when I no longer cared about Martin, not in the way I had cared before. For the first time in my life, I had to learn to give up. On one level, it mattered a great deal to me whether he lived for a few more weeks or not. On another level, it no longer mattered at all. There has to be room for everything, including death. Go if you must, I told him. I won't hold you back. Do what you have to do. Don't worry about me, as I'll no longer worry about you. We're out of each other's hands.

If those words sounded like a prayer, it was because they so completely contradicted my usual personality.

"WHEN did you and Kurt decide to have a child?" I asked Karen on the phone one night, while the baby was sleeping for a little while at least. Carrie had colic; she was by no means an easy child. Karen was surviving on snatches of food and rest.

"Who said we decided?"

"You mean you didn't want one?" I tried not to let her hear that I was appalled. "Or you didn't want one now?"

"Of course we wanted one." She sounded irritable, either because she heard me all too well, or because she had to decide what to tell the carpenter who was coming the next day to partition the storage closet in the second bedroom into two sections, one for the baby's clothes and the other for their own out-of-season things. "That's not the same as deciding to have one. We let things happen, that's all."

"You mean your mother never told you about birth control?"

"Look, you don't want to have a baby, you don't have one." It was important to me to picture my daughter always in command of what she was doing. "But if you have no real reason not to have a child, you just let go. You don't do anything to prevent it. You go with the flow."

So she'd never made up her mind to become pregnant. She'd become pregnant first and decided afterwards that this was the best possible turn of events, which was the answer to the question I wanted to ask her.

"You know what my friends said when I told them I was pregnant with Peter? 'Opinion in the neighborhood is divided,' they said. 'Half of us think Martin is crazy, and the other fifty percent think you are.'" And yet Pete's was the most deliberate conception of the three, I failed to tell her.

The other day I saw some old snapshots in a plastic cube on Karen's bureau, and tried to remember where our decisions came from. Who went upstairs and grabbed a camera, why were we living in this house, why had I given birth when I was almost forty, and what made us buy the puppy I saw climbing into the wading pool I'd forgotten we ever set out on the terrace? The only decision that came through as undeniably mine was the outfit I wore. Yes, I said. I acknowledge that pants suit. I remember picking it out.

This is the feeling I've come to lately: that I don't reach my decisions at all, but wait for my decisions to reach me, pretty much the way that my children reached me, fully formed, with nothing left for me to do but work out the details. The trouble is that I can't feel a decision coming toward me when I need one, although I can feel one creeping up on Ted, just as I used to sense a day in advance, when he was a child, that he was coming down with a cold, because he turned cranky. He isn't cranky now. He's riding high. He has lost so much weight on his diet of yogurt and bran that he went to Barney's and bought three new suits (I hope he let Felicia help pick them out), so that he can't afford to gain it back. Can he be thinking about switching jobs?

So Ted grows thin. And Karen grows motherly. But what about me? My children expect me to develop a new life for myself as cheerfully as they used to expect me to set a good dinner on the table every night. Everyone expects it, including me. I don't know how to admit that I can't remember how the trick is done.

At this point, I'm supposed to give birth to myself as my own last child, a self that may have a life-span of thirty, even forty years stretching ahead of it, assuming that Victor's genes are my genes— which is more time than Keats or Masaccio spent on earth, I remind myself, maybe as many years as the Brontës or Chopin or Pascal. But how am I supposed to become pregnant at my age? Homer says that mares turn their backs to the north wind, and are impregnated in that way without the help of stallions. Something can only be born out of nothing, out of north wind and darkness, out of what chills our bones, at the instant when we turn our backs to it.

I'll go to India and work with Mother Teresa. I'll find a job. I'll find a lover. I'll read John Donne. I'll sail to the Marquesas. I'll find six lovers, I'll sail to the Marquesas reading John Donne to my lovers on the way. I'll run for the board of the League of Women Voters. I'll run a shelter for bag ladies. What I need is to be needed.

"DID I tell you I took Peter to the Ground Round for a hamburger last night for his birthday?" I asked. "His choice, needless to say, not mine." On Saturday—this was Wednesday—we were going to have a family birthday celebration at a French restaurant in Greenwich Village for Ted and Peter and now for Carrie as well, even though she wouldn't be at the table this year.

Peter hasn't been the same since his trip West this summer. He won't eat lunch, for instance, at least not at home, or not where I can see him. He won't eat dessert at the dinner table. If he takes a Good Humor from the freezer, he eats it sitting on the back steps with the kitchen door closed. And I'm not allowed to go into stores with him any more if he needs clothes. In he goes by himself, but not until he first comes home after school and combs his hair and changes his T-shirt. If he can't get home first, he runs his fingers through his hair in the car, then in he goes to the shoe store to ask the salesman if he carries Tru-Form or Adidas or Nike. He goes into the record store and comes out wearing a shirt with a female skeleton painted on it, crowned by a wig of roses. He has discovered name bands and brand names. He's getting ready to leave me for good.

The night after we went to the Ground Round, I came home after having dinner with friends and went into the bathroom while Peter was brushing his teeth before bed, holding the brush vertically and rotating the tip at the base of his gums. He wore jeans and a leather belt, nothing else. Pajamas seemed as remote as sunsuits. As of this fall, I no longer tell him when to go to bed. "Say, how did you do in your cross-country meet today?" I asked.

"Not bad."

"Who won?"

"We did."

"Terrific. And how did you do?"

"About the middle." He spat, then attacked the back teeth so he couldn't talk. For some reason his face looked pinched with suffering.

"But that's wonderful." Is that the tone I'd have used if he'd been six inches taller, if his face had been pimpled and intermittently bearded already, like others in his class, if he'd been less beautiful, less pained, less obsessed by the evils of plaque?

He glared. "So why's it wonderful?"

"If you can place in the middle when you're only in ninth grade, you ought to be varsity for sure by the time you're in eleventh or twelfth." By the time your legs grow longer, I meant. "You must have beaten a lot of eleventh and twelfth graders today."

"So what?"

"Well, I think that's great."

"Well, it's not. A lot of ninth graders beat me." I straightened up the shelf where he kept calamine, Cutter's, shoe polish, even though I knew this would annoy him. He finished his attack on the inside lowers and then cupped water in his hands and took a mouthful, which he swished through his teeth for a full minute. Ever since he returned from his trip, he has refused to use a bathroom glass, which he considers unsanitary.

"You haven't told me the single important thing."

"What's that?"

"Did you have a good time at the meet?"

He frowned, while genuine wonder seeped under the edges of his anger. "What do you want to know that for?" he asked. "What difference could it make to you?"

KAREN was thoughtful. "I'll do it the cheap way. It doesn't pay to put too much money into remodeling a closet. If we have another child, we're going to need a larger apartment anyway."

"Listen to yourself," I said. "You're planning another child already. And you wouldn't have moved into a two-bedroom apartment in the first place if you hadn't counted on having one. Didn't I tell you that you were nothing but a salmon heading upstream to spawn?"

"Well, we certainly didn't plan on not having one. We made ourselves available. That's all there was to it." She began telling me about a friend who gave her newborn baby eight ounces of milk, and the baby threw up. "Nobody told her not to give a newborn that much. Nobody tells you anything. She had to stop and figure out if that's why the baby vomited." She wanted me to tell her that she wasn't the cause of her daughter's stomach pains. Suddenly her voice lifted, like leaves showing their pale undersides in the first gusts before a storm. "Just listen. Carrie's fussing. Now I've lost my chance to sleep."

"LET ME look at the debutante. Out at this hour of night." Marion held open her arms to her great-grandchild for the first time. Never had her apartment seemed so dark. Karen and I might have been passing from a city street into the subway when we wheeled the carriage out of the elevator, negotiated the tricky turn in the hallway and passed through the unlocked door of apartment A. We hung up our coats while the baby slept in her carriage in the foyer. "I've been waiting for you all afternoon."

"Well, it takes a lot of time for Mom to pick me up from Westchester, and then I had to wake Carrie and change and dress her," Karen answered placidly.

"Aren't you going to bring her in here?" But Karen had already gone back to the foyer while I trailed after her to watch as she rolled the baby over, unzipped the pram suit and picked her up with flips of her wrist that went straight through my heart.

"Not that way. The other way," Marion said, her eyes not on us while she gestured that Karen should come around to the other side of her chair and put Carrie in her left arm, instinct pushing its way through the brambles after all.

Karen drew up the dressing-table bench and laid the diaper bag on it. It was the bench that my great-grandmother and I used for a card table—we were pretty close to the same size, when I was six—when she taught me the difference between big casino and little casino, both of us in awe of the two full-size women who talked in another room, and happy to be out of their way.

So here we were once again, where three of us have been before: four generations of women in one room, a ladder of women on which I've climbed to the third rung. But what keeps us here together? Who needs whom?

Karen doesn't need me for anything: not for money, not for advice, not even for baby care (she has already hired someone who'll come in by the day when she goes back to work) any more than I need Marion, or would take help from her even if I did. For that matter, Karen doesn't need Kurt. She has a job, which means she has two strings to her bow. She can quit her job or she can quit her husband—granted, it would be tough—or she can hold on to both.

Carrie needs someone, but, for the next six months anyway, it needn't be her mother. She'll let anybody pick her up and care for her, because nature protects her during the time when she and her mother are most vulnerable by seeing to it that her need is impersonal. The first time that she smiles because she knows whom she's smiling at, the first time she cries when I pick her up because she recognizes that I'm not her mother, I'll know that she has fallen from the freedom of angels into the bumpy world of love and need along with the rest of us.

The only one of us who needs her parents is Marion, whose mother and father are in the room with us right now. Her father is a chifforobe; her mother is an armchair. Between them, they support her. She doesn't need a husband. Thank God for that. She doesn't need her daughter or her grandchildren, either. She can hire nurses to do whatever children are supposed to do, without giving her any back talk while they're at it.

How lucky we are, how exposed to risk we are, a twentieth-century phenomenon but not common even now, four generations of women who live in three separate households supported by four incomes, freed from gratitude toward one another as we are from obligation. We are a set of unmatched Royal Worcester cups. Nothing can be taken for granted among us. Everything becomes possible. Even rupture. Even tenderness.

"Wake up," Marion said to Carrie, who was asleep in the crook of her arm. "I've so many stories to tell you." She stroked the infant's cheek. She ran her long bent knuckle over the indigo sole of the baby's foot. Carrie stretched her arms up, one at a time.

"See how she's reaching?" Karen whispered to me. "That's insecurity. Like a monkey. She's grabbing for the next branch."

"You want a lollipop?" Marion said. "Is that what you're reaching for, because you know I'll give you a lollipop? Yes, I will." She wagged her head from side to side, prepared to bury her face in assent to the sweet new flesh, great-grandmother at last, but also grandmother and mother at last, transformed for a golden minute into the mother I never thought I would have. A minute is enough. It brings a new self into existence that may be snuffed out in the next minute, but that can never afterward be said not to have existed, equal in authenticity to all the other selves that appear and disappear inside our bodies. "Oh, yes I will. And I'll tell you so many stories. I've been saving them up for you."

Carrie hovered between sleeping and waking, then seemed about to settle back to sleep again. Marion rubbed the side of her finger over the soles of her feet this time. "Let her sleep," I said.

"She should sleep on her own time." The baby lay crumpled like a leaf on her lap. I could feel Karen, who'd moved over to the dressing-table bench, grow tense. "Isn't that right? What else do you have to do but sleep and eat? You're just like me, aren't you?"

"She should try a little more sleep," I said. "Karen hasn't had more than four hours at a stretch since she got out of the hospital."

"Four? I haven't had two."

"And whose fault is that, if you wouldn't have a nurse? What else did you expect?" But Marion spoke without her usual fire, peering into the baby's upturned face while she talked. "A little night owl, that's what you are, aren't you? You want to go nightclubbing, is that it?"

"She didn't have to expect colic," I said sharply. Couldn't she see how tired Karen looked? The sparkle had vanished from her surface—she hadn't even taken enough time to brush her hair. Her regular clothes didn't fit yet. She was wearing an old gray wraparound skirt of mine that made her waistline look puffy and shapeless. "Lawzy, Miz Scarlett, you done gone and had a baby," I'd told her. "You never gwine to have a sixteen-inch waist again."

"And that's the way you're going back to your job?" Marion asked her. "Leaving a colicky baby at home? You'll make yourself sick for sure."

Karen's face was broader, in spite of the lines of fatigue, but it was her eyes that had changed, focused and yet flickering, as if they were satellite stations for the third eye, the one that had developed during the past two weeks, stationed inside her child's body from which it sent her a constant stream of messages.

Karen stared at her child, who was beginning to clutch the air again. Marion stared at Karen's child. I stared at my own child, who'd always been thin but who had never looked as thin and tired as she did at this minute, deprived of her food and rest by this colicky newcomer who was no daughter of mine. This was the way I used to feel when Karen was a little girl playing in the sandbox in the park with the other children, who were so much lustier and bigger than she was, even if they were no older, that they were bound to grab her toys. But for some reason they never did.

"They lose those monkey reflexes when they're a few weeks old," she murmured. As she turned toward me, I noticed spots on her blouse, the first I'd ever seen on her. Even as a child, she'd been immaculate. The spots were as much a declaration of a change in status as the first time she let Kurt kiss her in front of us.

"I'll keep a box of lollipops in that drawer just for when you come to see me," Marion said. She jiggled her knees, she patted the infant with her free hand, but she knew it was no use. Carrie was making unhappy noises. Karen put her hands on the bench, ready to rise.

"My turn," I said, taking the baby out of Marion's arm and hoisting her over my shoulder.

The baby drooped her head beneath my chin. I'd moved because

I wanted to rescue not only Carrie but Karen, not because I chose to move. All the same, I'd brought something to an end. Something had gone out of the room, a grace that had hovered over Marion for a while the way a hawk hangs over a hill, motionless for a moment before sliding away down a current of wind.

"That's the way you hold a baby when she's restless," Karen explained as she watched me walk around the room. If I dared to sit down, the baby was sure to fret again. But no, she seemed to like my gait. So far, I was doing all right. Karen made no move to take her away. The hand resting on my shoulder was uncurled.

But Marion had slumped in her chair and reached for a cigarette. All that jiggling and tickling, why couldn't the woman ever hold still? Now I understood why she'd put on the most appalling clothes she owned, the same old gray sweater and skirt. Before we came in, she'd known that she was heading for another defeat. The family had one more member now who was due to turn away from her. "Carrie," she said. "Whatever made you pick a name like that? Sister Carrie. Carrie on. Carrie me back to old Virginny." Karen lowered her eyes, as Marion blew smoke from her cigarette in our direction.

From the bed to the chifforobe, from the chifforobe to the bureau I walked, and as I walked it seemed that the spaces between the rungs of the ladder were far from equal. Between Carrie and Karen the space was enormous. Between Marion and me, the distance seemed very short, with the foreshortening of time which is so cruelly opposite in effect to the foreshortening of space. From Carrie's point of view, Marion and I would seem equally ancient.

When I got to the bureau, I stopped in front of the mirror that hung above it. In order to see the baby, I had to turn my back and look over my shoulder, a bad angle for any woman my age but especially for a gaunt one like me, all tooth and sinew, the view of myself I sometimes catch in store windows. I hadn't realized I was smiling so broadly. I would be the first woman in the family in three generations to be called Grandma.

"What did you do for Peter's birthday?" I could hear from Marion's tone that she was afraid she'd been left out of something.

"Not a thing. I took him to the Ground Round for dinner."

"And that's all?"

"Tuesday was a school night, remember?" I didn't choose to tell her about the family party we were going to have tomorrow. "But you want to know what he's doing right now? As one of his birthday treats, he wanted me to buy him a saucepan at the five-and-ten, so he could melt marshmallows and make some godawful marshmallow-and-Rice-Krispies concoction he got off the back of the box." Peter was fooling us on his fourteenth birthday by pretending that he was a little boy who wanted treats, at the same time that he proved how cheaply he could provide them—nothing but a box of cereal and a bag of marshmallows. I got the message about what I could do with my offers of cakes from Carvel. But how quick I'd been to bring this piece of news to the city, proving that I too was the mother of a young child.

"I can hold the baby on my shoulder like that," Marion said. I laid her in position on Marion's left shoulder and sat down opposite them again. Karen and Marion began talking about bath towels. Marion didn't have any that weren't frayed; Karen had bought a stack of irregulars at the white sales in July. The air in the room was ringing with the old wives' rhyme: "A son is a son till he gets him a wife, But a daughter's a daughter for all of her life." Ted and Marion and I would never sit in a room alone with his baby.

"If I give you three or four, you won't have to send your cleaning woman down to the washing machines in the cellar so often, so you wind up saving money in the long run." But Carrie, who'd been growing increasingly restless, broke into real crying at this point. "It's your time, isn't it?" Out of a yellow plastic diaper bag Karen produced a yellow insulated container that looked like a thermos but held a bottle of cold milk, bottle and all—only it didn't hold milk, it held a soybean substitute.

I waited to be sure that I wouldn't make a fool of myself by assuming that the baby was going to drink the formula ice cold. "You think I could feed her?" When Karen said of course I could—I got the feeling that she'd thought this out beforehand—I scooped Carrie off Marion's shoulder, while she rolled herself into a ball like a caterpillar that has just been touched. Food was on the way, I tried to tell her with my hands. What's more, I was going to be the source of it.

Carrie frowned when I nudged her lips with the nipple, as if I'd given her something obnoxious to taste, before she decided that she recognized it and settled down to feed. I could feel the bones and the fold of hot skin at the bottom of her skull, like the pulsing triangle underneath a cat's chin.

"Nothing like my child," Marion commented. "I never saw her clean a plate in her life."

"Or like me," Karen added politely. "I suppose she eats so well because I don't expect it."

No, she was nothing like her mother. This granddaughter of mine, with the jowls of a middle-aged bridge player, laid her hand on the bottle as if to make clear her claim to it.

"Give her a piece of candy for every meal she keeps down, that's what the pediatrician told me," Marion said. "Even if it's breakfast. And spank her every time she throws up."

Carrie thrust her toes against my side, climbing me as if I were a tree, while I put her on my shoulder to burp her. Her left foot pushed too hard against my nipple, sending a thrill through my pelvis. I moved the foot a couple of inches, but still felt a painful pressure. But whoever thought that a newborn baby was small? Only a man could have said that, looking at a baby as an object in space, comparing her fingernail to his fingernail, her foot to his foot.

" 'You'll only have to spank her once,' the doctor told me. After all the pediatricians I'd taken her to."

Inconceivably large, that's what an infant was, looked at across time the way a woman would look at her—not only large, in fact, but immense to have crouched between my daughter's hipbones only a little more than a week ago. By another one of those miraculous coincidences, she'd been born exactly the right length to rest between my elbow and my palm, or else my forearm had been designed to be exactly the right length to support her.

"Nothing but bananas when she had whooping cough," Marion was saying. "Because it's impossible to throw up bananas. Remember I told you that. No one can throw up a banana."

A flood of thankfulness poured through me for what Karen was allowing me to do. Had she noticed how neatly I'd burped the baby? "See?" I held up the bottle in triumph. "I never let them drink the last half ounce. Too many bubbles in it."

It was too much for Marion to endure. Karen went into the foyer to get Carrie's pram suit and then laid her on the bed to dress her. "Put your own coat on first," Karen instructed me. "I don't want the baby to sweat."

"I'll walk Karen home and help her get settled and then come back here," I said to Marion. I was having dinner at her house.

"You know why the baby cried when I held her, don't you?" Marion said, in the tone of someone who'd been waiting to have the last word. Her jaw pointed forward, to show us she was prepared to take it on the chin for speaking the truth, but at the same time, she peered at us through half-shut eyes, like a child, to see if we believed her. "I may have soiled my underpants. That's why, if you must know. The baby smelled it and thought her own diapers were dirty, and that's why she started to cry."

"I'll bet you're right," Karen said.

BY THE time we got to Karen's apartment, Carrie was asleep. Karen took off the pram suit while the baby was still lying on her stomach in the carriage, and prepared to lift her like a poached egg into her crib.

"Don't you want to change her first?"

How many furious excuses would I have tossed out in Karen's place? Can't you give me a minute? I want to wash my hands. Will you let me get to the bathroom first? What do you think I was just about to do when you interrupted me? Interrupted us, I'd mean. Came between mother and child.

"Oh," said Karen, speaking to Carrie with a lift of pleasure in her tone, as if she'd just heard a piece of remarkable cleverness. "Isn't it lucky for you that you have a grandmother?"

SO HOW does a woman achieve easiness of soul?

Through the knowledge as a child that her mother admires her. After all these years, I'm sure of that with the same conviction that makes my mother sure nobody can vomit up bananas. No other source matters, not even a father, who's bound to be so happy having his little girl sit on his lap that his judgment doesn't count—particularly not my father's judgment, because another of my mother's lessons was that his judgment wasn't to be trusted, and most particularly not where it concerned me.

Admired, I insist, not just loved. The mother must see qualities in the child that she herself lacks, as I see Karen's spirit, contained and containing as a lake, as Karen already sees and will admire her daughter's stubbornness and fire. But here's what I find hard to grasp: that my daughter can be easy with me in a way that I've never been able to be easy with my mother.

For such a long time now, I've been afraid. In fact, I've been afraid all my life. I was afraid of my mother when I was little, I was afraid of losing my husband's love, and ever since they've left home I've been afraid of my grown-up children, which is the worst fear of all because it's another word for loneliness, which is another way of saying that I'm growing old and one day I'll be just like my mother, and there's nothing on earth I can do to stop myself.

No. The truth as I see it now is more awful than that.

I won't be like my mother at all, but I'll be sitting there in my mother's place, wearing a velour robe and waiting in front of the window for the day to pass, and when my children see me silhouetted against the light, how will they realize that I'm not the person they take me for, my name isn't Marion or even Mother or Mom, I'm Joan and I'm thirty years old and taking a boat around a windward mark?

By some miracle I don't understand, all three of my children seem to be able to tell my mother and me apart.

"YOU don't mind that I didn't wait to have my drink?" Marion asked, when I got back to the apartment.

"Of course not. Let me turn on the light."

"So what do you think of that baby?"

"What do you mean, what do I think? What's to think? She's a wonderful baby."

"That's not a baby. That's a doll." She landed heavily each time on the word "that," sensing that I can't stand it when she turns a baby into an animal or, worse yet, a thing. The doll, she says. The butcher, the baker, the candlestick maker. The Pot. *Das Kind.* This afternoon she called me Karen again, although she never calls Karen Joan. She calls Sylvia "Sonya" more than half the time, but when speaking to me she refers to her as Rachmones—sometimes she calls her that to her face—which is a Yiddish and Hebrew word meaning pity, compassion, one of the Attributes of the Divine, derived from the root *rechem,* meaning "a mother's womb." This is the term she has corrupted to mean "poor slob." "Don't you dare tell her what Rachmones means," she warns me, laughing at her private joke. "That's my secret."

"All right. Have it your own way. She's a doll."

Sylvia came into the room and brought me a drink.

"You think it's all right that Karen's going back to work? Who's she found to mind the baby?"

This subject could take care of us for twenty minutes, if I nursed it along. "A young woman from Honduras, who used to be a schoolteacher. She doesn't speak much English, but she's smart. She and Carrie can learn together."

I gave her a few bits of gossip about green cards and FICA taxes and their effect on the new generation of babies, and she gave me back her comments. We were doing fine. The sight of Karen and her child, so recently seated here, had freshened the air in the room like a summer shower. We were left behind in this clearing, but left behind together.

"Did I tell you about Pete? He's been put on the staff of the school magazine." I knew she'd like me to say that in front of Sylvia. Her lips puffed in and out, as if she were trying to blow up a balloon. "Why don't you use your inhalator? Get some oxygen." The tank stood in the corner behind her chair.

"She don't use it right," Sylvia interjected. "She don't breathe deep, she puffs and pants."

During these past weeks, the insides of Marion's cheeks had drawn closer together. Her eyes had sunk deeper into their sockets. She seemed to be caving in from all directions at once. Either Karen's visit had exhausted her, or else she no longer felt the need to try to sit up straight, now that Karen and Carrie were gone. She was guttering out in front of me.

"I thought you told me last week that the doctor was going to send up a physical therapist. To teach you to use it."

Sylvia grimaced behind my mother's chair, to indicate that her patient had never called the doctor or the therapist to make the arrangements. I chose to ignore Sylvia's complaint.

Marion swatted these accusations away from behind her head. "Peter's on the school newspaper? Does that mean he was elected?"

"Magazine. For a ninth grader, that's not bad. They have a school-wide competition."

She sighed to show that these fine points were beyond her, but she could salute the general result all the same. "A toast to all our children!" She raised the drop that was left in her glass.

"I'll drink to that."

"We have a lot to be thankful for."

"With all our children. And you have one more than I do." For once I was pleased to grant her an edge.

"That's right. I do."

"And I hope I'm included in your toast?"

What ever made me say such a thing?

And what made me say it with just enough of a rising tone at the end so that it sounded like a question, or implied that a question might be present? Why couldn't I leave well enough alone, and raise a glass in a pleasant toast for once? Above all, what made me say it at such a time, just when we were leaning toward each other at last, if only because the role I played was no longer so different from hers?

There must have been a devil inside me, who'd waited for the first sign of weakness to pounce. The moment that her guard was down, I had to come rushing in to show her how she'd wounded me in the past. Or else there was something that I'd wanted from her for such a long time that I had to lunge for it, by hook or by crook, while I still had the chance.

Her eyes were on fire. Her back straightened. Her breath whistled through her teeth and puffed out her upper lip. Her hand slapped the arm of the chair. "How dare you say such a thing!" she raged. "You better take that back right away!"

So I had done it. Accidentally or not, I'd uncovered what it was she wanted from me, and no, it wasn't the assurance that I loved her, I'd been right on that score. What she was after was something much more humiliating to ask for, not to mention demand, from her daughter, and yet I was the only person from whom she could get it. In fact, she wanted what Karen had just given to me unasked. She wanted to be told that she'd been a good mother.

It wasn't enough for me to say that I knew now I resembled her, even if I could bring myself to do that. She needed me to tell her she'd done a good job in the only job she'd ever held. She wanted me to create a brand-new past for her, in which she'd been a well-loved, if abandoned, wife, a proud and attentive mother, a loving mother-in-law. She wanted a past sufficiently worthy that she could bear to leave it without shame. She wanted a life that hadn't ended at nineteen, or ended when her mother died, but had touched the life of at least one other person, who now ratified her existence.

My mother wanted me to write her a letter of references, so that she could leave the house carrying it in her hand. It was typical of her to ask me in an outburst of anger, in order to make sure that I wouldn't give her what she wanted through pity or self-reproach.

Chapter 9

*T*HERE was no need to wear my flat-heeled driving shoes or the old sailing jacket that I used as a driving coat while my good coat lay folded on the seat behind me. I wasn't going to take the car into the city this evening, I was going to take the train for a change. This man had insisted on it. He'd drive me home, he said, after which he'd turn around and drive himself straight back to New York.

So right from the beginning our reacquaintance had the flavor of the period when we last knew each other, back in high school in the forties, as if I'd taken an angora sweater out of the drawer and smelled L'Heure Bleue on it—as if I'd taken it out of the refrigerator, I should say, which is where we stored angoras in those days to keep them from shedding. At least that's where the other girls told me they stored theirs, and I chose to believe them, if only to share their lives to that extent.

If I wasn't driving, I could put on my good shoes and study the relative proportions of my skirt and heels in the bedroom mirror. I wouldn't need a wallet; I'd only need a few dollars for a train ticket, which meant I could carry the small black lizard pocketbook I liked. So many habits were disrupted at once. The smell of my perfume when I sprayed it on came as a shock to me. I put a real handkerchief with an embroidered monogram that matched my dress and a compact that had no powder in it, only a mirror, into my pocketbook, faithful to the forties and fifties myself, but neglected to take a tissue in case I wanted to wipe my lipstick off. But then I never took precautions. I'd never learned the proper way to date. I'd also forgotten to shave my legs. At the last minute I took off my engagement ring and left it in my drawer.

Why was I so terrified, then? Why the headache and gripy bowel when I woke up this morning, and all day since, if this man was already part of my past, and if I was only doing what Martin would have urged me to do long ago, what he urged all his matrimonial clients to do, in fact, the gaggle of the about-to-be-divorced, most of them females who were half in love with their lawyer? "Move to the city," he'd have said. "The suburbs are no place for singles. Give some dinners. Make friends. Make yourself available." Like most extravagant people, he couldn't bear the idea of an opportunity going to waste. He'd have thought of me as one more matrimonial client who needed prodding to get back into action so that she wouldn't be left hanging on the vine.

For a moment I was pleased to think that I hadn't moved into the city, I was doing this my own way and still doing what Martin would have wanted. I'd enhanced my value in his eyes, I'd confirmed his judgment (he never needed his judgment confirmed by anyone else) by attracting another man, not turning into a recluse as I so easily might have done, not given myself to my books and boat and walks to the beach in winter with Ralph.

No, I'd kept myself up to date—in both senses—so as not to humiliate his memory with a woman no other man wanted to have. I was wearing a paisley wool skirt and blouse. My hair is cut short nowadays; it's allowed to curl as much as it wants. My lipstick is pale. I wear practically nothing but separates, generally slacks or jeans and generally with sneakers. With all my heart, I refuse to look like my mother.

But none of these decisions has been come by easily. How can I forgive myself if the lines in my face are lighter than they were three years ago? Too many hours of sleep, too much night cream with collagen in it, have given my face the buttery quality of a nun's, and only my neck is thoroughly real to me, strained and windworn from sailboat racing, with a pale half moon under the chin that stands out against the rest, which is dark with a noticeable grain in it, like weathered teak. I'm learning to cruise. I pack my clothes in a duffle, and off I go on a bareboat charter as skipper with people I hardly know. This affects the way I walk as well as the texture of my skin. Martin would have approved of the fact that I do as I please.

So when I see my friends and neighbors and they let out glad cries about how well I look, in the tone they reserve for widows and the terminally ill, I'm filled with shame. Despite their best efforts to deceive me, they happen to be right. Three years ago, I was a middle-aged housewife. Now I'm an adolescent widow, leaner, tauter, sharper, more defensive, more vulnerable to sick headache and gripy bowel—how lucky that I'm not driving myself to the city tonight, I don't think I could make it—but also lighter on my feet, more sure of myself, less frightened by error and change.

Uncertainty is a subtle cosmetic, acting like a blusher to make me look heartier, more vibrant than I feel. Loneliness is an effective fashion consultant. Had I been aware of the imminence of death every moment of my life (as I should have been, of course), how much more raptly I might have worn paisley wool challis and colored beads.

No, I don't look well for any of the reasons that my friends or neighbors think. I look well because little by little—and this is the reason I'm ashamed—after all this time, with nothing at risk because I've already lost what I was afraid to lose, I'm turning myself into the sort of woman that Martin would have wanted to marry in the first place.

WE MET again at our high school class reunion. He looked exactly the same—well, not the same of course, not sixteen, which was when we last knew each other, but thirty-five or no more than forty at the outside, with the same head of curly hair, nothing to jar the sensibilities there. Our past was between us, and yet our past tactfully declined to come between us. We'd never dated each other in school or even thought about each other "that way," as we'd have put it, not because we disliked each other, but because neither of us was part of the crowd that thought such thoughts yet. I knew he was spectacular in math, but I'd never seen his wristbones. All the same, he was part of my history, and since Martin had accepted me, in a sense he'd accepted this classmate who was so much like me. He'd set his seal of approval on him.

No, he hadn't become a lawyer or stockbroker, he'd become a professor, not of math but of history, he told me, socioeconomic history, with a special interest in technological developments before the Industrial Revolution in relation to social change. He'd been a bit of a radical, if I remembered right. So had all the boys in our class, but none of the girls; it was like playing football. I thought he had an uncle (I was pretty sure he was the one) who worked for Norman Thomas. "Charlemagne conquering Europe because he learned about stirrups from the Arabs," I said, to prove that Bryn Mawr was every bit as good as Princeton. "I've often thought it must be great to live in a college community."

"Did you come alone this evening?" he asked.

"Is it a wonderful life?"

"Not at John Jay, it's not." It was easy to understand why he'd come to this reunion. The school had been a force in his life. His name was on all the word-processed letters I got asking me to contribute to the alumni fund or come to a party in honor of a retiring teacher. I supposed he was still paying off his moral debts as a scholarship student, or maybe he took on those jobs everyone else was too busy to handle just because that's the sort of person he was. From the tone in which he mentioned John Jay, I suspected that this building we were in, these classmates milling around us, had marked the high point in his life, when everybody, students and teachers alike, loved not only him—his brightness, his honor, his smile—but also his future, the luster he was about to shed on us, even if no one was specifically in love with his body. John Jay was what happened to him afterward. He'd brought it to the reunion, his tone of voice told me, because he couldn't leave it home, the way some of the men had to bring along dumpy wives.

But why was I here? Had I liked the school that much? he asked, in a voice that brought those days back in a rush.

"I hated it."

"Then why did you come?"

Before I could answer, an announcement was made that we should please come in to the lunchroom for the buffet supper. The two of us remained where we were. Behind me, the door of a metal coat locker crackled under the pressure of my back. The school population must be larger. I didn't remember lockers this close to the lunchroom. "Mine was at least a mile from any of my classes," I said to the man I was with.

"And you kept going back there to get rid of your books between classes. So you wouldn't be seen carrying them, and we wouldn't think you were as smart as you were."

"I don't remember any such thing." I remembered being invisible, that's what I remembered. He must have imagined the rest. A surge went through the crowd, as one of our classmates was pushed toward the buffet line in her wheelchair, propelled by her husband and surrounded by the girls who'd been her special clique in school. I held my weight on the balls of my feet, making myself as light as I could, not wanting this man to feel obligated by my presence.

"Have you anyone to eat with?" he asked. I looked around the room, as if I could identify his wife without having met her.

No, he was separated, he told me while we ate ham and cold pasta salad and drank wine out of plastic cups—well, he wasn't legally separated, but his wife had spent the past four-and-a-half years on Corfu with an American sculptor of Armenian extraction. She came home for their son's longer vacations from college, at which time she also visited their married daughter. As for him, he was still in a classroom where I'd left him, and alone. I was still working at a typewriter at home, and alone except for Peter. The years in between had left astonishingly few traces visible in our lives, as if we'd gone into separate movie theaters on Eighty-sixth Street on a Saturday afternoon while we were single, then come out and met again on a street that hadn't changed noticeably in our absence. The difference between us was that I couldn't keep Martin out of the conversation for two sentences—he might as well have been sitting at the table on my other side—while my companion never referred to his wife by name.

W H Y was I so uneasy then, a couple of weeks later, when he called and asked me to have supper with him in New York?

Now that I had a chance to study him, I saw that he didn't look thirty-five at all. He had two distinct faces. One of them—the face I saw waiting for me at the information booth on the suburban level at Grand Central, before he knew I'd arrived—had eyelids weighted down with disappointment, and an expression as smooth and strained and bitter as that of a turtle. The other—the face that appeared when he caught sight of me and broke into a smile—belonged to the curly-haired boy of fifteen. It was the average between the two faces that was thirty-five.

After dinner, when we walked into his apartment house between Columbus and Amsterdam, the janitor was mopping the floor, a hairy man dressed in a zippered sweatshirt. The man I was with stopped in front of his mailbox and unlocked and emptied it. There were two names on the box, I could see that much, but had no chance to read the second. We got into an elevator that had a porthole in its metal door.

He took my coat and went into the bedroom to hunt for a hanger. A fierce-looking Siamese cat with one eye, a tough veteran of the street wars, prowled across the top of a leather couch. "I never intended to adopt him," he said when he returned. "He battered his way into the apartment. He's stronger than I am. What could I do?" As he spoke, he tore a sheet of newspaper in half and crumpled it into balls for two less intense cats, who were lightly cuffing each other under the chairs, to play with. "What can I get you to drink?" The kitchen had five or six liquor bottles and an electric coffee pot lined up on top of the refrigerator. A plastic dishpan rested on a living-room chair.

So here it was, the academic shabbiness that shamed me, the fraternal charm of objects that belonged together because no one could afford to replace them or would be bothered to do so anyway, the bare bones that I'd always coveted. (That I'd ruin, given half a chance, by curtaining windows and bringing in hanging plants.) Those wrought-iron chairs must have been salvaged from a friend's porch. A quarter of the floor was taken up by a king-size mattress covered with a heavily napped black blanket that was loaded with pillows. I could think of only one reason for keeping a mattress in the living room. I couldn't take my eyes off it.

He poured me a Spanish brandy. His wife was Spanish, he said as he handed me the glass, though there was no connection with the liquor. Her father had been the consul general. She'd rebelled as a teenager and stayed in this country after the rest of her family went home. When he met Alex—her name was Serena Alessandro, but the first name obviously didn't suit her, so she'd kept her nickname from college—she was a dancer with Merce Cunningham, a very good one, he said in all fairness, but the life of a dancer doesn't mix well with motherhood, or with middle age, either.

Alex Alessandro. As I sipped, I imagined her (there was no picture in the room): dark, sweeping, impatient. Vainer than I am. Braver than I am. Ready for anything that would take her outside her own home. After she was replaced by younger dancers, she got herself jobs as an instructor with one group, an administrator with another, her husband told me.

I wasn't the only person in the room looking at a different life I might have led. He'd been offered first rate professorships, at least one of them at an Ivy League college, but of course Alex had refused to live anywhere except New York, until she met her sculptor, that is, just as she refused on principle to mind their children over weekends, even if she wasn't working at the time. Martin would have detested Alex. I decided that Martin would have been wrong. Alex would look down on me, if we ever met, which was one of the reasons that Martin would have detested her, but this didn't lessen my pity for her husband, who'd never written the books he ought to have written.

"I'm doing an outline right now," he said in a graduate student voice. "Most of the research is done. I may get a chance to go to Europe and finish it. In fact, I may even get lucky and get a Guggenheim." He was free of wife, children, orthodontists, college tuitions, dislocations and despair, he was telling me. He was going to get that Guggenheim; he was going to write more than one book, he had ideas for a string of them, he might retire from teaching altogether—with more than twenty years' seniority, he'd get a decent pension—and move to the country, where living was cheap, and devote himself to nothing but writing. Or to writing and carpentry. He happened to be quite a competent carpenter. We were both twenty-five years old and graduating to another level. We were primed for new careers.

But we couldn't sit there and talk forever. I stood up and went into the bathroom, where I smelled the litter box and saw a line of used margarine containers on the floor, with crusts of canned cat food that had dried around their sides. "Why do you need five dishes?" I asked. "You running a cat house here?"

"They like to pick their own kinds," he called through the bathroom door. I flushed the toilet while I used it, and then again afterward. Slowly I washed my hands and dried them on the back of his bath towel. Without thinking, I took off my blouse so that I could spray myself with perfume from my purse atomizer. Then I put the blouse back on, doing up the buttons before I combed my hair and wiped off my old lipstick, which had crusted in the outer corners like the cat food, replacing it with a fresh coat. I might as well have been a maiden aunt patting talcum on her armpits, I reproached myself. But there were no maiden aunts these days. I must be the only woman in the country palpitating in a bathroom at a moment like this. To make up for it, I considered taking off my earrings—but no, the act was too blatant.

What could he see in me? Less than a lay. More than a friend. Only one thing: I was a woman who'd remained faithful to one man for a long time, and taken pleasure in it.

When we sat down on the couch again our pasts sat down with us. I could sense that this man gave me too much credit for the happy years of my marriage and too much pity for the end of it, as if I'd gotten the right answer to some test question that he'd mysteriously missed. What he loved in me was Martin's wife.

But who was Martin's wife? An oyster with only one shell. Martin's shadow self (as Martin was my shadow self), who could afford to be a writer, sailor, recluse, so long as she had a husband who earned a good living, knew his way around the world, sang Gilbert and Sullivan in the bedroom and made more than enough friends and judgments for two.

But who would I turn into in response to the man who sat next to me on the couch? Alex? Was that what he brought out in a woman? Or Alex's opposite? And would I shape him, all unconscious if not unwilling, into the eager ghost of Martin's ghost?

What I needed at that moment was Martin to give us one of his long-winded funny stories. There was no more conversation between my date and me.

He moved his hand across the cushion. His palm lay on top of my palm. He stroked the underside of my fingers. He knew I was afraid.

That was what I didn't expect. If he'd tried to get me down on the mattress, I'd have gotten up and left, and we could have seen each other again or not seen each other again, even gone to bed—to mattress—or not, as we pleased, and it wouldn't have mattered much either way. Instead, he slid his hand along mine and put his fingertips against the pads at the base of my fingers and pressed, until after a while I couldn't tell which pulse was which.

Why did I cry? I suppose for the same reason that Karen cried when she gave birth. Martin had been dead, but now he was buried.

I'd forgotten until it hurt that I was wearing my wedding ring. A hand, any hand, is a history in itself, telling too much at a time to be bearable. Two histories were finding each other out. A finger tested my finger's responsiveness by bending it back and forth; rode over a knuckle that had been smashed on the boat; found out for itself that the platinum circlet would have to be sawn off, that's how much bigger the fourth knuckle had grown since the ring was put in place; discovered that the tip of the fourth finger cocked inward toward the third at a crazy angle, because of arthritis (oh, are there any of us who reach the age of fifty unmutilated?—which is another reason why I cried, that we could only come to each other as damaged goods). Then the finger slid along the mound of flesh at the base of my thumb, the mound that measures a girl's passion, the same thing as the pubic mound, the boys in our high school class used to assure us.

If his hand had been smaller, it would have been feminine. If it had been larger, it would have frightened me. But it was right, which meant it was the same size as Martin's hand, as if Martin had reached over from his side of the bed and found me again. The temperature of the hand was what it had always been; the fingertips pressed hard, they didn't graze or tickle; there wasn't too much hair on the knuckles. Martin's hand wore a big gold ring, which I'd given him for our twenty-fifth anniversary. This hand would have detested a man's ring. Martin had beautiful clean fingers. This thumb had a shattered nail. A slip of a hammer, a weight that dropped? A fight, was that conceivable? A penchant for self-destruction? An old injury, in any case; the skin had puffed up and covered the edges of the nail, which was opaque and faintly blue and cracked down the middle.

Above our shoulders, the one-eyed cat yowled and stalked along the top of the couch. My date stood up. "Excuse me," he said. "I'll take just a minute to open up a can of food for him. He's too good a friend for me to let him go hungry."

A good man, Martin cried out to me, as the man and cat walked into the kitchen. A kind man. Clever ones are a dime a dozen, but you've found yourself a kind one. Don't play the fool and lose him.

Martin never waited for his opinion to be asked.

Poor thumbnail. Poor hand. I had no idea what the erotic impact of chastity might be—on either of us.

Chapter 10

A F E W weeks after my great-grandmother died, when I was six years old, she came to visit me. I was spending Friday night as I usually did, sleeping in my grandparents' apartment. When I opened my eyes, there she was, sitting in the small rocker in the second bedroom, waiting quietly with her hands in her lap. I closed my eyes and shut her out, and by the time I opened them again she was gone forever, as I'd known she would be. She was never one to cause any trouble in the family.

Well, these experiences are quite common, maybe more the rule than the exception for all I know, even if nobody wants to talk about them. It never occurred to me to be honored that I was the one, or I was one of those, whom Grandma chose to visit.

Martin came back to visit me too, not long after his death, in the middle of the night. He didn't sit in a chair, though. He floated on top of me in bed, his face a foot or two above mine, and I wasn't frightened, quite the opposite, while he told me it was a terrible mistake, this story I'd heard that he was gone. He wasn't gone at all—which is why I was so shaken afterward, and had to beg him never to come back again, because I knew he could do just that if he wanted to. For a while at least, he could keep in touch, until he moved beyond visiting distance, just as he could get his corner table at Le Madrigal at the last minute, even when the place was fully booked. But that would be too much to bear, waking up and finding out all over again where I was in my life. He couldn't expect me to go through that more than once.

Other lovers, I'm sure, particularly other women, have had the courage and resilience to make the opposite choice.

Not once in all the years of our marriage did Martin do anything I specifically asked him not to do, but still I couldn't entirely trust him. After all, we'd never been separated before, except for short business trips, and then he telephoned me each evening and flew home at an ungodly hour rather than spend another night away. Not quite trusting him, after his visit I read in bed so late every night that I virtually fell unconscious instead of falling asleep, and never had dreams of any kind, at least none that I could remember. I gladly sacrificed my nights in order to salvage my days.

The question in my mind at this moment is how—or who—will my mother choose to visit after her death?

"WHEN did you hear the news?" Marion demanded, when I visited her in the middle of January. For two weeks I'd been more or less laid up with bronchitis.

"The same time you did." We'd already had this conversation several times.

"What are you talking about? He didn't tell me a thing until last week."

"Nonsense. I told you myself before the holidays. As soon as I heard. Anyway, you knew Felicia wasn't with us at Christmas." If it was going to happen, it had to happen before the holidays; that sequence was clear. It was too much the calendar imposed on us at one time: early darkness, and twilight soaked up by wet snow that wouldn't stick yet, and gifts to be decided on and cards written, love and all my love and love always, never anything less. It was too much to expect us to keep going.

I could see Marion trying to place herself in my living room at Christmas and remember who else had been with us. "Should I have sent Felicia her present anyway?" she asked, meaning her check. In her mind, there had never been a sharp distinction between her family and her in-laws, which might be one of the redeeming graces of her form of motherhood. She'd always found fault with us and preferred our friends. Of course her concern might reflect the fact that Felicia, out of all her relatives, had been the most tactful, the one most willing to touch her, certainly more willing than Pixie, for instance, which was what she currently insisted on calling her great-granddaughter. "Who'll get the engagement ring?" she wanted to know. It had been her mother's. "And that Limoges pattern she picked?" She wasn't going to be the only divorced person in the family any longer. Unhappiness was being served around a bit more equitably. Marion and me, Peter, and now Ted and Felicia—we could all divide up the pie. "She could have had my china. God knows I offered it to her often enough."

"All I know from Ted is that she's got the stainless-steel fish poacher. Never mind who gets the apartment, he has to buy a new fish poacher. The lawyers will work out the details when they do the separation agreement." I couldn't tell her that Ted wanted to give Felicia the apartment, the engagement ring, anything and everything including the fish poacher, as if his love, which had never diminished, had doubled at the sight of her distress.

Marion's eyes lit with interest at the mention of the separation agreement, which was a subject in which she was versed. Maybe her heart went out to Felicia, who would also have to do battle against a lawyer.

"At least I could give the poor boy a dinner," she said.

"Poor boy? Don't waste your time worrying about a good-looking bachelor in New York." Who's solvent and not even gay, I said to myself.

"I'm sure he doesn't bother to cook for himself."

"And I'm sure he doesn't have to." The poor boy was kicking up his heels, acting the part of a boy indeed now that he'd passed his thirtieth birthday a week after his younger sister gave birth to a baby. Was it the birthday or the baby, I wondered, that told him that youth was the opposite of a bar exam or partnership? It wasn't something he passed but something that passed him, or passed through him like beer, whether he'd done anything about it or not.

Marion put her emotional gears in reverse. "He could still find a few minutes to call me," she said. "He could tell me about it himself."

"Maybe he's depressed," I offered, to cheer her. "Remember that he has to start all over again. He never had much time to date, he met Felicia while they were still in college." I tried to visualize his new crop of women, not knowing what to call them, since the terms "girl friend" or "date" were almost as archaic as "sweetheart." All I could conjure up was the image of a sixteen- or seventeen-year-old girl who'd walked across our lawn one August afternoon, home on vacation from her boarding school in Pennsylvania, if I remember right, her long blond hair hanging straight down her back, the ruffle of her cotton dress brushing the grass; she wore a straw picture hat but no shoes. Clearly it was an image from the end of the 1960s. Martin never forgot the vision of her as she walked past the porch where he was working. It changed the way in which he saw his son, for sure, and possibly the way in which he saw himself. It may have been the equivalent of the moment when I heard that Karen was going to have a baby. Years later, we heard that the girl had become a porn star.

"All I can say is, I hope he plays the field for a good long time," Marion said, meaning she hoped he'd stay single forever.

I could understand that she thought I'd known about Ted's trouble for a long time and failed to tell her, but the truth was that I'd known nothing until they split up, at which time Felicia reached me first. Her phone call wasn't meant simply to tell me the news, but also to ask me to recommend a lawyer. Not only had I known nothing, I hadn't even guessed what I should have guessed: what a diet, a new exercise machine, a change of barber have to mean in the life of a man who has just passed thirty.

But if I didn't know, what did that say about the assumptions I made about my children? What sort of mother was I, anyway?

An aging mother, that's what sort. Or, to be accurate, a mother of aging children. A mother rendered obtuse as well as obsolete.

TED had described his furnished sublet in Greenwich Village, on the top floor of a brownstone, as a cubbyhole of unremitting charm. I saw what he meant. It had a working fireplace in the living room, topped by a carved mantel; a vase full of peacock feathers in one corner, and a bedroom so small that the floor space had been reserved for a bureau and a single French Provincial armchair. The bed itself was a bunk hung from the ceiling by chains, with a ladder leading up to it.

"How do you get the *Times* up there on Sundays? With a block and tackle?" By this I meant, Don't think of me strictly as your mother (as strictly as I think of my mother). Don't suppose that I can't envy your adventures up there on a Sunday morning in that improbable bed, your face not four feet below the ceiling.

"Can I give you some Perrier? Or tea?"

"Tea would be great."

"Herbal? Lapsong souchong or Indian?" He drinks nothing but

coffee himself, so this was his way of disclosing that he'd stocked up for guests of varied tastes. "What I can't figure out is why the sort of flake who owns a nice place like this always sticks peacock feathers in a vase. Do you suppose it's some secret code?"

"Did you put together that Christmas decoration yourself?" I asked, looking at a group of pine boughs artfully trimmed with pinecones and plaid ribbons. He couldn't have. He didn't move in until after New Year's.

"Nope, I found it here. I haven't gotten around to throwing it out yet." His voice had an edge to it.

Did he imagine I was criticizing his housekeeping, my Prince of Wales who will never grow thick-skinned enough to be impervious to his mother's comments? "First children are like pancakes," I used to say to friends in the neighborhood, in the deprecating style required in the suburbs. "The pan's never hot enough. You ought to be able to throw the first away." On his bureau lay a package of shirts fresh from the laundry, the paper ripped open, next to a mountain of change thrown into an ashtray. "Don't get rid of the branches. I mean, I wouldn't. For a month or two anyway. They give the place a personal touch." Put there by another young man (middle-aged men, old men, don't sleep in bunk beds) who then left home before the holidays.

"Actually, the agent tells me he may have killed himself. The apartment is owned by his estate, but his father—he's the executor—doesn't want the death talked about. He's afraid of repelling buyers."

How much does my son think about his predecessor while he lies in his bed? "So the apartment's for sale?"

"Yep. Or rather, it will be. If I buy it—there aren't many in the city like it—you know what I'll do? Open the ceiling and put in a skylight. There's this fantastic advantage, nothing but the roof above me, cool off the place in summer—otherwise I'm sure it's a hotbox—get some light in here. And get to see the clouds. Also the pigeon shit."

What does it mean, then, if he thinks of settling in an apartment only big enough for one person? Never mind what I told his grandmother. I have no way of knowing whether he's more miserable or less miserable than he was before, or how long it took him to decide that he was miserable in the first place. Does he believe that suffering is temporary by nature and directly proportional to eventual happiness?

He gets to Weiser's bookshop these days, he tells me. He's been to a seminar at the New School on co-opping brownstones. He brings home fresh pumpkin soup from Balducci's.

It's also true that he has had more colds and sore throats this winter than in any previous year of his life. Up to now, it was Felicia who had the colds and Ted who was the staunch one, the protector, but rough going has turned the two of them inside out and shown new patterns, like the linings of stormcoats.

We resemble each other more than he'd like to believe, this son and I, as proof of which I'm willing to bet that both of us dream in terms of houses. He has left the Upper East Side apartment, which was just like the apartment where he was born and the apartment where his sister lives now. He has taken an apartment, he is thinking of buying an apartment, in Greenwich Village, home of the perennially young and uncommitted. He sleeps in somebody else's bed; he survives on take-out food. The take-out food is better than anything the rest of us cook.

But what is he saying in this dream of a skylight? Is he telling me that at this moment what he wants is to raise the roof and let in the sun, or is he flexing his muscles, eager to show that he can improve any situation by making radical and undreamed-of—which implies expensive—changes that will astound us all? If he wants to take a cramped space and burst through its limits, is that the metaphor of a firstborn son, first grandchild on both sides, who suspects that he can't possibly measure up to our expectations unless he bursts through the boundaries of our ordinary physical selves?

Improvement. Renovation. Expansion. Breakthrough. These are the metaphors of a young man who conceives of improvement in terms of design and planning, R and D in his own life, whose energy exacts a high price from him. No matter what he thinks he thinks today, I don't see him living in a cubbyhole of unremitting charm five years from now, nor does he, or he wouldn't have signed up for that course at the New School. I can see him in a Charles Addams grotesquerie in a Hudson River town (not too different from the Berkman house, come to think of it), or maybe a piece of turn-of-the-century splendor set in the middle of a Newark slum. But whatever form it takes, I see him in a house that's grandiose and yet dilapidated, carved, paneled and leaking, a house crying out for historical tact and new pipes in the cellar.

Karen is the opposite, of course, as Karen is always opposite to her brother. Karen doesn't see her apartment or even the building it's in as a set of walls and floors, but as the center of her sphere of convenience: a washing machine beneath her in the basement, a doorman out front to accept her packages while she's at work (she wouldn't take Ted's sublet in a brownstone rent-free, she says passionately), the Y nursery school and playground and supermarket within easy reach of her stroller.

No, Karen doesn't see her apartment from the outside (as Ted would see it), nor does she see it as an investment and an address (as Kurt and Ted do), nor as a home fifty minutes away from her mother's home in Westchester (as Peter would wish his to be, right now, anyway). Her metaphor is time, translated into how much of it each of her activities requires, while Ted's metaphor is space. This strikes me as exactly in order. Karen, the new mother, knows herself to be a conduit for time. Ted, the young male, is required to be a tamer of space.

And what about me? In my light-headed moments, I talk about buying a house in the woods, maybe with a view of the water, but up in real country that wouldn't be too far from the city for easy visits in both directions. I see myself standing at a window and looking out. A point of view, I seem to say. Surroundings. Trees or waves, wind and shadows in place of people. Meanwhile, I cling to my mock-Tudor home with its thirty-year mortgage that's nearly paid up, to my astonishment. What's more, I preserve and improve it more lovingly these days, exactly the way I cream my face more faithfully now that the wrinkles have come. But none of this matters. Neither my real life nor my fantasy matters. What matters are my dreams.

In my dreams, time after time I find myself exploring a house that I know to be my own, even if it looks entirely different, discovering a corridor or stairway I never noticed before, that leads me to a studio or sometimes an attic, in either case an enormous room filled with light, and I ask myself why I've been living in quarters so cramped by comparison, while all these years this light-filled space has been standing empty, waiting for me.

In a way, my dream complements Ted's vision of a skylight. He dreams of self-improvement, which is the fancy and goad of the young. I dream of transformation, which is the dream, the only proper dream, of old age.

THE OTHER day my mother told me that she plans to leave me her apartment in her will.

"You apartment? Why? What would I do with it?"

"Well, *I* for one think it's a beautiful apartment."

"Of course it is." Valuable, too.

"Don't you think it's time you lived in the city?" Would I sell her apartment? That's what she wants to know, because if so, she won't leave it to me, she'll leave it to the grandchildren, who'll sell it themselves, needless to say, but on their part it won't be so clearcut a piece of treachery. In fact, it will be the only way to divide it in three parts. "You're not getting younger, you know. It's time you stopped batting your brains out."

"But everything I love is up in the country. Except you and the children, of course, and I drive in to visit you."

"Those terrible stairs." She shakes her head. Those stairs are one of the barriers that prevent her from visiting me, a flight between the driveway and the living room, and then another half flight, the cruelest section, to the closest bathroom. Sometimes she suspects that twenty-seven years ago I deliberately picked out a house with so many stairs in order to emphasize the difference between us.

"Anyway, there's no reason we have to talk about wills now. I hope it's a question that won't come up for years yet."

"Then you're even more of a fool than I thought."

Does she mean that I'm a fool to pretend that she's going to live long, or that she wants to live long? Or does she mean that I'm a fool not to keep quiet and accept the apartment, and then sell it after she's gone and pocket the money, even if it's my children who lose out? She always takes the part of the older generation against the younger. For that, I'm occasionally grateful.

No, she means neither of these things. Only later, while driving home, do I understand with terrible clarity what she means. She means that I must take her place in the pink plastic armchair, just as she took her mother's place. I must give up my car pools and my sailboat and my collie, my barbecue grill and the dogwood tree that's been hit recently by the blight that has swept through Westchester, because it's my turn to be hit next, not only by age but by some steadily worsening chronic condition.

What I mustn't do is insist on a multistory home above a drafty garage at the end of an icy driveway and icy steps, fifty minutes away from my grown-up children.

THEY understand nothing about this; they're too young. I understood nothing about it myself until this winter, when the bad weather settled in and I came down with bronchitis that refused to go away and discovered that I have no mind at all, only a body, and that body has only one implacable idea, which is sleep.

I read until one, two in the morning. I slept late. There was no commuter in the next bed to wake me. Peter made his own breakfast and left on the school bus long before I opened my door. Had I found the natural rhythm of my body, or had I found a way to avoid half of the normal day, lying in bed on my left side? The house was a xylophone, and I was in the center of it. A slow rain, left over in the trees, sent a streak of shallow patters down the dormer and gutters beyond my bed. Water dripped onto the air-conditioner case in sharp pings. From time to time, the control of my electric blanket let out a declamatory click. After a while, the radiator pipes built up a head of steam and expressed themselves in a series of clangs. All these sounds Martin had drowned out with the hum of his seasonless air-conditioner.

So now I know that this languor is all there is, this torpor is our natural condition, and anything else—what we choose to call consciousness, character, purpose—is frail, temporary, maintained only with effort, basically foreign to our tropical selves, imposed on us terribly late in human history and only on a limited, cold and rocky patch of the globe, where men first preached the fantastic doctrine of salvation through work, *"Laborare est orare."* Small wonder that in the Middle Ages, when consciousness was even less firmly entrenched than it is now, *accidie*—torpor, sloth—was recognized as the fourth cardinal sin. *Accidie,* acidic. The sourest view of life for sure, even if the etymology is false.

Listlessness. Indifference. Apathy. Nothing is as exhausting as apathy. We are animals; we are more, but not so much more as we imagine. We stir only for the sake of food, shelter, bowels and the care of the young. When those needs are satisfied, we stretch our limbs in front of the fire and doze, as Ralph dozes. ("Is it any wonder that dog looks so well?" Martin used to ask. "Look at the amount of rest he gets.")

Either we have too much pressing on us, we yearn for a break—like Karen, like Ted—or we have nothing at all to do, nobody needs us or wants us. There are only the pursued and the pursuing, the busy and the tired, said F. Scott Fitzgerald.

"Depression," Jack Nordlinger says about my mother these days. "Combined with weakness from emphysema and minor strokes. Nothing we can do about it." When I complain about the gloom in her apartment, he warns me that we have to be careful. We don't want to overstimulate her nervous system, he says, meaning I mustn't assault her with my demands that she wake up toward the end and pay attention to her life.

Have I been obtuse for years then, not to understand that her apartment is dark for some good reason beside her penny-pinching? Darkness may be as lawful for her development as Carrie's crib mobile is lawful for hers, intended to wake her up to life for a few minutes more each day. I see the two of them, Carrie and Marion, as opposite ends of a bell curve of consciousness.

"You know how long she sleeps?" I ask. "Twelve hours a day, not counting naps in her chair. If I call at nine in the morning, I wake her, and if I call at nine at night, I not only wake her, I scare the living daylights out of her."

"I'm only happy when I'm asleep," Marion herself says.

In my own way, I know what she means, although I've never told her this.

When the telephone call came at a few minutes past seven that morning, I did a curious thing after the voice stopped talking. I let the phone receiver dangle (or else I hung up, I can't be sure which), and then I went back to sleep. I didn't faint. I went to sleep, as if I had nothing else to do. The doctors have a name for this behavior, I've been told. They call it the Desdemona syndrome.

"What reason is there for me to wake up?" my mother asks, not unreasonably. "Why can't I die when I want to?" She speaks of death as one more acquaintance who refuses to pay her a visit, like her husband, like her former bridge partners, or visits her only at the end of the list, like the last of the women who promise to come play a hand of Spite and Malice, but cancel at the first threat of bad weather—or she equates it with her daughter, who has a reputation for not arriving for hours after she promised to come, by which time the expected pleasure of the visit has curdled from waiting too long.

"Remember," I said. "I'll see you next week, but I won't see you the week after."

"And why not? What's happening?"

"Don't you remember? I told you. I'm going away for two weeks. Get over this cough, I hope."

"You're going away sick?"

"I'm going to sail a boat on a bareboat charter in the British Virgins."

"Alone?" The vowel hung in the air, pointing at my shame.

"Of course not. How could I sail a thirty-nine-foot boat all alone? As a matter of fact, I've never handled a boat this size before. I'm going with a friend who sails with me in the summer and his two daughters."

"Ah." It was all right, then. There'd be a man on board.

"But I'm skipper." She didn't choose to hear this. "I'm going down a week early to get some rest and get over my cough."

"Going to your father's, you mean?"

"Not to my father's. I have to go to Tortola anyway, to pick up the boat. You know I don't like to be a houseguest anywhere for more than a few days."

"Two weeks?" She hates beaches, heat, hotels, weekends and holidays. She has a daughter who abandons her home and son, not to mention her sick mother, even rejects her father in Florida—pays good money to reject him when she could get the southern sunshine free—and goes to sit alone on a beach, exposed to the sympathy of strangers. "And who's going to be with Peter all that time?"

"I'm hiring a baby nurse to take care of him," I cried out in my fury.

While we sat there, letting the anger die down in the room, I could feel her chewing up my words and turning them into something her body could use. "I should've known," she said in resignation when I bent over and kissed her good-bye. "I should've realized you don't have that good a time when you visit your father."

ALONG the railroad bank the forsythia sprays turned golden, while everywhere else the countryside was gray and dormant; even the contract gardeners on the first of their monthly visits looked gray and dormant as they bent over to rake the debris from the flower beds. It's always this way with the forsythia, because the railroad bank is fully exposed to the sun, but the effect is of good news hurrying north along the right of way, carried by an electric charge that runs through the rails and pulls the rest of the season behind it.

Kurt had to go to London on business for a few days in March, so Karen and Carrie came to spend the weekend at my house, Karen back in her old room and Carrie in the den, with an intercom connecting them. "I'll be glad to give her the six-o'clock bottle," I offered, eager, if only for one morning, to have back the teenage daughter with her collarbones sticking out, who used to rise at noon and drift into the bathroom in her flannel granny gown, to peer in the mirror and see if her crop of hickies had grown greater or less in the night.

"It isn't six, it's more like five," she said. "And she'll get hysterical if she wakes up in a strange room and cries and you come in to her."

Water was running in the bathtub by the time I'd had breakfast. "Can I come in and talk?" I asked from outside the door. With an electric heater steaming up the room, Karen was sitting in the tub in a few inches of water and soaping her hair, with Carrie propped in the vee of her legs, dabbling her hands. The two of them in their tropical lagoon had turned pink from the thighs down. Why hadn't I thought of so obvious a way to keep my babies happy while bathing myself, instead of doing everything that mattered to me late at night and alone? Carrie nestled inches from the spot from which she'd emerged six months earlier.

"Marion's going downhill fast," I said. "Have you spoken to her lately?"

"She can't be too bad. She said she was having the leak in her living room wall next to the window patched up, because she's having the painters next week." Karen sounded smug at having done her duty and called her grandmother in spite of the demands on her time.

I tried to think of having the painters as a hopeful sign. "She called twice last week to say she's been going over her will but she can't find any mention of what-do-you-call-it, the payment for the cemetery—she means perpetual care, of course. She knows she made her mother pay for it, but how can she be sure the payment will take care of another grave?" Karen couldn't hear me for a minute while she ran the hand shower over her head, carefully tilting it back so that no spray would fall in Carrie's face. Bubbles streamed past her legs, to the baby's amazement. "I asked if she'd ever gotten a bill from the cemetery for annual upkeep, and when she said no, I said that proves it. Her parents must have provided for perpetual care in their will."

"Hand me the shampoo, will you?"

"You don't have to bring your own shampoo. Don't you think I have any? But you don't understand. She wouldn't be worried about perpetual care if she thought I was ever going to visit the plot."

"Well? Who's to say she's wrong?" The top of one breast reflected pink and lavender lights through a film of soap.

Two weeks earlier, when I came back from my sailing vacation and went to New York on the first mild day of the season, wearing a short-sleeve blouse and white wool skirt to show off my tan, I found my mother lying in bed, which was a shock in itself, both arms outside the blankets, but only one of them covered by a flannel bed jacket.

"The left is colder than the right," she explained. Her hands were no longer claws, but lay open on top of the blanket cover. "We've just come back from the doctor's," she said. "I had to be up at the crack of dawn." She'd had to wait two hours, she hadn't been allowed anything to eat, not even a cup of coffee, she'd lost her bowels again, as she phrased it, this time in the taxi coming home. Her coat was hung over the back of a chair to dry. Sylvia had washed the lining in the bathtub. "And after that, all he did was prick my five fingers." Her eyes were red circles with a set of furrows above them. She had the look of a frightened child who supposes there's something she ought to be doing, but has no way of being sure what it is.

"She miss you something terrible while you gone," Sylvia said in front of her. "She talk about you all the time, say how homesick she is for you. I tell her over and over, but she don't believe you on vacation."

"Where was I supposed to be?"

"I thought you'd gone to the hospital secretly. Because you didn't want to worry me. That cough of yours." I couldn't be sure whether the shame on Marion's face rose from the foolishness of her idea or the suspicion that she'd undermined my health so seriously that finally I'd been driven to a hospital.

My mother missed me—that's what I heard—which was something I'd never heard before.

It was so late. It was too late in our lives, wasn't it? I was the daughter born in her sleep; I was the child whisked away to stay in a hospital nursery for two weeks, carried home in the arms of a highly recommended baby nurse, taken care of by Fräulein, by Nanny, by housekeepers; I was off in school all day; I was taking a Sunday walk with my father; I was in my room reading with the door shut; I was away at college; I was working; I was married; I was visiting my father and Sally in Florida. Why shouldn't she miss me? Or maybe none of that was true, maybe she'd never had a daughter at all, I was only a dream, or, more probable still, I was real enough but I wasn't her daughter, I was the baby sister with whom she'd been saddled while she was still in her teens.

It may be that every change of spirit from one level to another is marked, more abruptly than we believe, by a change of name, as Abram became Abraham and Sarai became Sarah with the covenant, as lovers drop their worldly names and become "dear" to each other at some point in their relationship. After that day, I couldn't think of her as Marion any longer. I thought of her as Mother, which was ironic, because that was the afternoon when I acknowledged that she wasn't a mother now and probably never had been—in fact, couldn't have been a mother, no matter what she intended—since she was only a child herself. But what had I done to frighten this child so badly that she got out of bed, when she obviously didn't want to, and sat in her chair, looking at her lap and waiting to be scolded?

KAREN climbed out of the tub and knelt wet and naked on the mat to dry the baby, Carrie's legs kicking against the bush that was so much lusher than mine had ever been, a place for a baby to get lost in or to have emerged from, like Moses from the bulrushes. When she bent forward to dry the fold beneath the chin, Carrie's face was inches below the aureoles of Karen's nipples. Did I imagine that this bottle-fed infant cocked her head and looked up fondly at them? Powder came next, Johnson & Johnson's, but it wasn't talcum any more, it was cornstarch, better for babies because they didn't breathe the light talcum dust into their lungs. (What did I do to my babies' lungs?) It gave out a faint crisp sound like taffeta when Karen rubbed her palm over it, and it rested on top of the skin in a layer so fine that the individual grains caught the light. My granddaughter shone like a fish. I handed over her undershirt, but no, it wasn't time for that yet. Lotion had to be spread on her cheeks and under her chins and in the creases of her thighs.

"Diaper first," Karen said. Of course. I'd been thinking of the old days, when diapers had to be pinned to the tabs of undershirts. No question about it, everything for babies was better these days, not only the powder, and the shirts with snaps instead of strings that tore off, and paper diapers, which had improved (except for the scent) even since Carrie's birth and now had resealable tabs, but also—but especially—the parents.

"Shall I hold her on my lap?" Karen used to be light as a pocketbook, easily overlooked as she coiled inward against my stomach for shelter, a thumb-sucker, an ear-puller, curled smaller than small. This child could never be overlooked. As Karen connected the blower and started to dry her own hair, Carrie looked at her mother suspiciously to make sure she didn't plan to leave the room, but sat solid and quiet, happy with the familiar sound of the blower. Her hair held traces of tearless shampoo that slightly cleared my nostrils as I nuzzled her. Her body smelled like the dishwasher when it's opened while the dishes are still hot. But it was her feet that captured me as I held one in each palm, pink and lavender, with maps of unvisited countries etched on their unused soles.

As Karen switched off the dryer and turned around, Carrie lifted her arms with an aggrieved air, suddenly aware that her mother had been busy with something else. She was scooped up and lifted to the level of the mirror over the sink.

"See?" Karen said. "Who's in there? Who do you see?" Carrie stared, first amazed, then amused by the image. "Who's that in there?"

"Ba-by," I expected her to say, as I'd said so often to the face in the medicine-chest mirror.

"Mother and child. That's who you see." she answered. Whatever else may happen, Karen isn't likely to wake up one day and discover that she's lost track of herself and a younger woman who has every right to call herself her daughter.

WE WENT to market together, the three of us, and then we went shopping for spring clothes. I wanted to buy Karen a dress for her birthday, which was coming in two weeks. By the time we got back to the house, Kurt was waiting for us, having taken a taxi directly from the airport.

"Will she come to me?" I asked, while we snatched at our supper. Carrie was growing impatient. She demanded to be taken out of her high chair. I undid the Velcro strip that fastened her bib, and sure enough, she sat on my lap while I watched avidly as Karen ate her own lamb chop.

"Give her room!" Karen cried. "You mustn't cramp her." I rubbed noses with her, I licked her behind the ears, but even I could see that the meal had better end. We hadn't had dessert, Karen had barely started her potato, but Kurt was already rising to bring the suitcase down from the bedroom, while Karen still had to go through the house to gather up toys and bottles. "I'll change her for you," I offered.

To my surprise, Carrie laughed on my shoulder as we climbed the stairs to Karen's old room, where a bath towel had been spread on top of the bureau to make a changing table, and where Karen had already laid out a clean diaper. I sat the baby on top of the towel and began to peel the stained suit off her. Nothing that I was doing was strange to me. There was no greater gap of years between Carrie and Peter than between Peter and Karen, after all.

See how good I am at this, I said to her, see how gentle I am now that I'm older, and it doesn't spoil the effect a bit if I'm aware that I'm gentle with you as I was never gentle with my own children, because I realize that I'm on probation. If you howl when I grasp your ankles and lay you flat on the towel to change your diaper, why, that's only to be expected.

I was ready for her. I handed her the cap from the Vaseline jar. She batted it away, furious as a turtle at finding herself on her back, even more indignant when she remembered that the hands overpowering her were unfamiliar. Don't howl like that, I said. They'll hear you. They'll think you don't like it here. And I have my last bedtime story to tell, not to you but to my own children, especially the one who's your mother, about what a wonderful parent I was, how kind and loving I was, as well as dexterous.

In my hurry to slip the dirty suit out from under Carrie, I rolled her too far over and her cries grew louder.

Just a minute and we'll be done, I said to her, as I put her feet into a clean terry stretch suit for the trip home. I'll have you up on my shoulder and laughing while we look out the window together. Grandparenthood is a deceit and a delusion, you see, and the past that I'm trying to create with you is for my benefit and my children's, because we need new pasts more than we need new futures as we grow older (my mother wasn't wrong about that), and we need our own children more than we need anyone else's. This past, this bedtime story I'm creating with you, is a wonderful story in which I'm as tender as ever I was passionate, a story in which my attention and desire—even my efficiency—focus on a single figure, a baby, whose name changes and changes again, until finally it becomes you, Carrie. You. So let's hurry and get your other arm into this suit, because then I can pick you up, and you'll be happy and clean and pretty as a picture to go with my story.

But Karen burst into the room as I was zipping the zipper. "What are you doing to her? The child's hysterical. You should have called me!" She seized her. Carrie stopped crying. In the silence I heard a car trunk slam in the driveway.

"There's nothing in the world wrong with her."

"Kurt heard her screaming outdoors." It was her mother, her house. Kurt would lay the blame on her. Was that why she was so upset?

I have to do it, she was saying across her baby's body. Don't you see? I'm not your daughter. I'm my baby's mother.

"She'd have been quiet in a minute, as soon as I picked her up." You're my daughter. The fact that the relationship between parent and child is inevitably doomed makes no difference at all.

"Not if she got hysterical first."

"Suppose she did? So what?"

"And what would that have taught her?"

"She'd have learned that she can survive being taken care of by someone else."

"You think she'll learn by being hysterical? At eight o'clock at night, when it's past her bedtime already?"

"You think it's good for her to get the idea that she's been snatched from the hands of a monster?"

Karen softened. "Next time we're up here, we'll start earlier."

SO I was right: this is the final bedtime story I'll tell my children, but it's not going to be the pretty story I'd like it to be, at least not in Karen's presence. At this minute, both of us see me grappling with my firstborn all over again, mine as well as Karen and Kurt's, tearing the membrane of my experience, making it easy for others to follow. But I see what they don't see, that I'm not the irrelevant figure I thought I was a few minutes ago. I have a role. Which is why Karen and I are standing in her old bedroom while I fight fiercely for something I haven't earned yet, for divided custody, even if my portion of this child's time amounts to no more than one percent (which may prove to be heaven-knows-what fraction of my own emotional energy).

Beyond her mother and father, this child has me. This child needs me. As I need her. I stand for the rest of the world, and what she learns from me is not unimportant.

I am the other woman in her life. I am difference and separation and possibility and therefore risk, while her parents offer only identity and safety. I am the past, which is magical and mysterious, which shifts every day, while they are merely the demands of the present. I am what is, and I am what isn't. I am the old woman who sits in the attic, spinning her spinning wheel by the light of the moon, with silver hair that touches the floor and an embroidered gown. I sing as I spin, but only my grandchildren hear me.

Karen zipped the pram suit but left the collar unsnapped so that the baby wouldn't get too hot. "You two are a pair," she sighed, referring to the two tempers, her mother's and her daughter's, that sandwiched her in between.

"What about this receiving blanket?"

"I'm leaving it here. And these diapers." She laid Carrie on the bed and put on her own coat. "Why don't you bring her down to the car?" she suggested. "I'll get a bottle ready for her to drink while we drive."

"That's silly. I'll get the bottle, and you carry her. She's peaceful now. It would be a shame to disturb her."

Love, like water, always flows downhill. Children cannot love parents the way that parents love children. Men cannot love God in the way that God loves men. Honor thy parents; love thy child. What choice are we given? My love for my child is so overwhelming that nothing, not even my love for my grandchild, can stand in its way.

Karen and I begin again, as the two of us will always know how to begin again between us.

Chapter 11

*A*s it happened, we got out of the station wagon just as Pete got home. I drove it into the garage so that Karen could get out on a flat surface while carrying the baby. There was Pete, putting his bicycle away after a magazine staff meeting at school. Now that spring was finally here, he wouldn't let me drive him on Saturdays and wouldn't take the bus to school during the week, if he could help it. *"Infra dig,"* I said to the others. "Either a senior editor drives him or he rides his bike. In two years he'll get his license." This wasn't true, of course. He'd get his license in eighteen months.

Ted was helping a young woman to get out of the wagon. In order to close the garage door, Pete leaped up in the air to trip the rope that was tied to the door hinge; he liked to tuck his knees up under his chin and swing back and forth on the rope when he did this.

"Hey, Quasimodo. Come over here," Ted called. "I want you to meet Hilary."

"Just a minute. I have to lock up my bike first."

"For heaven's sake, take Hilary in through the front door and not through the kitchen," I said.

In spite of two weeks of snowstorms and unseasonable cold that had passed since I'd seen the children, I'd been sure that it would be a day as fine as this when I planned Karen's birthday celebration for the first Saturday in April. At the moment, she was carrying the baby, who was wearing a dress for the first time in her life.

"You're driving all the way to New York to pick up the children?" my mother had asked me the evening before.

I said I was. There was no reason not to be honest. She'd been invited, after all, but hadn't the strength to come. "Ted's bringing a girl—a woman—who works for the company that does their legal printing. Tomorrow they're going up to Connecticut to look at some houses for a possible group rental this summer." I was lucky; she didn't ask for an explanation of group rentals.

The girl was English. Her name made me think of bone-china eggcups and nursery teas, but she turned out to be an athletic-looking young woman with an attentive face and straight hair that she slicked back, first behind one ear and then the other, as if carefully balancing her thoughts. She didn't flinch when we came into the house and Ralph leaped all over us in ecstatic confusion as to whether he hadn't seen me for a month and had seen Ted two hours ago, or the other way round. When Ted made him sit down and hold up his paw, Hilary squatted in front of him before she shook it and flipped her hair back like a swimmer getting ready to plunge, which made me sense in her a great hunger for family surroundings. Carrie blinked her eyes every time Ralph barked.

As soon as we were settled, Ted put on shorts and went jogging with Peter, while Karen and Kurt pushed Carrie in her stroller to the beach, everyone cheered by the first spring day. Only Hilary drooped. She was exhausted from working overtime all week, she said, so I put her to sleep on my bed and covered her up with a quilt.

Before we sat down to dinner, while Karen gave the baby her bath, I phoned my mother. She didn't feel too well this evening, she said, which was a relief of sorts for both of us, freeing us from the reproach that she should have been up in Westchester with the rest of the family for the birthday celebration. "Can't quite hear you," she said. "Water running in my ears. I may have had another stroke."

"Have you called the doctor?"

"What do you expect him to do about it?"

"You ought to call him. You ought to let him know."

"You think he's waiting for me to call on a Saturday?"

I could hear Ted hunting through the house for a free bathroom. Hilary was still sleeping, which meant he couldn't go into my room. Kurt was using the guest bathroom. I could hear his sister yell at him, when he looked into Peter's bathroom, to shut that door immediately, couldn't he see that the baby was wet and naked and lying in a draft?

"Did Karen get my card?" my mother asked. "I couldn't get out of the house to buy one. And there's no sense telling my nurse to pick one out. What does she know? It was the best I could do."

"What? You sent her a birthday card? How very nice. Do you want me to ask her?"

Ted banged the flat of his hand on Peter's door. "Hey, Pete. Can I come in and piss on your rug?" As I went in to finish dressing the baby so that Karen could come to the phone, I could hear Peter explode with delight.

"I'm going to buy myself something special with it," Karen was saying, when Carrie and I came into the kitchen a few minutes later. "A silk blouse, maybe. But what I liked best was the card."

"Ask her if I should come into town. She isn't feeling well. She may have had another stroke." The answer must have been negative, because a minute later Karen hung up the phone.

"What kind of card did she send?" I asked in a voice that I tried to keep casual.

"It wasn't a card. She drew some flowers on a piece of stationery. From the box that you gave her, I think. Do you know, she must've had real talent once?"

"That was ingenious of her. That must have taken a lot of effort."

"She drew them on the envelope, too. But I could see that her hand was shaky."

"YOU should've let me go upstairs and give the baby a bottle before we started to eat," Kurt said to Karen as we gathered in the dining room for the birthday dinner.

"Too late now," I said. "We have to sit down right away. This is timed like an America's Cup start. Roast beef and chocolate soufflé."

Hilary had come out of her nap heavy with sleep, although I couldn't tell whether this was due to the work week she'd just gone through, maybe with a cold coming on—and with Ted keeping her up late at night?—or whether it was a sign of indifference to a house that was only a stopping-off place, after all, on the way toward renting part of a house for summer weekends that would itself be nothing more than a stopping-off place. On the other hand, her exhaustion might mean the opposite: a visit so significant that it took more strength than she could muster to sit up and stare it in the face. Ted gave me no clue. He may have enjoyed his role as mystery man. Pete was playing up to Ted, trying to prove himself worthy of having a brother who wanted to piss on his rug.

"You could've done it half an hour ago. But I think she'll be okay until dinner's over," Karen suggested, torn in her loyalty. Carrie, who'd been fed in advance, sat in a corner of the dining room and played with her toys, surrounded by sofa cushions like a Buddha on a lotus pad, because she couldn't balance firmly yet and tended to topple over from time to time in unpredictable directions, particularly when she was tired.

"I'll give it to her and get her to sleep before the meat's carved," Kurt said, picking her up and marching to the kitchen.

Your father would never have gone upstairs to give any of you a bottle, I said to myself. "Hurry up. Guests wait for soufflé, not soufflé for guests."

There was an interval of bobbing up and down for wine bottle, Coke bottle, peanut butter, ice cubes, telephone, all of this bobbing and the instructions and requests and complaints that went with it accomplished even faster than usual to dazzle Hilary, who studied her surroundings with a waif's hunger for details. Her face was pale and damp with perspiration.

Looking around the room at chairs and candlesticks and silverware, all the patterns I'd picked out, she must have supposed that I knew what I was doing when I chose them, just as she supposed that I'd foreseen, or even designed, this mix-and-match set of three children, one son-in-law and one granddaughter, who shone in the light that sloped down from the chandelier. I could feel her pain, which was equal and opposite to my own. She supposed that these sets I'd acquired represented an accumulation of wisdom as well as time. She supposed that whatever was real was also deliberate. She supposed that a future as blank as hers was at this minute must be more painful than a past as rich as mine.

"Not a Swiss Army knife," Peter was saying indignantly to his brother. "No way. Who're you kidding? I want a real one."

"He doesn't mean a switchblade?" Karen asked in alarm.

"We'll buy a knife as soon as I get the list of required equipment from the trek group for this summer." I wouldn't let them think that my child was being shortchanged. I was a sailor who carried a stainless-steel rigging knife myself on a lanyard around my neck whenever I was on the water. "I'm only afraid the one he wants has too short a blade. I'd rather see him use a good, sharp blade, not hack around with a toy. That's the way you get hurt."

"Nothing wrong with a Swiss Army knife," Ted said. "He doesn't want it for heavy-duty cutting."

"Well, sure I do." Pete protested. "I want a knife for cutting too. Like sharpening pencils. But mostly a knife is for carrying in your pocket, it's a fashion thing."

"Of course," said Karen.

Peter leaves his black leather belt dangling on the hook on the back of his bathroom door these days, long and phallic. In his room, the closet door stands wide open. Both doors of the stereo cabinet are left open, with a sign posted on the cabinet warning me not to shut them, something about letting in air, as if he kept canaries in there. His records are stacked on the floor; any letters he has gotten recently are clipped to his desk lamp. He'd like to be out-and-out messy, but can't nerve himself to that point. Still, the geography of his room has shifted. No longer a series of closed surfaces, cliffs and plains, it juts out now, a landscape of indecision, showing an unwillingness to shut the door on any possibility.

Hilary was telling Karen and me about her job, which was meant to lead her into book publishing one day, although the connection seemed remote. I carved the meat. If Hilary and Ted became lovers, or if Hilary and Ted were already lovers, and she moved into his apartment, and a few years passed and they had a fight, she'd turn right back into a waif again. Nothing would belong to her; not even the pots and pans would be in her name. Ted earns so much more than she does that the lease on the apartment, or the deed to the co-op, and all the furnishings in it would prove to be his contribution to the household, and her contribution would consist of the bedding she'd changed and maybe some shepherd's pie.

Martin was right. I always tended to side with an outsider against the family, any outsider, not only an in-law but even someone I'd never met before, a waif who would probably never become an in-law, not even in Ted's most casual flights of fancy.

But what about the divorce? Would Martin have been surprised, or did he suspect that it was coming all along? Would he have thought we picked the right lawyer from his firm for Ted, the one he himself would have picked? Was I wrong to recommend a lawyer for Felicia too, from another firm? It didn't matter. If I'd made a mistake, or been blind where I should have been most perceptive, Martin would never know about it. The thought reassured me.

Kurt returned to the dining room and plugged in the intercom, which buzzed peacefully on the floor, the other end connected in the bedroom where Carrie's crib stood, while he announced in a tone of reproach that she was asleep now. Ted began telling him the inside details about the week's stunning merger of two major security firms. "Are you two going to be boring again?" Karen wanted to know.

"Do you think you'll be able to handle it, taking care of a baby and keeping your job?" Hilary said to Karen.

Do I still love Martin? I asked myself, wondering if Hilary was asking herself at that moment if she was in love with Ted.

We speak of loving "forever," but we make promises only "until death do us part." But how long is forever? Once again, lawyers, or rather lawmakers, have the last word, more poetic than poets: They tell us that oral contracts cannot bind the parties if more than a year is involved. To a lawyer, by definition, the word "forever" means twelve months or less.

But who says I have to stop loving a man just because he's dead? Out of sight, out of mind? No, our affair goes on, feeding on a rich diet of revelations. We're getting to know each other at last, we're stripped of our clothes, as if our first honeymoon was a period of moonshine, while this second honeymoon, this final chance to explore each other, takes place on a mountaintop, some peak of almost unlimited visibility without moisture in the air, because I've discovered that's what death is: Death is the opposite of darkness. Death is a dazzling white light. Death isn't obscurity or fading away or blurring, but clarity, perspective, totality. Death is sex with the bedroom lights on.

And I'm as liberated as my lover. For the first time, I can see that he had faults (no, he couldn't have had faults, but maybe he had a few little flaws in his makeup), and I can acknowledge those faults without trying to change him (but I always try to change everyone in the family, in particular I try to change the picture of me they hold in their heads), just as I acknowledge my own deficiencies in front of him now without being afraid that I'm about to lose him. He can't leave home. He can't move further away than he has already moved, so I needn't hang on to him with an embrace that may, in another period, have turned into a squeeze.

I can even face the fact that I'm changing. I have my own concerns and habits these days. I'm no longer half of a pair. In a few more years, it's possible that life for me without Martin may be life for me without quite so much of Martin in it.

"We ran the dinner for the acquisition team, twenty-four of us, down at that new restaurant in the Village, Le Petit Prince," Ted went on.

"Seth Weil was one of the partners kicked out in the merger?" Kurt asked.

"Early retirement, you mean. He's forty-two." Ted sounded depressed. "I never figured out why the newspapers had to print their names."

"Did they?"

"All seven. Along with some sharp shots as to the amount of money they got. As if they'd been indicted." While he spoke, he slipped a piece of meat to Ralph under the table and petted him. "The restaurant let us bring our own wine, because they don't have a license yet. We saved a bundle."

So I heard an answer to a question that I would never have dared ask. The use of the pronouns "I" and "we" served as a report card and told me not to worry, both my son and son-in-law were about to be promoted to a higher grade. They'd become partners soon—they'd make partner, was the way they'd put it—and what's more, from the way in which the two young women were chatting while the men talked, I could be pretty sure that Karen, at least, was clued in to what was coming.

The young dogs chase the old dogs in a circle, Martin said, who would have been one of the old dogs himself by this time, counting on his fingers the years remaining until compulsory retirement. Now the circle has come round. Ted and Karen have acquired lovers, leases, professions, colleagues, insurance policies of their own. Karen has a child. Ted will have a child one day. Ted and Kurt will be partners soon. Karen will be a partner's wife. Everything that Martin and I had together is theirs, everything with this single exception, this romance after death, which will be theirs too one day, of course—this intermittent, ultimately truthful weaving and baring of two spirits, now that I've grown more provocative, more desirable, because I've found out that I can manage without him, in fact now that I've turned into the woman he should have married in the first place. Two spirits at two different levels of being, we're bound to each other by our wish that we had been something finer than what we were. Well, it's not bad that this wish should be the part of us that survives.

"Get the dog out of this dining room while we eat, will you?" Peter said, glaring at Ralph, who had made himself conspicuous by picking up one of Carrie's toys in his teeth—her teething ring, unfortunately. "I can't stand the stink." Karen leaped up to rescue the ring and put it in the kitchen to be sterilized. Kurt stood up and led Ralph by the collar to the kitchen door, while Ralph drooped his tail between his legs, the tail that used to be a golden plume, full of bronze glints and burrs and seeds, now become a rat's half-naked coil.

"He can't help it," I said, as he went through the door, shamed in front of his family. He was far from young even in the days when

Martin said he was still too young to learn to talk. "His breath is bad because his teeth are rotten. I brush them for him, but his breath still smells. He passes gas. He's getting old. What do you expect?"

"I'll bet you use my toothbrush on him. I expect to eat my dinner in peace," Pete said. "You should put him outside before we sit down at the table."

"I'll put you outside instead." He was your father's dog, I meant.

"Fine. I'd rather eat in the yard, so long as I don't have to smell him. Why don't you shoot him? He'll only get worse and worse." He spoke with the fury, the terror of an adolescent trapped in a body, surrounded by other bodies, all of them decaying minute by minute. I had betrayed him by accepting into the family circle a body that was bound to age and smell and grow offensive and disintegrate at its own accelerated rate, while he was still moving toward his prime.

"Poor Ralph," Karen crooned, with the impersonal croon that she uses for any living creature other than her daughter.

"Such a beautiful animal," Hilary said.

"Watch out, Pete." Ted leaned across the table and spoke in a warning voice. "We have a curious tradition in this family. You mean no one ever told you? When the dog of the house dies, we have a solemn ritual. We slaughter the youngest child and bury him in the dog's tomb."

There was a single sharp cry on the intercom. Karen sprang to her feet. The rest of us froze in place. "Wait a minute," Kurt said. "Don't go up. She may go right back to sleep."

"She may have had a bad dream." I wanted Karen to finish what was on her plate for once.

"She never does that. She never wakes up and settles back to sleep."

But the intercom was silent. We stopped talking for a minute, to be sure. "You see?" Karen sat down again. I tried to remind myself that Martin, like his dog, would be older now, his hair grown sparser and his nostrils wider. Like the dog, he'd pass gas more often. But thinking of his flaws made me miss him more vividly rather than less.

The phone rang. "Let it ring. People ought to know better than to call on a Saturday night at dinnertime. We can't hold up the soufflé."

Gitte said that she was finished anyway. She carried some dishes into the kitchen as she went. A minute later she called me to the phone.

"Marion's nurse," I reported to the children. "The weekend nurse. She said I'd better come."

"I'll drive you," Ted said.

LIGHT was what I saw, blinding light on bare and damaged walls. A crime must have taken place here. Police floodlights throw off such a light. The windows were black. There was no furniture in the room, no pictures or ornaments on the walls. The bookshelves were stripped. Robbery. Rape. The front door was unlocked. No, there was furniture, I saw now, but it was huddled in the center of the floor under a dirty canvas. The carpet was covered with more canvas. My mother had moved out or been moved out of her apartment, and no one had told me.

Jack Nordlinger was standing in front of me in the entrance hall, putting his coat on. He grasped both my hands with a practiced grip. "I'm so very sorry," he said, his voice ringing against the walls which had great cracks in them, I saw now, outlined in white. In the corner next to the window, where she'd complained for years and years of a leak, there was a swollen scar. Two strange men walked softly around the edge of the room. Police. Detectives. A young black woman, dressed in tunic and pants, stood behind the doctor, paralyzed with fright—the new weekend nurse, I assumed. We'd never met.

Couldn't we turn the lights down? Or angle them so that they didn't blind me? Was someone being grilled?

"It was over before I could get here," the young doctor said. "I'm sorry to be the one to tell you."

"We realized before we left home," I said.

"Thank you for coming so quickly," said Ted.

"There was nothing I could do."

The painters, that's what I'd forgotten. They were doing a good job, especially in the corner with the persistent leak, which had been patched from outside, I remembered now. The problem might finally be solved. A floodlight was clipped to a portable aluminum stand that must belong to the chief painter, a man she'd used for twenty years.

"Are the remains in the bedroom?" one of the strange men dressed in a dark raincoat asked.

"We're grateful it was quick and easy," Ted added. Scrapings of old paint littered the floor. We had to be careful not to trip on the folds of canvas as we walked toward the bedroom.

"Is there anything I can do for you?" Jack asked. I said we'd taken enough of his time on a Saturday night, but he refused to leave at least until I'd seen her. "I've put it on the bureau," he said, nodding to the nurse as I went into the bedroom. The death certificate, he meant.

Death is, without doubt, a dazzling white light, as I said before. In a bed immaculately made, the pillow puffed up, the sheet and blanket tucked under her chin, my mother rested, not the mother I knew but the mother I'd always wanted to know, her head tilted to one side in sweet, good, girlish compliance, sweet as a good child put to bed, stripped of her quarrels as she was stripped of her clothes, the bruises and tobacco stains hidden underneath the covers. Looking at her the way I looked at her now, I could so easily have told her that I loved her. I could have called her Mother to her face.

But she was always like this, I heard her tell me. Death is transformation. She was transformed back to what she was meant to be in the first place.

I don't believe people who say that they're overwhelmed by grief in the first minutes. What I felt wasn't grief or remorse. It was the surge of energy I'd known when my children were born, when my granddaughter was born, when I was in danger of drowning in a small sailboat in a storm, when I first knew that I wanted to marry Martin. What I felt was deeper than the grief or fear I'd felt on some occasions, deeper than the joy or thankfulness I'd known on others. Feelings come afterward, when there's time for them, like high water that rolls over the sand in the wake of a storm, when the worst of the wind is over.

Death is the knowledge that there's no place further to go. This is what is; the center of the labyrinth has been reached. Now the survivor must hunt for the way out again.

"I wanted to call you sooner," the nurse said, obviously terrified of death, or of me, or both. "I wanted to call the doctor and I wanted to call you, but she say no, she don't want me to call you, she don't want to be taken to the hospital, she want to die at home." What was the girl's name? Rose, I thought. She was a college student, but none too bright, nothing like Sylvia. My mother had complained constantly about her, was planning to replace her, in fact, but weekend nurses were even tougher to find than weekday nurses. All the same, she'd chosen to die with only this girl for company.

"She died in her sleep?"

The girl shook her head and pointed to something at the side of the bed. "She die on that." She couldn't say the word. She was pointing to the commode.

Jack Nordlinger glared at her. "That's not unusual. Matter of fact, it happens more often than not." He stopped, examined what he had said and corrected himself. "I mean it's not unusual for the sphincter to empty. At the last moment, the pelvic-floor muscles contract. What's unusual is for somebody to muster the strength to get to the commode."

Like childbirth, I thought to myself. At the moment of giving birth, while the doctor's voice calls out in triumph "Here it comes!"—still forced to say "it," because all he can see is the crown of a head—what the woman on the table feels, with her knees pulled up, is an urge to unblock her bowel of the biggest movement of her life, a movement that will never come out, that's how big it is; and she strains without a toilet until suddenly the head slips through, and the shoulders and body seem so soft by comparison that the baby slides out like a fish.

Now I knew the other part of the beautiful symmetrical secret: that death is the complementary movement, the parallel scene at the other end of a life, the final triumphant evacuation, a cleaning out complete enough to satisfy even my mother. At birth and at death, what we feel when we can't speak is that we're being turned inside out. What was inside us, invisible, unreachable, not created by us and yet undeniably ours, has waited its time until it can wait no longer and comes out, cries out, takes over, exists on its own. Deathbed, the poets say, stripping the scene of its grandeur. But death isn't a bed. Death isn't darkness. Death isn't going to sleep. Death toilet, let them say more accurately. Death commode. For those who have the strength of will my mother had. The others make a toilet of their beds.

The nurse avoided the doctor's eye, aware that she'd said something wrong. He'd arranged the body so nicely. There was no need to delay him any longer, so Ted and I walked him to the front door and waited until the elevator came. I wondered if he was the one who ought to tell the elevator man the news.

While Ted was drawn into discussion with one of the representatives from the funeral chapel, the other accosted me. "How about clothes?" I'd already decided on the raw silk dress and jacket that she'd worn at Karen's wedding. But what did I do about underwear, stockings, shoes? No one had taught me such things. All I knew was that I mustn't give these men any jewelry. My mother often said it never went under the ground.

I went back to the bedroom to get her clothes. But the bed was empty. She wasn't there any more. I almost tripped over something that had been left lying on the floor, a stretcher with a black plastic cover over it. Then I realized that it wasn't quite flat. The body under the cover hardly raised the surface. My mother was lying at my feet. I'd almost fallen over her.

She didn't let anyone call me. She didn't want me with her. I was only fifty minutes away, and she knew I was home having dinner with the children, but she didn't allow her nurse to call me.

I could have come without being called. I didn't need an invitation. I suspected, when we talked before dinner, that she'd had another stroke, in fact she said so herself, but I didn't think too much about it. I didn't want to break up Karen's birthday party. Love flows too readily downhill. Parents love children more than children love parents.

She could have told me she wanted me. That was all that was needed. She didn't have to be dying to say that.

I was in New York anyway this afternoon, picking up the children. She knew that. I'd planned to leave home earlier and stop in and visit her first, but I didn't do it. An hour would have been plenty of time. Half an hour would have been enough. We come so heartbreakingly close to doing whatever it is we ought to do.

"Who sent the beautiful tulips?" I pointed to a vase that stood next to Karen's picture.

"Your son. What's his name? The one in the living room."

"Ah, yes. She told me. I'd forgotten. She was so pleased." She hadn't even mentioned cost. I sent her lilacs every year, but hadn't gotten around to it yet this season.

The girl was still ruffled by Jack Nordlinger's displeasure. Undoubtedly this was the first time she'd been alone in an apartment with a dying person, much less a corpse. She wasn't even a practical nurse, after all. She was a student who worked her way through college by living in sick people's homes on weekends, taking the place of absent daughters, so to speak. By now, she was thawing out. "Know what she say to me? Her very last words?" She needed to be praised for what she'd gone through. For all I knew, she might have had to sit alone in the apartment afterward, waiting for the doctor to ring the bell, then help him lift the body back into bed and arrange the sheets. "She say 'I think I'm dying. When I get there, I'm going to tell them what a good girl you been.' "

The words that I'd waited so many years to hear her say to me, my mother gave, in her last minute, to another girl. She held on to them until the end, and then gave them to someone she didn't even like. At that last moment of her life, was she counting on the fact that they'd be repeated to me? Was she showing her old skill in Scrabble, using an opportunity no one else would have spotted to put across a message that no one expected, scoring enough points horizontally, vertically, diagonally to win the last game?

That other girl was holding her hand and acting the part of her daughter. The girl was thin. Maybe my mother felt the narrow bones of her forearm and imagined it was my arm she was grasping.

No, never. I could imagine almost any ending for my mother, but not befuddlement. The explanation had to be simpler. I'd often been in the room when she reviled one nurse or another behind her back, then patted her arm as soon as she came in. She'd learned the lesson of old age: the need of the flesh to be cared for, and the fleeting fleshly love for the person who fills the need. That's all she meant when she told Rose she'd been a good girl.

What cause had I given her to tell anyone her daughter had been a good girl? Two hours ago I spoke to her, but I didn't take it on myself to call her doctor, or go in to see her myself.

Probably that was for the best. She wouldn't have wanted to die in a hospital. Quit while you're ahead, she'd have said. Still, I hadn't intended to do her that good turn.

She sent Karen a check and a card for her birthday. My birthday was forgotten two months ago. Time after time, she'd insisted she was about to give me the silver water pitcher or the porcelain pigeon from the coffee table, but she never gave me a thing. She sent Karen's card a day early, and it was a card that she made herself. She drew pictures on the envelope as well as on the notepaper.

I meant to send her lilacs, but didn't do it. It was Ted who sent the tulips.

Carrie cried out in her crib, loud and sharp, and went back to sleep, or else never woke up in the first place. Such a thing never happened before. What could make an infant cry out like that, without cause? Was it her great-grandmother's spirit entering the house, rushing past the dining room where the rest of us were partying without her, and traveling upstairs—swifter than we were, for once, getting up those stairs without trouble—to say good-bye to the person she couldn't resist saying good-bye to, the only one in the house who wouldn't remember her?

No matter where I looked, my mother's last thoughts passed over me and headed for somebody else.

Of course she picked Carrie. Who else would she choose? She was her mother's daughter, and she was mother of a daughter. And her daughter had a daughter, who in turn had an infant daughter. Where else would Marion's spirit linger, if not in this line of female succession?

But did she see her own daughter—me—as anything but a necessary link in a chain?

Does it matter? Can't that sort of love be as real as any other?

It occurred to me that the men in black suits were gone, and so was the stretcher. They hadn't come past us, so they must have gone down in the service elevator. Between them, my mother and her mother before her had lived in this apartment for almost forty years. As she grew older and weaker, the doorman had taken her arm and steadied her whenever he put her into a taxi. But now, the moment she was dead, she had to be bundled out by way of the back elevator—summoned by some special signal, no doubt, to make sure that it would be empty—and then taken through the cellar into a van waiting to get her at the side door.

She had committed an offense worse than ringing for the back elevator man in her nightgown. No one should have to see the depths to which she'd sunk.

H E R life had been turned inside out like a glove. The part of her that was cracked and discolored had become invisible, while a fresh, unweathered part was exposed to view.

Her belongings were turned inside out, too. By the time that the estate appraiser had done her work, the contents of the silver cabinet and dish cupboards and linen closet were strewn over the floor, to be divided into three piles for the children, who had to take those aspects of their grandmother seriously which up to now they'd deplored, for they too—the older children, especially—had been transformed by death. They were no longer the weightless generation, critical as angels. Every death brings about a liberation, a divesting, but it also brings about a shift of burdens, and with those burdens come decisions, desires.

Ted was avid for old carving knives and his grandmother's Dutch oven, but above all for big wooden cooking spoons dark with age, objects that can't be bought in Macy's Cellar. There's nothing he doesn't need, including an apartment, but before he commits himself to accepting the pair of massive dining-room chests fronted with marquetry, he either must or must not consult Hilary about her taste and plans. Either way, a decision hides inside every decision.

Karen won't agree to load up with damask tablecloths and sterling napkin rings and silver salt cellars with blue-glass liners that she swears she'll never use. It's our family mealtime argument all over again: Take a little more, I urge her. It's such good stuff. You'll wish you had it later on. No more, I can't handle any more, she insists, and pushes herself away from the group, which doesn't mean that by turning toward Carrie she can escape a transformation of her own.

The three children are to share what will be left of their grandmother's money after estate taxes are paid, and this prospect brings problems, or at least changes, in its wake. Until now, Karen has kept her job because she and Kurt will need a larger apartment soon, if they ever want to have another child, and The Detwirth-Manning Foundation can be counted on to help with financing, but soon she'll have enough money of her own. Her employer will be replaced as fairy grandmother. If she goes back to work on Monday morning, it will only be because she chooses to go to work. If she delays having a second child, it will only be because she chooses to delay.

We sit on the dining-room floor, building our three piles, while Carrie sits on a sheet spread on top of the carpet and plays with an old bronze dinner bell. Karen gets china and crystal. Ted gets flatware. A diamond engagement ring has been reserved for Peter, to make up for furnishings. The silver candlesticks, very old, family heritage, provenance uncertain, are allotted to the firstborn. A silver bowl goes to Karen; the repoussé water pitcher I thought I wanted I've put aside for Peter.

But what's that look in Peter's eyes? Ted and Karen have a lifelong habit of splitting rather than sharing, Jack Sprat and his wife, who need each other right now to empty the silver cabinet the way they used to need each other to wield the broom and dustpan when they cleaned up the playroom, but Peter has no such background. Until today, he has successfully defended himself from having too many good things thrust at him. Is he wary all of a sudden because his brother and sister are making off with armchairs and tables and lamps, while he's left out, or because he can't envisage a future in which he'll have a house or apartment of his own, a shell large enough to hold such objects? There's no nourishment in the idea of a ring sitting in a bank vault, waiting for him to find a woman to wear it.

THE ESTATE appraiser was here this week, a beautiful woman with long blond hair—thirty-four years old she told me, but she looked younger—just Ted's type, I couldn't help thinking. "So sunny!" she exclaimed when she came into the living room. "So brilliant." I'd refused to put back the curtains and drapes after the painters left, so the spring sunlight poured over the roofs of brownstones and water towers and washed through the room, hiding the stains in the carpet with its glare.

"These shades and curtains haven't been raised for years." I opened the door of the guest closet to show her where they were hanging. It was her job to catalogue every item in the house and find as many flaws as possible, so that she could appraise it at a low value for estate tax purposes.

"Of course they haven't. Old people love darkness. They love their own disorder. But this apartment is so clean."

Old? My mother was seventy-four. I'd never thought of her as old.

"You should see the clutter I usually walk into. You know what we found in an apartment the other day? At the bottom of the laundry hamper, under the dirty clothes, the janitor of the building found the dead woman's diamond jewelry. Well, I warn you right now, I won't go pawing through dirty clothes."

My mother was disintegrating in front of my eyes, turning into one of "them," turning into another customer for this girl the age of her grandson, turning into an old woman who wasn't radically different from other old women, more cantankerous than most, certainly, but not monstrous, not the dragon-goddess breathing scorn through her nostrils, capable of annihilating or annealing me with her flames.

While the recording angel went on with her chant, I emptied the desk drawers, thumping down unused return envelopes one after the other. Inside a Con Edison envelope, I found half a dozen stamps that had somehow passed through the mail uncanceled. Inside another, I found limp and dingy foreign stamps, left over from the days when Ted collected them. "You want a present? Here's a blank engagement diary from 1958. Useful, in case 1958 comes around again."

"Scratch paper. They're all the same." The appraiser nodded. "The men save old pens that don't work. They die of self-neglect and malnutrition. The women hoard everything, but especially envelopes."

"Freudian, don't you think? Male pens against female envelopes?"

She took a pen of her own out of her pocketbook, along with a notepad. "But before I begin, tell me if there's anything here that didn't belong to your mother." This was the point at which I was supposed to name the most valuable items, so that they wouldn't be included in the estate. I glanced at a Meissen shepherd and shepherdess standing on gilded brackets and simpering at each other across the back of the couch, the position of honor in the room.

"Not a thing," I said. "Everything in the apartment belonged to her." The recording angel looked surprised. She scratched a metal figurine with her diamond ring. "Bronze," I told her.

She went to the window and examined the scratch in the light. "Pewter," she said with satisfaction.

"Wait a minute." I sounded angry. "I forgot. There *is* one thing in the apartment that belongs to me. That white porcelain pigeon on the coffee table, that was my last birthday present from my mother. I hadn't gotten around to taking it home yet." I was afraid to categorize it as Nymphenburg for fear I'd find out it was something less splendid.

The appraiser nodded with even greater satisfaction and licked a hairline crack on the underside of a plate. "I can always taste glue if it was broken and mended." She picked up a bronze-and-ivory statuette of an Egyptian princess, held it upside down, studied it at length in front of the window. "Oh, thank goodness. I found a tiny break in the foot," she said with relief. "Otherwise this piece would've been quite valuable."

I'd come to the bottom drawers of the desk. From behind the

ledgers I drew out a box full of photos and letters and picked up at random a snapshot of a girl three or four years old, wearing a bathing suit and carrying a pail and shovel. At first I couldn't understand what I was seeing. The child who refused to raise her head and look at the camera, much less smile, was obviously Marion, and yet her expression of fear—fear and the desire to be loved—was an expression I'd been sure that I'd caused. But in front of my eyes, this little girl with her sand toys hung her head at the same abject angle as the old woman who'd sat in a pink vinyl chair in this apartment a short time ago, looking as if she was about to be scolded. I wasn't the cause of my mother's unhappiness after all. Or I was only the most recent cause.

Recognizing my father's handwriting on an envelope, I drew out a letter and unfolded it. "Angel Wife," the letter began. "Today it is two years that we have been united in the holy bonds of matrimony. Your unswerving devotion during these two years, your indefatigable efforts to maintain peace and comfort and happiness in our household, have served to increase my love for you (if it be possible to increase it) to the utmost heights. . . ." His style, I observed, had changed less than his sentiments.

I pulled out the other snapshots and letters, one by one.

SO THE time has come at last when we begin to know each other, my mother and I—as Martin and I begin to know each other—the one I needed too much and the other I needed too little for them to be happy. We want nothing from each other any more. And so we're free to talk. The dead talk in lighthearted tones, full of the mockery and superiority of upperclassmen dealing with freshmen, telling about many periods of their lives at once, since all truths are contemporaneous from their vantage point, all truths are of equal value, now that they are moot. Little by little, we piece together what happened. We find out the plot of the play we've just seen. For all I know, this may be what their deaths are for.

Shouldn't a little girl be happy on a beach in the first summer that she's big enough to build a sandcastle on her own? If she hangs her head, it's undoubtedly her father with his terrible temper she's afraid of, but it seems to me that it has to be her mother as well, her charming mother who was so much fun, who was such a bundle of laughs, who threw a bronze bookend at her husband's head only once, whose fury was never expressed after that single heave, and yet was strong enough to contain his. Would this child want to make herself the rival of such a mother by acting the part of a mother herself?

The dead woman I nearly tripped over when she lay underneath the black plastic cover on the bedroom floor was still my grandmother's child, I see at last, and I see that this is my grandmother's apartment I'm cleaning out, now that the intervening tenant has departed. This chiffon blouse with handmade buttonholes up the back, too small for my fingers to manage, these suede gloves that reach up to the elbow, with beaded embroidery and cutwork on their backs, these marcasite shoe buckles and mirrored buttons salvaged from a discarded black dress—all these things belonged to a woman of style. I claim these things. I'll hang on to them for myself and for Karen and Carrie—where could we ever find such quality these days?

But above this layer I find the midden my mother has left behind—plastic rain bonnets in little slipcases, and imitation ivory chopsticks with the names of Chinese restaurants printed on them—and I want to weep for the woman who tucked these away and thought them worthy of being saved; I want to rage at that woman's mother, who couldn't help what she did, either.

In a way, my grandmother has reached the next-to-last stage in her dying. The last stage will come with my own death, or maybe with Ted's and Karen's deaths, if they remember her well enough, as mine will come a couple of generations down this path.

"You'll have yourself a picnic going through those drawers some day," my mother used to say. She turns out to be right, although not in the way that she meant.

I also find what I don't find. What I don't find is any trace that this woman ever had a daughter. There's no copy of the book I wrote, nor a single one of my articles, even though I brought her the magazines they appeared in. I'm struck in the pit of the stomach when I think of the effort it must have cost her to stand above a wastebasket and let each magazine in turn drop into it, while she was incapable of throwing out a pair of plastic chopsticks.

In the end, nothing is forgiven. Nothing is wiped clean. Everything is accepted. If I had been handed the picture of the little girl with pail and shovel on the beach years ago, would I have really seen it? And if I'd been capable of seeing the look in those eyes, would I have loved my mother any more out of pity and understanding? If I had been told years earlier that it was possible for me to live a life without Martin, not as desirable, certainly, but possible all the same, would I have loved him any less?

No. Only with greater pain.

We are never capable of acting better than we did. We are never capable of finding a solution to a problem, because we exist on the same level with the problem. Then one day, something or somebody transforms us, moves us to another level. The problem isn't solved; it ceases to exist.

A GEOLOGICAL change had taken place in the apartment. The better pieces of furniture that the children didn't want had been carted off to an auction house. The rest would be picked up in a few days by a thrift shop. My mother's beds had been given to the back elevator man, who took them away in his lunch hour, uncovering a six-foot square of carpet that turned out to be a surprisingly deep mauve, with a shell pattern woven into it that I'd long forgotten. Where the chifforobe used to stand, there was a black rectangular depression an inch deep that no vacuum had reached in twenty years. Closing my eyes, I walked across the room and traced my mother's history with the balls of my feet, from the thick turf under her bed to the path flat as lichen that led from bed to chair to bathroom and back again.

Only a man could suppose that our possessions stay the same as they were, after we leave them. Two weeks ago, these objects made up a Park Avenue apartment, rundown maybe, but decent looking, even impressive enough in its own way. Now the cracked figurines and the porcelain bird that stood poised forever in one direction, because the hidden wing was broken, are wrapped in tissue paper and packed in hat boxes for the thrift shop. The Meissen shepherd and shepherdess are in disgrace; they are as ugly as I thought they were, but they aren't Meissen. ("On the bottom they're stamped 'Dresden,' and then there's some sort of seal and then 'Bavaria,' and we know Dresden isn't in Bavaria, don't we?" the recording angel said to me.)

These objects can't forgive me for their loss of status, or else I can't forgive them because I have to deal with them. In any case, we're on the outs with one another. When I took an etching off the wall so that the appraiser could see it, the frame fell apart in my hands. When I rolled the Sheraton-style card table to the station wagon in order to drive it to Karen's apartment, the wheel dropped off one of the legs. I picked it up and put it in my coat pocket, but now I can't find it. My mother was right once again. Her possessions have suffered more at my hands in the first two weeks after her death than they did staying with her for twenty-five years.

And I'm like the rest of her things. The cracks in me show up more obviously than they did a couple of weeks ago. I'm not irritable any more, now that she's not here to provoke me. I don't sound rebellious or scornful these days, I don't strain either to please or displease her, I don't make unkind remarks that cause me grief later on, but only now that the irritation and rebellion and scorn are gone from my voice do I recognize that these were signs of youth, or at least of immaturity, and I was young, I was immature only so long as I stood in contrast to somebody else.

From now on I'll have to be careful to wear nothing but jeans and sneakers in front of my children.

WHEN we finished dividing up the linens, the children packed what they'd decided to take home with them that day. Ted carried an old Electrolux, its hose draped around his neck like a snake. Karen couldn't carry much, but she'd loaded the back of the stroller with placemats and napkins, a couple of bathmats and Carrie's bell. Peter was ecstatic because he'd discovered a portable typewriter that had been mine twenty years earlier.

"All it needs is a small repair," he said. "The carriage return that moves you to the next line doesn't work."

"In that case, better make sure that your first sentence is a lulu," Ted said.

"I'll pay for the repair myself." Peter sounded somewhat huffy, not so pleased any more to be teased by an older brother. Teenagers grow more in height in the spring, and more in body weight in the fall, I'd read, and almost imagined that I could watch the early May sunshine, coming through the window, as it stretched him out.

"I'm ringing for the elevator," Karen announced, the minute that she had Carrie's jacket buttoned.

"This typewriter'll last forever," Pete went on. "Think what it's worth in terms of scrap metal alone. Besides, I like it because the keyboard's so small."

"Whereas on my typewriter, I keep the "q" in the bedroom and the "m" in the living room," I said, as we got into the elevator. I'd already made up my mind to get him a self-correcting electric for his birthday, whether he wanted it or not.

We said good-bye to the elevator men and doorman, who'd watched us strip the apartment. Good-bye, the children said to me and to one another, and I said to them, after we were out on the sidewalk again, while I bent down to kiss Carrie, after which Ted headed downtown to his apartment, maybe to join Hilary for the evening, and Karen walked home pushing the stroller, and Peter, my calendar of years, strode ahead of me toward the car, so that no one should think he was with me.

In my tone, I was astonished to hear that I can live without the dead, and I can live without my children also. I'm free of the lot of them. I can live without anything except my work, which is another way of saying myself, and my work was what waited for me at home.

As the children moved off in their own directions, carrying their new possessions, I watched their lives grow denser, more humid every minute, clotting the air around them, at the same time that mine grew thinner and more rarefied, harder on the lungs, sustaining less effort, and yet—occasionally—translucent.

Good-bye. I am your past, I said to my children's backs. But I am also your future.

ABOUT THE AUTHOR

Joan Gould's literary apprenticeship began at Bryn Mawr College, where she studied for two years with W. H. Auden. Her work has appeared in many publications, including *The New York Times*, where she was a "Hers" columnist, *Esquire* and *Sports Illustrated*. *Spirals* was completed while she was a fellow at Yaddo.

She is an ardent sailor who races her own boat, which she keeps near her home in Rye, New York.